Scheming Women

Scheming

Cynthia Hogue

Women

POETRY, PRIVILEGE, AND
THE POLITICS OF SUBJECTIVITY

STATE UNIVERSITY OF NEW YORK PRESS

Photograph by Esther Bubley, reprinted with permission
from Esther Bubley.

Published by
State University of New York Press, Albany

1995 State University of New York

For information, address the State University of New York Press,
State University Plaza, Albany, NY 12246

Production by Bernadine Dawes • Marketing by Dana Yanulavich

Library of Congress Cataloging-in-Publication Data

Hogue, Cynthia.
    Scheming women : poetry, privilege, and the politics of
subjectivity / Cynthia Hogue.
        p.   cm. – (SUNY series in feminist criticism and theory)
    Includes bibliographical references and index.
    ISBN 0-7914-2621-1 (HC : acid-free). – ISBN 0-7914-2622-X (PB :
acid-free)
        1. American poetry–Women authors–History and criticism–Theory,
etc.   2. Lesbians' writings, American–History and criticism-
-Theory, etc.   3. Feminism and literature–United States–History.
4. Women and literature–United States–History.   5. Subjectivity in
literature.   6. Authorship–Sex differences.   I. Title.
II. Series.
PS310.F45H64   1995
811.009'9287–dc20   94-47463
                                                                            CIP

10 9 8 7 6 5 4 3 2 1

For my family,
far and near

Contents

Acknowledgments

Writing is a quest of sorts that often begins with one goal in mind and ends up surprising the writer by arriving at another. As a poet and scholar, I began this journey as a personal quest to study how a few exemplary women poets, whose work I admired, had "found their voices." But gradually, as I found my way, the path turned out to be in another, though related, direction, taking me by a more circuitous route through a consideration of class and race privilege as well as a criticism of gender oppression. My path became an inquiry into a peculiar position (or so it seemed to me) of strategy and strength: the equivocal subjectivity I came to think of, and finally to theorize, as an ethical poetic practice. My journey parallels many others, and my hope for the study it has produced is that it will participate in and contribute to a dialogue with those who have also traveled through domains of female experience, voices, lives, history, literature. Like all quests, universal in this one sense, mine could not have been completed without helpers along the way.

And so it is time now to thank all who have contributed in various capacities to the completion of this project. I am profoundly grateful to Susan Hardy Aiken, Tenney Nathanson, and Patrick O'Donnell, whose generous feedback has inspired and taught me, and whose wise counsel over the years, in conversation and in print, has contributed so much to this project, and to me personally. Likewise, my heartfelt thanks to Barbara Babcock, whose generosity when this project was in its early stages I well remember, and whose influence has continued to resonate with me through the years. I wish also to thank Jerrold Hogle and Herbert Schneidau, who first guided and galvanized my thinking about poetry and poetics. Members of a wonderful feminist discussion group a decade ago in Tucson, dear friends all—Julia Balén, Karen Brennan, Janice Dewey, Laura Hinton, and Nancy Mairs—first encouraged and then, through continuing exchanges long after the group had disbanded, inspired this project along the way, which I remember and for which I am at long last able to thank them.

I also would like to thank my colleagues in the Department of English at the University of New Orleans. Anne Charles, Nancy Easterlin, Jessica Munns, and, in particular, Carl Malmgren and Joyce Zonana all contributed to this project through discussion, feedback, and timely encouragement. My colleagues and friends in Women's Studies, especially Pamela Jenkins and Alice Kemp, have supported me at crucial points. Thanks also go to my research assistant, Michael Mahoney. I feel blessed to have taught the talented graduate and undergraduate students in three women's studies and poetry seminars at the University of New Orleans, who put my thinking-through of the issues addressed in this book to the test in our discussions, most recently in a very special American literature class this summer.

Without the opportunity to study at the following institutes and to work in the forums provided by two consummate scholars and teachers, this project could not have arrived at its present form: I wish to thank the School of Criticism and Theory for a tuition scholarship, and Wendy Steiner for her spirited seminar in post-modernism. I am also grateful for a National Endowment for the Humanities Summer Seminar Fellowship to the Institute for the Study of Women and Men at the University of Southern California, and to Lois Banner, not only for her lively seminar in the new gender scholarship in history, but for her generous support and critical help since. I wish to thank the University of New Orleans for the crucial support needed to complete this book: two semester course reductions from the Department of English facilitated my work during the academic year; two College of Liberal Arts Faculty Summer Research and Writing Fellowships and three University Research Council travel grants made it possible for me to conduct research in the H.D. papers housed at the Yale Collection of American Literature, Beinecke Rare Book and Manuscript Library, Yale University, and in the Marianne Moore papers housed at the Rosenbach Museum and Library in Philadelphia, and to complete this project. Elizabeth Fuller, Librarian of Literature at the Rosenbach, was especially helpful in guiding me through the Marianne Moore materials. I also thank Evelyn Feldman, Research Associate at the Rosenbach, and Patricia Willis, Curator of American Literature at the Beinecke, for their timely help, and Dorothy Prelinger, former librarian at the Yale University Art Library, for making both stays in New Haven as informative as they were gracious.

Colleagues elsewhere who helped me with encouragement, exchange, and friendship over the years, for which I am deeply grateful, are Kelly Coyle, Ana Dittmar, Judith Elsley, Gary Lemons, Joseph Parkhurst, Ted Parkinson, Diane Shoos, Jan Stryz, and Michael Wutz. I am indebted to AnnLouise Keating, who discussed extensive portions of this project with me, consistently offered information and advice, and read the whole manuscript at a crucial final stage: my deep gratitude to her for going the distance with me. I also thank Richard Dellamora, Suzanne Juhasz, and Cynthia Griffin Wolff, who encouraged me at important stages of this project. My gratitude to Lynda Zwinger for her abiding generosity to me. I am deeply thankful to her and to Cristanne Miller for their enthusiastic readings of the finished manuscript, and to my editor at State University of New York Press, Carola Sautter, for her belief in this project. Thanks also go to my production editor, Bernadine Dawes.

My thanks to the editors of *American Poetry* Vol. 8 (Fall 1990): 87–99; and of *Phoebe: An Interdisciplinary Journal of Feminist Scholarship, Theory, and Aesthetics* Vol. 3, No. 1 (Spring 1991): 59–65; who published portions of chapters 4 and 5, respectively, in much earlier versions. Portions of chapter 2 are gratefully reprinted from, *The Emily Dickinson Journal* Vol. 1, No. 2 (1992): 30–53. Reprinted by permission of *The Emily Dickinson Journal.*

Grateful acknowledgment is given as well to the following sources for permission to reprint material:

The poem, "Myth," from *Breaking Open* by Muriel Rukeyser. Copyright © 1973 by Muriel Rukeyser. Reprinted by permission of Random House, Inc.

Passages from *The Poems of Emily Dickinson*. Reprinted by permission of the publishers and the Trustees of Amherst College from *The Poems of Emily Dickinson*, edited by Thomas H. Johnson, Cambridge, Mass.: The Belknap Press of Harvard University Press, Copyright © 1951, 1955, 1979, 1983 by the President and Fellows of Harvard College.

Passages from *The Complete Poems of Emily Dickinson* edited by Thomas H. Johnson. Copyright © 1929, 1935 by Martha Dickinson Bianchi; copyright © renewed 1957, 1963 by Mary L. Hampson. Reprinted by permission of Little, Brown and Company.

Passages from *The Letters of Emily Dickinson*. Reprinted by permission of the publishers from *The Letters of Emily Dickinson* edited by Thomas H. Johnson, Cambridge, Mass.: The Belknap Press of Harvard University Press, Copyright © 1958, 1986 by the President and Fellows of Harvard College.

Passages from *The Complete Poems of Marianne Moore*. Reprinted with permission of Simon & Schuster from *The Collected Poems of Marianne Moore*. Copyright 1935 by Marianne Moore, renewed 1963 by Marianne Moore and T. S. Eliot. Copyright 1941, 1944, and renewed 1969, 1972, by Marianne Moore.

Passages from *The Complete Prose of Marianne Moore* by Patricia C. Willis, Editor. Copyright © 1986 by Patricia C. Willis. Used by permission of Viking Penguin, a division of Penguin Books USA Inc.

Passages from Marianne Moore's unpublished papers. Reprinted by permission of the Rosenbach Museum and Library, Philadelphia, and Bryn Mawr College. Permission for the quotations from Marianne Moore's unpublished notebooks and mss, *The Marianne Moore Reader*, and the poem "Roses Only" (*Observations*, 1924), granted by Marianne Craig Moore, Literary Executor for the Estate of Mariane Moore. All rights reserved.

Passages from H.D.'s *Collected Poems 1912–1944*. Copyright 1925 by H. D. Copyright © 1957, 1969 by Norman Holmes Pearson, Copyright © 1982 by the Estate of H.D., Copyright © 1983 by Perdita Schaffner. Reprinted by permission of New Directions Publishing Corporation.

Passages from *Helen in Egypt*. Copyright © 1961 by Norman Holmes Pearson. Reprinted by permission of New Directions Publishing Corporation.

Passages from *Tribute to Freud*. Copyright © 1956, 1974 by Norman Holmes Pearson. Reprinted by permission of New Directions Publishing Corporation.

Quotations from H.D.'s unpublished letters and manuscripts. Reprinted by permission of the Yale Collection of American Literature, Beinecke Rare Book and Manuscript Library, Yale University.

Passages from *The Fact of a Doorframe*. Reprinted from *The Fact of a Doorframe, Poems Selected and New, 1950–1984*, by Adrienne Rich, by permission of the author and W. W. Norton & Company, Inc. Copyright © 1984 by Adrienne Rich. Copyright © 1975, 1978 by W. W. Norton & Company, Inc. Copyright © 1981 by Adrienne Rich.

Passages from *Diving into the Wreck*. Reprinted from *Diving into the Wreck, Poems 1971–1972*, by Adrienne Rich, by permission of the author and W. W. Norton & Company, Inc. Copyright © 1973 by W. W. Norton & Company, Inc.

Passages from *A Wild Patience Has Taken Me This Far*. Reprinted from *A Wild Patience Has Taken Me This Far, Poems 1978–1981*, by Adrienne Rich, by permission of the author and W. W. Norton & Company, Inc. Copyright © 1981 by Adrienne Rich.

Passages from *An Atlas of the Difficult World*. Reprinted from *An Atlas of the Difficult World, Poems 1988–1991*, by Adrienne Rich, by permission of the author and W. W. Norton & Company, Inc. Copyright © 1991 by Adrienne Rich.

Finally, I am deeply grateful to my family, whose care and encouragement preceded as well as accompanied this project: my father, Earl Hogue, who taught me that comic relief is essential and regeneration possible; my sister, Christine Stegel, who intervened and gave me the chance to change my life; Elaine Hogue, my sister in spirit as well as fact, whose friendship gave me the courage to transform consciousness; and my mother, Evangeline Hogue, who instilled in me her own love of language, intellectual curiosity, and creativity, whose loving support and friendship over the years (including a stint assisting me in my research at the Beinecke!) has sustained me; in short, who catalyzed my journey in more ways than I can count.

To my husband, friend, and fellow traveler, Jón Haukur Ingimundarson, my love and gratitude. Engaged in his own theoretical and field research in anthropology, he spent many hours brainstorming with me on mine, reading chapter drafts, inspiring me, accompanying me on research trips, as well as covering household chores so I could bring the project to completion this summer while I was teaching. Even as our work has separated us in the past few years, I could always count on his support, his devotion, and his belief in me, and that knowledge has sustained me in darker hours. For all he has done, for who he is, I thank him. He has encouraged me with love and by example to seek, if not *the* truth, *my* truth, and so I have. And continue.

Abbreviations

DICKINSON

L – *The Letters of Emily Dickinson,* ed. Thomas H. Johnson and Theodora Ward (Cambridge: Harvard University Press, 1958). Citations are by letter number.

P – *The Poems of Emily Dickinson,* ed. Thomas H. Johnson (Cambridge: Harvard University Press, 1955). Citations are by poem number.

MOORE

P – *The Complete Poems of Marianne Moore* (New York: Macmillan, 1967).

CP – *The Complete Prose of Marianne Moore,* ed. Patricia C. Willis (New York: Viking, 1986).

MMR – *A Marianne Moore Reader* (New York: Viking, 1961).

RML – Moore's unpublished letters, notebooks, and manuscripts used in this study are housed at the Rosenbach Museum and Library in Philadelphia, cited as *RML,* followed by the appropriate file number.

H.D.

HE – Helen in Egypt (New York: New Directions, 1961).

TF – Tribute to Freud (New York: New Directions, 1984).

CP – Collected Poems, 1912–1944, ed. Louis L. Martz (New York: New Directions, 1983).

YCAL/Beinecke – H.D.'s unpublished letters and manuscripts used in this study are housed in the Yale Collection of American Literature, Beinecke Rare Book and Manuscript Library, Yale University, cited as *YCAL*/Beinecke, accompanied by the date.

RICH

ARP – Adrienne Rich's Poetry, ed. Barbara Charlesworth Gelpi and Albert Gelpi (New York: W. W. Norton, 1975).

ADW – An Atlas of the Difficult World: Poems 1988–1991 (New York: W. W. Norton, 1991).

BBP – Blood, Bread and Poetry: Selected Prose, 1979–1985 (New York: W. W. Norton, 1986).

DW – Diving into the Wreck: Poems 1971–1972 (New York: W. W. Norton, 1973).

FD – The Fact of a Doorframe, Poems Selected and New 1950–1984 (New York: W. W. Norton, 1984).

OWB – Of Woman Born: Motherhood As Experience and Institution (New York: Bantam, 1977).

LSS – On Lies, Secrets, and Silence: Selected Prose 1966–1978 (New York: W. W. Norton, 1979).

WP – A Wild Patience Has Taken Me This Far: Poems 1978–1981 (New York: W. W. Norton, 1981).

Preface

The poet, or "the man of beauty," as Ralph Waldo Emerson proclaims in "The Poet," "stands among partial men for the complete man." But what of his counterpart, the woman of beauty? She stands, of course, in a very different relation to poetic tradition. She is the object, not the subject, of poetic contemplation (and her death, as Edgar Allan Poe representatively, if excessively, states in "The Philosophy of Composition," is the "most poetical topic in the world"). In order to write themselves into the scene of such complete absence as subjects, women poets had to wrest the rhetoric of poetic power from the domain of exalted masculine selfhood in which it was inscribed and, as feminist studies have amply demonstrated, transcribe it for their own use.[1] Modified by aesthetic and cultural codes, female poets also transform them.

The inquiry that follows will examine the nature of poetic subjectivity in the works of Emily Dickinson, Marianne Moore, H.D., and Adrienne Rich. These poets—disempowered because of their sex, but privileged because of class and race—share a relation to white male hegemony that inflects the construction of their subjectivity in poetic language in discernible ways. None of the categories of masculine poetic projects (the Romantics' egotistical subject, the modernists' objective image free of subjectivity,[2] the postmodern desubjectivized lyric,[3] to name but a few) applies neatly to their poetry. Yet these four poets surely stand out as female counterparts to their male peers. They had similar access to the advantages, if not the direct line into attendant social and professional networks, of their class, and were able to claim powerful poetic identities.[4]

The purpose that unifies this book, however, is the concern to demonstrate how these female poets exemplify a destructuring of the very poetic power they assert, what I call, for the purposes of this study, an *ethical* poetic practice. Dickinson, Moore, H.D., and Rich, I argue, share a refusal not simply of the trivialized identity of "poetess," but of the socially idealized identity of "poet" and all that it can be said to represent symbolically. They variously unsettle and redefine the valorized discursive positions male poets have traditionally assumed, which Jonathan Culler in his analysis of the figure of apostrophe terms "poetic pretension":[5] the speaker's assertion in Walt Whitman's "Crossing Brooklyn Ferry," for example, that "what I shall assume you shall assume." In not reproducing positions of dominance indicative of larger cultural trends, these poets, I suggest, are paradigmatic of important alternatives. My project adds to the more densely realized historical studies of American women's poetic traditions by providing close readings that are informed by the semiotic attentiveness poststructuralist and feminist theories have taught us.[6] Because each chapter's discussion is grounded in and develops out of each poet's specific poetics, however, such theories amplify my approach rather than are imposed on individual texts. The following three schematic divisions, although not so discrete or equally prominent in the text proper, will serve to clarify the organizing features of this book.

First, I examine how poetic subjectivity is an issue of sexual difference because of the division instituted in female subjects by the split in identification between object and subject of poetic discourse. Beginning with Dickinson, I demonstrate how such a split schemes a female poetic subjectivity as divided (hence the book's title). These subjects are thereby able to resist strategically the ideology of gender purveyed through the lyric's pervasive image cluster: active masculine/passive feminine. All four poets can be said to displace woman as sign of lack and loss by foregrounding, rather than dispensing with, difference. My discussion of the various schisms at the level of figure, logic, and schematic structure that typify these poetic subjects is the basis for the hypothesis that such divided subjects decenter dominant tropes of femininity and hegemonic subject positions more generally.

Second, the conflation of femininity and maternity is such a broad cultural pattern that I have spent some time addressing the contradictions surrounding images of the maternal in the poetry under discussion.[7] If poetic language exposes the operations whereby we invest in fixed representations, and if it does so through a maternally connoted discursive register (the *semiotic chora*) apparent in poetry, as Julia Kristeva postulates, then images of and discourse on the maternal in these poets' work can be approached as sites of ambivalence evincing both rejection of and identification with dominant versions of the maternal. Although I argue that these poets refuse to reduce femininity to maternity, the "normative" pattern, they reject the conventions to which they were enjoined to conform. They do not refuse the mother, as in the masculine scenario. Rather, they either deconstruct that scenario, as in Moore's and H.D.'s work, or redefine "her," as do Dickinson and Rich. The maternal figures they inscribe are often revisionary, in Rich's well-known sense of the term.

Finally, I suggest that these poets share a rhetorical feature I have termed "equivocation," related to the specificity of their class position. Although I postulate that this poetic strategy is class-specific, I am not claiming that the methodology is solely employed by the class of women poets I treat (it is not, that is, class-exclusive). As an intervention upon the male control of woman's image and voice in the genre most concerned with those features, the strategy is open to all women. But in the composing process, I began to notice a similarity in ambiguous subject positions that seemed, finally, to indicate a method these poets might share in their relation to male-dominated culture and discourse. The notion of equivocation thus evolved from close textual readings. I expanded the idea to conceptualize it as a double linguistic operation that not only resists unified meaning, but refuses to occupy a position from which semantic fixity can be imperially proclaimed. Because my intention is not to stabilize a definition of a destabilizing strategy, my application of the term itself shifts in this study. My purpose is to characterize a discursive methodology that operates as a way of both disrupting and redefining relations of subjectivity to positions of power.

I came to associate equivocation, as a strategy of apparent compliance and actual resistance to the androcentric order, with Darlene Clark Hines's theory of black women's dissemblance and Gloria Anzaldúa's notion of latina women's *mestiza* consciousness,
which theorize strategies of doubling and masquerade that women
of color employ in order to subvert ánd survive white hegemony.[8]
Aída Hurtado contends that the difference between white women's
and women of color's relation to white masculine hegemony is
characterized precisely by their differing relationship to privilege,
construed, I should add, within the institution of heterosexuality.
She asserts that white women are seduced by their proximity to
hegemonic men, while women of color are excluded from even the
semblance of privilege (white women's actual status) by reason of
their unacceptable difference. Although Hurtado overgeneralizes
to make a point, her work has helped me to resist idealizing
assumptions of commonality among women, as well as to clarify
how these poets relate to privilege as well as to oppression.[9] I use
the term *woman* throughout to indicate the symbolic function of the
feminine, not women themselves (the same principle functions in
my use of the term *man*). When I do generalize about women, I
have tried to be consistent in making statements that might be
applicable to all women without conflating them into one entity
(women not woman). As such, I hope to contribute to our understanding of poetry as inflected by female subjects, as well as to postulate that the ways the poets here under discussion dismantle the
conventional lyric's valorized subjectivity exemplify revised relations to dominant structures of power.

Having summarized the general concerns of my study, I would
like briefly to turn to the substance of the individual chapters. Chapter 1 posits a gendered but provisional subjectivity through a critical
rereading of Kristeva's complex work on revolutionary poetic language and subject formation as it relates to poetic practice and theorizes the role that figures prominently as the register in poetic language that disrupts identity—the repressed maternal. Following the
first two sections' treatment of male- and female-authored poems that
reproduce or redefine the specular lyric tradition through its most
significant feature, the erasure of the feminine, the third section
stages an intertextual theoretical discussion of Kristeva, Teresa de

Lauretis's theory of female subjectivity as experientially constituted, and Paul de Man's analysis of the disjunction between grammar and rhetoric. I elaborate a notion of difference, the scheming women of the title, that will serve to ground the study's examination of how Dickinson, Moore, H.D., and Rich variously divest themselves of valorized positions of poetic power. They do so through the strategy I have termed "equivocation," a discursive methodology, I will be suggesting in that section as well, that does not reinstate the privileged status it effectively destabilizes.

Chapter 2 examines Dickinson's inscriptions of self-erasure and division within a heterosexual construct. The split speaking subject in many of her poems resists identification with predominant cultural notions of femininity (as well as with a nascent feminism). Based on this thesis, the chapter compares the Dickinsonian sublime to the tradition. In reinstating the maternal/feminine abjected in conventions of the sublime in order to reconsolidate the subject, Dickinson gestures toward a tolerance of internal alterity transferred to the reader via "maternal" writing. Marianne Moore also seems to erase "herself" and renders idealized images of femininity and maternity ambivalent. Chapter 3 argues that such a disappearing act is a performance, however, and considers her elaborate public costuming in relation especially to masculine epistemological and poetic systems as strategic masquerade. I contend that Moore works to change the inequitable social order through a reformation of that by which it is represented–language. She dialogizes poetic discourse, depriviliging her own status as poet. Through a subjectivity remarkably feminist, she restores to the traditionally monologic lyric other voices as well as otherness.

In placing the most (in)famous figure of Western white feminine beauty squarely at the center of her late-life feminist epic, *Helen in Egypt*, H.D. plays with the reinstatement of that valorized image. Chapter 4 analyzes how she nonetheless decentralizes Helen's voice. Originating in part from H.D.'s analytic sessions with Freud in the early 1930s, her poem extends and poeticizes her critique of his theories of normative femininity as masculinist. Her relation to Freud as represented as well in *Tribute to Freud,* however, epitomizes the strategy of equivocation: for H.D., whose rereading of Freud was, interestingly enough, contemporaneous with Lacan's, taking one's place in language requires fixing one's gender identity within androcentric constructs. H.D. sought to destructure them. In conjunction with this notion, chapter 4 extensively examines *Helen in Egypt*'s critical representation of hegemonic masculinity. Unlike Dickinson and Moore, in whose works masculinity functions in the main in the abstract, it has an urgent specificity for H.D. in this poem. She poetically retheorizes its terrors of the maternal as projection and imaginatively poses the transformation of its unconscious, as well as the woman at once exalted and debased in its imaginary structures.

Finally, Adrienne Rich, like Dickinson and Moore, begins her poetic career in "self"-erasure and discreet performances,[10] and evolves, like H.D., fiercely and persistently to write "our names" into the "book of myths" in which they "do not appear," as "Diving into the Wreck" concludes (*DW*, 24). Her poetic project is characterized by its attempts to name and to define honestly the unnamed or misrepresented: maternal and feminine experience. Rich's work shares with the other poets' an ambivalence about maternal conventions, which chapter 5 will address in a discussion of both the transitional poem "Snapshots of a Daughter-in-Law" and Rich's cultural study of motherhood as experience and institution, *Of Woman Born*. In addition, her work helps us to amplify those concerns, because Rich's career represents an evolution from a utopian belief in a common female identity transcending boundaries of class, race, and sexual orientation, among others, to a painstaking record of her ongoing confrontation with the specificities of her own positioning. For Rich the issue became not how to claim a (white-defined) feminine poetic power, but how to give it up by denaturalizing her position as subject, as well as by transferring power to the reader. The chapter closes with a brief afterword that takes up this creative alchemy between reader and text, which Rich contemplates as the possibility of changing *political* poetry to political *activism*.

Scheming Women proceeds from analyses of strategies of resistance within heterosexual constructions, epitomized by poetic structures, to the inscription of bisexual and lesbian subjects attempting to extricate themselves not only from the framework of sociocultural hierarchies, but from implication in them. Although their subjectivities cannot be reduced to a unified feminine "one," Dickinson, Moore, H.D., and Rich represent, as I hope to demonstrate, the promise of ethical feminist poetic practices. These poets' practices neither uncritically reproduce dominant poetic codes, nor, following Kristeva, invest in a totalizing unity of the subject. An examination of non-white poetic subjectivities is admittedly beyond the scope of this study; I address Moore's and Rich's exposure of the racism as well as sexism in dominant cultural constructions, however, in poems which take up these issues. In considering the implications that poetic subjects divesting their positions of privilege might have for new ways of being, new ways of relating to identity and the processes of identification, my hope is to contribute to the connections, poetic and otherwise, that continue to expand the thinking about and the dialogue among women, between men and women, and about feminisms.

1 Conceiving a Girl

INTRODUCTION TO A FEMALE
POETIC SUBJECTIVITY

STORY OF A WOMAN WHO

Indeed, if woman had no existence save in the fiction written by men, one would imagine her a person of the utmost importance; very various; heroic and mean; splendid and sordid; infinitely beautiful and hideous in the extreme; as great as a man, some think even greater. But this is woman in fiction. . . .

A very queer, composite being thus emerges. Imaginatively she is of the highest importance; practically she is completely insignificant. She pervades poetry from cover to cover; she is all but absent from history.

—Virginia Woolf, *A Room of One's Own*

. . . images and symbols for *the woman cannot be isolated from images and symbols of the woman.*

—Jacques Lacan, "Guiding Remarks for a Congress on Feminine Sexuality"

⋙

The failure to possess the woman of the West's poetic legends is often the occasion for a poem's coming into existence. Displaying herself in some way, on a walk or with her flock, the woman invites notice (in essence, asks for it). The resulting demand on the part of the male, as Lacan tells us in another context, leads to language: for the poetic subject, the displacement of unfulfilled demand (desire) produces the poem; for the subject-in-process, entrance into

1

the social contract.[1] This displacement is as true of origin tales of poetry as it is of psychoanalytic scenarios of gender identity and subjectivity.

But poetry practices poetic license, taking an imaginary detour off the symbolic path. The violent appropriation of the feminine figure by the masculine that so often comprises in poetic convention the originary enunciatory moment—rape sublimated as poetic ravishing—illuminates the ideological specificity of sexual difference and its relation historically to poetry and aesthetic representation. The ideology of gender is inscribed in poetry through such hierachized images as dominating male/dominated female figures. A solitary woman is represented as violable; that is, she is intolerable when she remains independent of the man.[2] He must make his presence *felt.* Her protests of violation are brutally silenced by/in beautiful language. This pattern of the woman's loss of autonomy from the male term, *voice* as synecdoche for *self,* reveals that for the masculine subject woman "is unnecessary in and of herself, but essential as the non-subjective subjectum," as Luce Irigaray observes.[3] The poem must replace her, because the poet must prove the durability, the potency, of his word: gender violation slips handily into a trope for the creation of poetry itself.[4]

Ovid's *The Metamorphoses* plays upon and tells its stories through this slippage, suggesting not only that "the politics of violence [is] already encoded in rhetorical figures," as Barbara Johnson suggests,[5] but that it is encoded in the structural patterns of a text as well. Nancy J. Vickers contends, for example, that *The Metamorphoses* both illustrates the gender violence in Western cultural constructions and helped to institute it as a canonical poetic feature.[6] The tale of Syrinx epitomizes the heritage of occulting gender politics within the rubric of a universal poetics. Famous for her charms, her elusiveness, and her "bird-like voice" (and thus closely associated with Philomela),[7] Syrinx twittered and sang, "slipped through the clutches of the most nimble satyrs," and because of this inappropriability was by some mistaken for the virgin goddess, Diana.[8] But one day, Pan sees and chases her. This time, Syrinx cannot evade her pursuer, but she does frustrate his worst intentions. Her prayer to be rescued is answered: Pan seizes not a nymph but a "sheaf of reeds." Her metamorphosis is the lesser of two evils: Syrinx is "saved" by losing herself.

Pan, too, would seem to come out a loser in this turn of events, and yet he is satisfied, for "Pipes are my pleasure; they are mine to keep."[9] If he cannot have Syrinx, she is nevertheless his kept woman, her altered body his instrument, the very medium for his song. Because Pan's (proliferating) pipes function in the genre as a trope for poetry itself, the tale quite literally replaces Syrinx's voice with Pan's lyrics. Unlike Diana, Syrinx is not inviolable, cannot punish her ravisher, and disappears in the process of her own rescue. The unstable status that her metamorphosis represents indicates that what gets restabilized in Ovid's text is the symbolic threat to masculine identity posed by an autonomous feminine voice (and all that it represents synecdochically). When she is overtaken, her body as well as voice are taken over: the reeds are "broken," her lips (and, we presume, other orifices) sealed with wax. She becomes the vessel that conveys "divine" inspiration that is, as it will come down to us through the Romantics, poetry. As inscribed in this tale, woman's disembodiment spells man's gain of poetic inspiration. The reason underlying this repeatedly represented failure to possess the woman physically, that the poem *requires* the absence it seems to lament, is the point of Lacan's observation of that "staggering thing," the "fraud" central to Western poetic tradition, that "courtly love is the only way of coming off elegantly from the absence of sexual relation."[10]

Vickers's feminist analysis of the specularization and fragmentation of the female beloved that characterizes Renaissance love poetry exposes the violence central to the tradition as well, which the term *courtly love* elides. The Ovidian context that Petrarch brings to his poetic portraits of silenced and partial feminine beauty, she asserts, suggests that the relation between masculine seeing and feminine bodily dispersion, Laura-in-pieces (a poetic *corps morcèlé*) scattered throughout, is castration anxiety projected onto the figure of woman. Vickers contends that such portraits became a conventional gesture in Western lyric tradition because the resolution, the substitution of poem for woman, displaces the threat.[11]

According to Margaret Homans, the Biblical tradition transmitted through Milton culminates in the "Romantic reading of gender," which most often identifies the feminine with nature and silence, an otherness a masculine self can absorb and dominate.[12] Extending Homans's insights about British Romanticism to the later American Emersonian version, Joanne Feit Diehl argues that in order to be the poet of the common man, Emerson claims the "common" (feminine) domestic sphere for poetic activities at the same time as he denies woman access to the soul's affective life. He thereby doubly disempowers women.[13] Mary Nyquist speculates that the figure of woman in poetry, especially as muse, has to some degree always been represented as "the other who makes possible the creative articulateness of the male voice," hence the obsessive representation of mute, dead, or silenced feminine figures.[14] The image of the male poet as seer and prophet—"Walt Whitman, a kosmos," to name but one example—has produced a fetishized version in the lyric of discourse that occults the ideology of gender, as Teresa de Lauretis asserts of aesthetic structures in general, as well as suppresses the material conditions of gendered experience. That image of the lone male poet as visionary purports to represent universal experience.

Joel Fineman's analysis of Shakespeare's sonnets elaborates the implications of the trajectory I am reviewing. Noting the emphasis in the lyric on visual imagery as well as on subjectivity, he examines Aristotelian metaphor, "to see the same," and characterizes this reflexive generic feature as "the orthodox homogeneity and homosexuality of the poetics of praise."[15] His thesis supports feminist critiques of structuralism—most famously, of Claude Lévi-Strauss's contention that women function like words and things, not subjects, in the symbolic exchange systems that establish bonds, networks, and alliances among men—and helps to confirm that aesthetic as well as social structures are, to invoke Irigaray, *hom(m)ological* in nature.[16] Similarly observing the paradox that characterizes Lévi-Strauss's thinking on this point, de Lauretis states that "One can only conclude that . . . this human subject is male."[17] Speaking of deep sociocultural structures and symbolic patterns, Irigaray has argued that woman is "never anything but the locus of a more or less competitive exchange between two men."[18]

Shelley's "Hymn of Pan," which portrays Pan as insisting on the potency of his songs after he has lost a musical competition to Apollo (a loss Pan suppresses), epitomizes such an exchange. The poem represents within its framework of direct address not only the symbolic structure that pertains to this discussion, but the violent process by which it is reified. Shelley's depiction of Pan suggests that desire posits poetic subjectivity, an implication that apostrophe exposes better than it conceals. Throughout the poem, Pan portrays Apollo as listening, "silent with love" and "envy" of Pan's "sweet pipings."[19] But by the end, it is clear that Apollo is "frozen," not with love or envy, but with indifference, a listener only because the device of apostrophe constitutes him as one. Culler examines how a poet employs apostrophe to posit an inanimate or unresponsive object as another subject, in order to assert "the condition of visionary poet who can engage in dialogue with the universe." The device figures the poetic subject's claim that he does not merely write verse, but embodies "poetic tradition and the spirit of poesy."[20] Although he has lost the contest, Pan can still win if his songs move Apollo to tears.

In the poem's resolution, Pan's recollection of his frustrated attempt to possess a "maiden" (he suppresses not only Syrinx's name but the reason for her metamorphosis) changes both Pan's line of thought, his *tune*, and the poem's theme:

> And then I changed my pipings,–
> Singing how down the vale of Maenalus
> I pursued a maiden and clasped a reed.
> Gods and men, we are all deluded thus!
> (lines 29–32)

The elusive maiden replaced by the reed becomes sign for the epistemological crisis that Pan, as representative of the male poetic subject, finally confronts. But in order to close with a universalized claim in the tradition of philosophical idealism, that appearances are deceptive, the text must suppress the literal violence, a discursive trace of which it restores at the end. The allusion, like the thematic interruption, creates a break in the formal surface of the poem through which the *other* frozen body surfaces: Syrinx's living body has been permanently "frozen" into the image of the dead reed that she quickly became in Pan's hands. Her fate is the inverse of Pan's attempted animation of Apollo: originally animate, Syrinx has been rendered inanimate.

Pan's suppression underscores the masculine creative investment in its representations of the feminine, the tendency to jettison woman in order to consolidate a unitary masculine subject (a point I will take up more closely in chapter 2 in relation to Dickinson and the sublime), as well as the revelation that it is Apollo, not Syrinx, that Pan wishes to engage in (poetic) intercourse. But in representing the real nature of Apollo's indifference to Pan, the homological, specular desire that occasions the Romantic male subject's entry into language, Shelley's poem endorses the masculine social bonds that Irigaray criticizes for being exclusionary.

Although surely ironic, his portrait of the artist rehearses the appropriation of the feminine in the service of poetry. Pan's desire for Apollo's rather than Syrinx's attentions is based on the generic tradition of a richly self-reflexive construct. Male poets in Western tradition have been free to ponder metaphysical and aesthetic "truths" (for example, the valorization of Apollonion constraint over Dionysian excess), without concern for whether such "universal truths" could in fact be true for all. Even those poets whose works are most associated with a radical revision and subversion of the lyric "I" illustrate the rhetorical blind spot of Western poetic tradition that figures woman but grammatically elides women.

Consider Whitman, whose poetry has significantly influenced twentieth-century fictions and inflections of Western poetic subjectivity. The Romantic speaker in "Out of the Cradle Endlessly Rocking" locates his origins as poet, as well as the source of the poem itself, in the disappearance of a female bird. The speaker construes a performative transformation of identity at the expense, in effect, of the feminine.[21] Through a series of curious reversals after the bird's departure, the "curious child" is able to pronounce himself "the outsetting bard."

The speaker's description of watching the nesting birds anticipates the poetic authority he will come to assume. Although he keeps his distance spatially, the speaker imaginatively violates the birds. Privy to their language, he is also privy to its meaning, "never too close, never disturbing them, / Cautiously peering, absorbing, translating" (lines 30–31).[22] The boy already stands in the privileged position of visionary poet able to comprehend the incomprehensible, which the transformation into bardic identity thus merely formalizes.

We should by now not be surprised at the dynamic that structures such self-recognition. The constitution of this self-creating "bard" rests on the boy replacing the lost mate. Listening to the male bird's lament unleashes "love in the [boy's] heart" (line 137) and arouses "the fire, the sweet hell within, / The unknown want, the destiny of me" (lines 156–57), awakening the boy's own "songs." Desire comes into being, not only as a function of his voyeuristic gaze, but as a relationship established between two male figures catalyzed by the departure of the feminine figure. The distance between the speaker and the birds collapses in an imaginatively reversed apostrophe that disguises its performative *léger-de-voix* (so to speak): the boy asks whether it is "toward your mate you sing? Or is it really to me?" (line 145). But if the boy seems now to stand rhetorically in the place of the beloved, his "translations" (the poetic text) have subtly replaced not only the vanished female bird, but the male bird's lament itself.[23]

The boy / bard's songs find their source not in the discovery of sexuality, as the text claims, but in the recognition that desire translates into poetic identity. The rites of passage into sexuality symbolize the boy's more significant passage into textuality,[24] as the speaker's earlier use of "translation" suggests. His coming into an authorizing relationship to words is consummated by the revelation that he can translate "The word of the sweetest song and all songs" that the "old crone" sea whispers to him: "death" (lines 180–82). The last line ("The sea whisper'd me") is ambiguous, suggesting both that the sea whispers to the boy and that "she" speaks, metaphorically *bears*, the bard into being. But either reading makes the poet present to himself. The speaker's capacity to pronounce the "final" word is the sign of his birth not only into poetic identity but into linguistic authority. The bard's newly attained poetic power to inspire, to put words in the mouth of, the omnipotent crone / sea, who can then be represented as speaking him into being, is the very sign of that authority (and, incidentally, the final ironic reversal of the poem). The text's proliferating voices–the speaker's "thousand . . . songs," his "translations" of the bird's lament, the sea's whisperings–arguably cannot be "contained" within a unified "one." But tellingly, the repressed of Whitman's poem, like that of Shelley's, is the sexual politics that structure it.

The claims for poetry, from its being divine inspiration to its being the unselfconscious expression of an individual voice overheard, have rendered it an especially idealized (or, to put it another way, defensive) discourse. While the work of such theorists as Culler and Paul de Man has helped to expose the idealizing tendencies of the genre, male-authored poststructuralist writing has itself perpetuated the dynamic of "the putting into discourse of 'woman'" to valorize a masculine activity in writing, as Alice Jardine aptly characterized the pattern she termed *gynesis* some time ago. Jardine's question, What do these discourses have to do with women?[25] is not simply rhetorical, since it poses the distinction between woman, as symbolic sign, and real women, as speaking subjects, on which de Lauretis has insisted as well.

A wry poem invoked by de Lauretis that raises this question as a grammatical issue is Muriel Rukeyser's "Myth," which I quote in full:

> Long afterward, Oedipus, old and blinded, walked the
> roads.   He smelled a familiar smell.   It was
> the Sphinx.   Oedipus said, "I want to ask one question.
> Why didn't I recognize my mother?"   "You gave the
> wrong answer," said the Sphinx.   "But that was what
> made everything possible," said Oedipus.   "No," she said,
> "When I asked, What walks on four legs in the morning,
> two at noon, and three in the evening, you answered,
> Man.   You didn't say anything about woman."
> "When you say Man," said Oedipus, "you include women
> too. Everyone knows that."   She said, "That's what
> you think."[26]

While the poem pokes lighthearted fun at masculinist fantasies of linguistic inclusion (as well as of odorless femininity!), it also draws very pointed connections between grammatical exclusion, rhetorical misreading, and the subsequent tragic (and implicitly *preventable*) consequences of inclusionary fictions. In so doing, it illustrates Craig Owens's assertion that women artists are concerned to address "what representation *does* to women (for example, the way it invariably positions them as objects of the male gaze)."[27]

The difference between two modern versions of Helen, one by W. B. Yeats and the other by H.D., further exemplifies Owens's point. Yeats's "No Second Troy" images Maude Gonne as Helen, it would first seem, to elevate her beauty to a mythic level: it is "not natural in an age like this" (line 9).[28] But the analogy excoriates Maude, who in teaching "most violent ways" has, we are encouraged to conclude, not only filled the speaker's days "[w]ith misery" but made a spectacle of herself. In suppressing the context of Maude's political commitment to Irish independence in order to lay a personal blame at her door (in addition, the final question, "Was there another Troy for her to burn?" [line 12], demonstrates a curious confusion of agency), Yeats's poem suggests how, in order to be rendered solely in relation to the male term, the woman behind the figure of woman must be decontextualized. H.D.'s poem "Helen" reproduces the process of such iconicization of woman, but is concerned to demonstrate that it has literally lethal consequences for women. Lingering over the parts of Helen's body (that is, miming the Petrarchan gesture), the text portrays her slow death beneath the castigating as well as fetishizing gaze of "All Greece," metonym for the force of the whole patriarchal history of blaming the woman (*CP*, 154–55). The pallor of this woman both damned and deified for her beauty is, as Susan Stanford Friedman has remarked, a deathly one.[29] By the final stanza, her perfect "white face" has turned to "white ash amid funereal cypresses," literally and figuratively dematerialized by the objectifying eye of scopic and cultural judgment.

Following Catharine A. MacKinnon, de Lauretis contends that because art has historically upheld women's socialization as sexual objects, reiterating as well as regulating the power differential between men and women that characterizes the institution of heterosexuality, aesthetics is a *political* subject.[30] Like Woolf in the epigraph that opened this chapter, de Lauretis emphasizes that the figure of woman is paradoxical, "a being that is at once captive and

absent in discourse, ... displayed as spectacle and still unrepresented or unrepresentable,"[31] and asserts the need to maintain the
distinction between woman and women. The Rukeyser and H.D.
poems discussed above confront the problem in grammar and representation that de Lauretis calls a real and irreconcilable contradiction: that "women continue to become woman."[32] Woman is
present in rhetoric, trope, figure; but women are absent in grammar, logic, scheme. Ironizing the (il)logic of women's place in relation to men, Rukeyser as well as H.D. find there is none—*nowhere* in
the conventional scheme of things other than for scheming woman,
who *is* present grammatically as well as figuratively, as the always-
marked term. What is a woman to say?

An example that will serve to illustrate an alternative is posed
by Elizabeth Barrett Browning, the poet who represented for Emily
Dickinson both poetic foremother and the proto-feminist claim to
female poetic subjectivity. Invoking Irigaray, de Lauretis asserts
that if women's perspectival difference, their "view from 'elsewhere,'" still seems invisible, it is not because women artists (or
feminist theorists) have not succeeded in producing it. Rather, it is

> that what we have produced is not recognizable, precisely,
> as a representation. For that "elsewhere" is not some mythic
> distant past or some utopian future history: it is the else-
> where of discourse here and now, the blind spots, or the
> space-off, of its representations.[33]

Barrett Browning's retelling of the Pan/Syrinx myth, "A Musical
Instrument," shares similarities with the male-authored heritage,
most notably the outline of its plot. But its differences prefigure de
Lauretis's insight that the "elsewhere" of women's perspectives is
already encoded in the "space-offs" of hegemonic discourse. The
repetition of the same story does not, that is, produce the Same
story.[34]

Like the Shelley and Whitman poems, Barrett Browning's
raises questions about poetic power, identity, and subjectivity. But
in dwelling on Pan's mutilation of the living reed to make his pipes,
"A Musical Instrument" dissects, rather than glosses over or roman-
ticizes, the violence of the originary moment. Pan "hacked and

hewed" until "there was not a sign of the leaf" (lines 15, 17).[35] He "cut" the once "tall" reed "short," "then drew the pith, like the heart of a man," and "notched the poor dry empty thing / In holes" (lines 23–24). As in the canonical tale, the reed is killed to bear art forth. It is imaged as masculine, not feminine, however first implicitly in the fourth stanza in the likening of the reed's pith to a man's heart, and then explicitly in the last stanza when Pan is described as "Making a poet out of a man" (line 39). In Barrett Browning's version, considerably more than Syrinx's body has been transformed. The chilling scene of "creation" that displaces the attempted rape in Ovid's tale characterizes the relation between poetry and poetic power as permanently disfiguring.

Paradoxically, the poet gains (rather than loses, like Syrinx) his identity through this process. The poem's explicit theme is whether the disfiguration that gain entails is worth the "pain" it cost the poet. As the reed's leaves are hacked off, its height cropped, its insides emptied, the poem visually associates it with the male "instrument" itself. It irreverently reproduces the homological poetic structure reviewed above, as well as the accompanying tendency in the lyric to homogenize voices. Because of the connections the text draws between poetic power, masculinity, and violence, Barrett Browning's insight in this poem thus seems a radical one.

Anticipating Vickers's compelling point, the poem suggests that the sadomasochistic fantasy of divine ravishment that defines the romantic poet is transfigured castration anxiety.[36] It inscribes the simultaneous reassurance of and threat to masculinity that, Barrett Browning's text indicates, writing poetry seems to entail for male poets (hence so many of the defenses of poetry are couched in the rhetoric of a revised "manliness").[37] The act that most establishes the reed as male, the hacking off of the leaves to reveal the reed's phallic attributes, also depicts the process that transforms man into poet as emasculating, producing an ambiguity of gender. No longer feminine, the reed is nevertheless not wholly masculine either: after cutting it down to size, Pan reintroduces the "holes" that Barrett Browning's version has previously erased. This effeminization of the reed suggests the fine line between the reed's masculinization and the poet's emasculation.

In the space between them, Barrett Browning implies that the engendering of violence is a defensive posture against castration anxiety (a point to which we will return in chapter 4), the masculine subject projecting fears of gender ambiguity onto the feminine. She thereby renders the invisible elsewhere a visible here-and-now, intervening upon the conventional image of woman as passive vessel through which lyric song is born. Pan's notching activity *re*inscribes the identifying feminine lack ("holes") as already within the masculine.[38] The "feminine" is symbolically altered, no longer a sign now for the male poet's empowerment but more accurately a screen image for a masculine hysteria, the male subject in crisis. Barrett Browning subtly re-presents poetic identity as emasculated, uncannily effeminized, indeterminately bisexualized (in a word, problematically *feminine*),[39] encoding the cultural heritage of gender asymmetry as an "empty" misrecognition.

Substantively rewriting the earlier versions of Syrinx's loss of voice, Barrett Browning exposes the sexual politics on which traditional lyric conventions are based. She transforms the textual implication that women were absent from the "divine scene" of poetic production, as she calls it elsewhere, into a critique of the scene itself. Her transsexualization of the reed shifts the perspective on the conventional codes. Although the poem astutely intuits masculine posturing as defensive, however, revealing its stature to be an illusion (though a grand one), Barrett Browning's "solution" to women's defilement by the signifier (to paraphrase Lacan) is, as it were, a dissolution. As John Fletcher observes, the poem leaves unanswered how one might make "a poet out of a woman."[40] It reproduces the historical silencing of women poets Barrett Browning otherwise decried, a protest with which the next section will open.

A WOMAN OF DEEP ACQUIREMENTS

England has had many learned women, not merely readers but writers of the learned languages, in Elizabeth's time and afterwards—women of deeper acquirements than are common now in the greater diffusion of letters; and yet where were the poetesses? The divine breath . . . why did it never pass, even in the lyrical form, over the lips of a woman? How strange! And

can we deny that it was so? I look everywhere for grandmothers and see none. It is not in the
filial spirit I am deficient, I do assure you—witness my reverent love of the grandfathers!
                                                    —Elizabeth Barrett Browning, *Letters*

-≫

Full of questions and exclamations, this famous passage from Barrett Browning's letters is a text at odds with itself.[41] The statement
about the erudition of women in the past is part of a coordinated
structure: a question follows the first clause that attenuates the
assurance of women's historical accomplishments ("and yet . . . ").
To be sure, the passage insists on the inexplicability of women's
absence from the "divine" scene of poetic production, but we look
everywhere for *authorial* assurance and see none except the insistence on "filial spirit."

But because we see nothing, is there nothing to see? Barrett
Browning protests too much. The grandmothers may be absent, but
she commands visibility ("witness my reverent love"). The grandmothers may have been deficient, but she is sufficient, for reasons
having less to do with of her reverence for the grandfathers than
with her striking rhetorical strategy. Her insistent questioning of
why poetry alone of all literary genres was not written by women,
and her choice of the exclamatory "strange" to characterize that
(uncanny) absence, are cast within the framework of the idealization of poetic discourse. That miming of the Romantic defense of
poetry calls attention to itself, at the same time as it deflects focus
from the implications of her meaning.

Barrett Browning poses the issue of the grandmothers' absence
as a rhetorical question ("can we deny that it was so?"). De Man has
usefully analyzed the specific ambiguity of the rhetorical question,
in reference to the last line of Yeats's "Among School Children"
("How can we know the dancer from the dance?"). The grammatical model of the question is itself devoid of ambiguity, he asserts,
but signifies through its rhetorical mode two mutually exclusive
meanings—one at the literal, the other at the figurative, level. When
grammar and logic support each other, de Man observes, linguistic
as well thematic coherences are maintained. But when two entirely
contradictory meanings prevail, it being impossible to decide

between them, rhetoric "radically suspends logic," opening up "vertiginous possibilities of referential aberration."[42] By means of her rhetorical question, in other words, Barrett Browning manages vertiginously to say not only that we can, but at the same time that we *cannot,* deny that the "divine breath" has passed women's lips. The question opens a space in which to interrogate women's absence.

It is no coincidence, of course, that sexual difference plays a part in both instances of this "rhetorization of grammar," de Man's term for the semantic effect, as that which is present but un(re)marked by de Man himself. Nor is it accidental that issues of thematic consistency, schematic and figural symmetry, and rhetorical balance arise in the context of an analysis of an intersexual dialogue about "difference" that he canonizes: Archie and Edith Bunker's (his first example of the rhetorization of grammar). One must not "yield," de Lauretis dryly remarks, to such "referential aberrations." De Man, for instance, goes on to erase the eruption of gendered differences by discussing Yeats and Proust, analyzing the grammatization (mechanization) of rhetoric and demonstrating finally that poetic writing is not irresolvably indeterminate (as perhaps is gender difference), though it be "forever the most rigorous and . . . the most unreliable language in terms of which man names and modifies himself."[43] There is "something accurate about [the] repeated dramatization of woman as simulacrum, erasure, or silence," Barbara Johnson remarks: "For it would not be easy to assert that the existence and knowledge of the female subject could simply be produced, without difficulty or epistemological damage, within the existing patterns of culture and language."[44] The rhetorical contortions of Barrett Browning's brief passage, like those in "A Musical Instrument," attest to her awareness of the threat to epistemological systems (and her male reader's comfort) were women to have drawn breath in that rarified masculine air of poetry. But the passage also dramatizes how Barrett Browning strategizes her position as speaking subject equivocally, within "existing patterns" of grammar and rhetoric, by logically suspending logic. She constitutes herself as the referential aberration contradicting women's absorption into symbolic figuration.

It is in such a radical suspension of coherence between logic, grammatical pattern, and rhetorical mode that I locate the pun in this study's title, *scheming* women. In classical rhetoric, which de Man redefines as poetic writing, tropes are semantic deviations, while schemes are syntactic deviations, deviations of normative grammatical patterns. But schemes as well as tropes have been classified as figures, because such mechanical deviations also can influence a text's meaning. It is fairly self-evident that the basic distinction between schemes, nonsignifying deviations of word order (chiasmus, for example), and tropes, signifying semantic deviations (metaphor, for example), can blur, as a passage from Mary Jacobus's brilliant reading of Charlotte Perkins Gilman's "The Yellow Wallpaper" readily illustrates. Noting a moment in the story's climax structured by a chiasmus, Jacobus asserts:

> The figure here is the grammatical figure of chiasmus, or crossing (*OED*: "The order of words in one of two parallel clauses is inverted in the other"). "I pulled and she shook, I shook and she pulled" prepares us for the exchange of roles at the end, where the woman reading (and writing) the text becomes the figure of madness within it. Gilman's story hysterically embodies the formal or grammatical figure. . . .
> . . . Since chiasmus is at once a specular figure and a figure of symmetrical inversion, it could be regarded as the structure of phallogocentrism itself, where word and woman mirror only the presence of the (masculine) body, reinforcing the hierarchy man/woman, presence/absence.[45]

How can the syntactic inversion of the "order of words" (scheme) become a "grammatical figure" (a "mechanized" trope)? Throughout the passage, the borders between structural and figural features, scheme and trope, are chiastically crossed and confused. In order to theorize a female-authored text that represents chiasmus as a figure for the prison house that symbolic structures have been for women, Jacobus must perform the very rhetorization of grammar whose significance she is, in fact, analyzing. In order to read a woman's lines as lines written by a woman, in other words, Jacobus must read between them.

Julia Kristeva's theory of poetic language does not purport to conceptualize female subjectivity, but she does provide us with a linguistic pattern, a schematization of linguistic registers, that theorizes the feminine's (or more precisely, the maternal's) place in subjectivity as well as text. A scheme is a syntactic pattern, but a deviant one. Kristeva arguably does not allow for female subjectivity. In de Lauretis's view, as well as that of others, Kristeva's human subject—indeed, Kristeva herself—is thus "male."[46] Kristeva theorizes a *pattern*, perhaps a normative (shall we say "masculine"?) pattern, but one from which a woman can deviate. As the phrase *scheming women* implies and Johnson reminds us, however, it isn't easy to produce a female subject without epistemological damage to existing patterns of culture and language. Recognizing the specificity of women's differences is far more difficult or threatening than is the mimetic revelation of woman as sign (the substance of the first section's discussion).

As we have seen, rhetoric and grammar do not always support each other. Nor do Kristeva's analogous linguistic modalities of semiotic (nonsignifying) and symbolic (signifying) in her theory of subjectivity. Rather, rhetoric and grammar oscillate between support and subversion, and, in that schematic deviation from the normative order of things, form not only affects but resemanticizes content. De Man's anxiety about, as well as interest in, the resulting indetermination of this suspension of fixed meaning (an anxiety both Johnson and de Lauretis note as well) might suggest why, in the age of second wave feminism, he so fully erased the possibility of female subjectivity. (It is, for example, the last sentence of "Semiology and Rhetoric" that defines literature as the language in which "man names and modifies himself.") To recall the passage that opened this section, Barrett Browning's letter indicates that standard, or "masculine," techniques are of course employed by women as well as men, but when they are, both Owens and Jardine assert, they are "modified." Words, images, structures are resemanticized.

Women have functioned in the symbolic order not only as objects of exchange analogous with words and things, but in the social order as surfaces reflecting and augmenting masculinity, behind which they disappear. If representation conditions feminine sexuality and subjectivity, as Lacan implies in the quotation serving as an epigraph to this chapter; and if, as Jardine and de Lauretis have noted, women become conflated with the androcentric representation of femininity; and if the implication of that insight is that woman is represented but women are not; then how, one might ask, "can a girl be conceived?"[47] To respond to that question in terms of women's poetry, we must think what the Oedipus of Rukeyser's "Myth" and Johnson's "de Man" could not: we must reconsider the specificity of female subjects, and relate that particularity to the grammatical and rhetorical schematization sketched out above.

TO MAKE A POET OUT OF A WOMAN

The psychoanalytic staging of subject formation within the heterogeneity of language paves the way for grammatology, Kristeva claims.[48] Like many materialist feminists, as well as other "French feminists," Irigaray and Hélène Cixous among them, Kristeva assumes that representations are historically situated and ideologically produced. To change the socioeconomic scene, it is therefore necessary to alter radically the representational system. For the Kristeva of *Revolution in Poetic Language*, an alteration of master signifiers in the culture can potentially transform the social order and thus change the subject, which is constituted in symbolic discourse and lives through its representations. Because of the transference entailed in the act of reading (the reader identifies with the subject of the text), the *reading*, as well as writing, subject is altered by this revolutionary subjectivity.[49] Beginning in the nineteenth century, Kristeva asserts, avant-garde poetry articulates such a subject. My approach to the work of the poets on which this study focuses is to a great degree framed by this definition of poetry and subject.

Framed indeed. Kristeva forecloses on the possibility of women writing revolutionary poetic language. For her (at least in one incarnation, "Stabat Mater"), women's identification with their mothers causes them to lose themselves when they enter the symbolic order. Men, of course, must separate from their mothers in order to establish their identity. They gain from the abjection that establishes them in the symbolic order; women lose. Women poets are

Kristeva's blind spot, which can be usefully exposed if one reads her against as well as with the grain (a methodology her theory invites). She writes in a note to the translator, for example, that because the subject of *Revolution in Poetic Language* is "universal," she employs *he* to signify both sexes. She adds, however, that in "reality, feminine 'subjectivity' is a different question."[50] If the subject is universal, why is feminine subjectivity a "different question"? Although it is now a truism that "feminine subjectivity" is not a linguistic position that necessarily denotes female subjects, Kristeva's employment of the third-person masculine pronoun throughout *Revolution in Poetic Language* is remarkably consistent with her discussion of male poets. I am interested in examining the substance of this aside, this "different question," which is also, obviously, a question of difference in relation to poetic subject and text. To do so, I would like first to consider briefly her notion of universal subjectivity and revolutionary poetry.

Revolution in Poetic Language concurs in broad terms with Lacan on the subject's constitution. The child must separate from the mother, through the mirror stage and the discovery of castration, in order to introduce "the signifier/signified break" productive of both subjectivity and social communication. Identity is first experienced as both specular (the child's image unified in the mirror) and separate/divided (the image is not the child). In Kristeva's mirror stage, unlike Lacan's, the child mistakes neither its image nor the mother wholly for itself. It differentiates itself from, as well as identifies itself with, both. It is already instituted in processes of separation and identification that will be transferred to language, eventually enabling the subject (the signified) to acknowledge that it is not present in that which constitutes it (the signifier).[51] According to Kristeva, there is no seamless imaginary plenitude of maternal/ specular identification for the child. Although, as in Lacan's scenario, the father's intervention in the mother-child dyad inaugurates the child's entry into the social contract, Kristeva does not give his role the weight of initiation that Lacan does; she redistributes it to the mother. The Kristevan father merely fills a position in a structure already in place in the subject-to-be.[52]

Kristeva terms the subject's necessary but provisional assumption of a positionality (identification) the "thetic." The thetic is the "precondition for signification" because it recognizes the place of the Other (separation) in the processes of identification. The thetic marks the threshold of heterogeneous contradiction between the semiotic (nonsignifying elements) and the symbolic (signifying processes). The *Symbolic,* "an appropriate term for this always split unification," is comprised, then, of both *semiotic* and *symbolic* modalities.[53] This important distinction explains how Kristeva can locate the mirror stage in the Symbolic order, before the subject takes its place in language.

Her theory restores the repressed, the significance of the mother's role in the development of the subject. She casts this development as an early function of intrasubjective differentiation, which the mother regulates but into which the child does not assimilate her, that precedes the mirror stage and entrance into the symbolic. The confrontation between these actions prepares the subject-to-be for the transfer to the linguistic level of the negativity ("drive rejection") already present at the physiological level (for example, in bodily functions). This transfer institutes the symbolic rejection that undermines identity even as it is posited.[54] Kristeva brings the speaking body back into structuralism, Kelly Oliver explains, by reinscribing not only the body within language (biological drives), but language within the body: "For Kristeva, just as the pattern and logic of language are already found within the body, the pattern and logic of alterity are already found within the subject."[55]

Kristeva builds on Lacan's notions of fantasy, separation, castration, and division as integral to positing the subject in language. Rather than rejecting the symbolic order (because such a rejection would "open the way to psychosis," as Jacqueline Rose explains),[56] she concurs that it is the social realm and that our condition as split subjects is "the common destiny of the two sexes, men and women."[57] She agrees that men and women share a *linguistic* destiny. But in theorizing the place of the maternal function, her work diverges from orthodox psychoanalytic theory in a number of ways useful in thinking about gender, subjectivity, and poetry.

In postulating the semiotic *chora*, she attempts to theorize the importance of the mother all but absent in Lacan's and Freud's thinking. The *chora* is tied in with the preoedipal drives that "con-

nect and orient" the child's body to the mother, which are transferred to subjectivity. There is something "nourishing and maternal" as well as disruptive about the semiotic.[58] Although it
"logically and chronologically precedes the establishment of the
symbolic and its subject,"[59] it can only be "designated" by discourse, which "regulates" it. It precedes as well as underlies figuration and thus identification ("specularization") in and by language.
The *chora* marks the symbolic with the negativity that produces it
(the moment within linguistic unity that shatters it).[60] The *chora* and
the symbolic are, in sum, mutually constructive and destructive of
the subject.

Revolutionary poetic writing demonstrates this structuration.
Poetic language is a heterogeneous, signifying "process . . . a structuring and de-structuring *practice.*"[61] The text puts the interaction of
symbolic and semiotic modalities into a form that makes possible
the articulation of psychic processes and an engagement of the limits of meaning without becoming nonsense. Kristeva contends that
poetic prosody is not the representation of the unconscious (or, for
that matter, of the "real" in any of its senses), but "its expenditure,"
its discharge. Prosody "recalls," spatially and musically, the dialectical moment of signification, the subject-in-process, the double
articulation of signifier and signified.[62] In poetry it is obvious,
Oliver observes, that the meaningful but nonsignifying aspects of
prosody—rhythm, tone, music—are just as important as the signifying elements of language. (And to a poet, of course, it is obvious that
the distinction between signifying and nonsignifying meaning is
very difficult to maintain.) In the poetic text the heterogeneity in
the signifying function is at its most apparent: "Poetic language is
language that is also not language, language that is other to itself."[63]

Kristeva's poetic theory is reminiscent of de Man's grammar/
rhetoric split (or the reverse, as she claims). Poetic language "demonstrates that it is possible for a signifying process to be different
from the process of unifying conceptual thought."[64] Poetry is associated with social practices that unsettle bourgeois hegemony—eso-
tericism, shamanism, carnival—because, like them, poetry demysti-
fies the unifying operations of language and the symbolic bond
itself.[65] It is revolutionary in the sense that it articulates a crisis of
meaning to which it submits language that supports sociocultural

constructs. Rose recounts that in Kristeva's challenge to totalizing (and totalitarian) subjectivity and identity, in politics well as aesthetics, the question for her became "not how to disrupt language by leaving its recognisable forms completely *behind.*" Rather, psychoanalytic and deconstructive interests meet in her concern to examine how the psychic processes that language normally glosses over in the name of meaning and sense are nevertheless articulated in the symbolic order.[66] When the maternally connoted semiotic does not support the paternally connoted symbolic that "regulates" it, vertiginous possibilities of referential aberrations open up:

> Art—this semiotization of the symbolic—thus represents the flow of jouissance into language. . . . In cracking the socio-symbolic order, splitting it open, changing vocabulary, syntax, the word itself, and releasing from beneath them the drives borne by vocalic or kinetic differences, jouissance works its way into the social and symbolic. In contrast to sacrifice, poetry shows us that language lends itself to the penetration of the socio-symbolic by jouissance.[67]

Without this breakdown of meaning (*jouissance*), which for Kristeva maternity as well as poetry mobilizes, the subject-in-contradiction is invisible and complicitous with dominant bourgeois ideology.

The totalizing tendencies of both the symbolic bond, in Kristeva's sense of the term, and the imaginary subject, in Lacan's sense of the term (as indicative of unity, however illusory), are ruptured by the action that the semiotic *chora*, not desire, exerts on it. Because the oscillation between semiotic and symbolic modalities both precedes and exceeds the "stases of desiring structuration,"[68] the framework of intersubjective identification, for Kristeva the Lacanian notion of desire cannot satisfactorily account for all the features of the signifying function. Kristeva suggests that Lacan, unable to see beyond the externalized Other (productive of "phallicization of the mother," as Kristeva puts it),[69] misses the grammar of the internal other, maternal *jouissance, ek-stasis.*

Rather than fetishizing or abolishing the mother, Kristeva situates her notions of the significance of the maternal role in lived experience. She translates her personal experience of maternity as "self-division" and "forgetting oneself" in relation to another into a theory that proposes a paradigm shift that would transform the subject, its material practices, and in turn the "implacable violence" of the symbolic order. To suggest the maternal *chora* as a trope for internal alterity brings light to the dark continent of Lacan's and Freud's androcentric thinking. Her aim in such early work, as well as in the later *Tales of Love, In the Beginning Was Love,* and *Nations without Nationalism,* is increasingly therapeutic: to conceptualize an ethical subject that takes the psychic into account, where the Law is not simply internalized but shattered-within-unity. In confronting the internal "strangers to ourselves" (the title of one of Kristeva's recent books), subjects can mobilize a radically ethical (Kristeva's term is *herethical*) tolerance for external differences.

The theory of the semiotic, under the rubric of which she attempts to account for the mechanisms of signification in the Symbolic, has drawn heavy fire from some feminists for its perceived heterosexist emphasis on women's reproductive function. De Lauretis, for example, criticizes the Kristeva of "Stabat Mater," "Place Names," and "Motherhood according to Giovanni Bellini" for idealizing motherhood and heterosexuality, arguing that Kristeva confuses women's narcissistic identification with the mother and desire for other women.[70] Oliver, on the other hand, characterizes Kristeva as a melancholic within the institution of heterosexuality, an interpretation that neither idealizes Kristeva nor precludes consideration of her theorization of maternity as paradigm for an ethical subjectivity, on which this study builds. Not only does Kristeva posit the tolerance of difference, as Oliver asserts, but she undoes the hegemony of the unified subject privileged in Western conceptual thought at least since the Enlightenment. Because her theory doubly articulates the maternal as vocalic register and symbol, it suggests (as Oliver and de Lauretis very differently observe) that a distinction between maternal function and women, including between women who are mothers and their maternal role, needs to be kept.[71]

In "Women's Time," Kristeva opens a space for the consideration of female difference described with images of, but not synonymous with, the maternal. She attributes to women, particularly to those feminists who identify with the "archaic mother" a (maternal-izing) concern

> to lift the weight of what is sacrificial in the social contract from their shoulders, to nourish our societies with a more flexible and free discourse, one able to name what has thus far never been an object of circulation in the community: the enigmas of the body, the dreams, secret joys, shames, hatreds of the second sex.[72]

In suggesting that the psychic processes of the one sex have been symbolized (lack, threat), and that those of the other have yet to be put into circulation (a gap that she, like the women about whom she is writing in this essay, attempts to fill), her closing allusion in the passage above implies that Kristeva is taking up where her own intellectual "archaic mother," Simone de Beauvoir, left off. Another important essay postulates:

> It is probably necessary to be a woman (ultimate guarantee of sociality beyond the wreckage of the paternal symbolic function, as well as the inexhaustible generator of its renewal . . .) not to renounce theoretical reason but to com-pel it to increase its power by giving it an object beyond its limits.[73]

The implication of this passage is that women not only retain their reason, but wish to apply it to renovating the paternal symbolic order. Kristeva employs a discourse in these essays and elsewhere that at once associates women with mothering and sustains the dif-ference. In the latter passage, for example, women are both the social's "guarantee" and its (re)generator, poetically identified not simply as mothers but by that *role*. The maternal connotations of Kristeva's language construe an "unwrecked" symbolic that women potentially actualize. Because they may have less psychic invest-ment in defensive unifying identifications and power structures than do men, having very different relationships to those structures, women are positioned, Kristeva suggests, to change the symbolic contract.

In the following passage, she considers the relationship of the body to sexual difference, to the subject's constitution in language, and to power:

> Sexual difference—which is at once biological, physiological and relative to reproduction—is translated by and translates a difference in the relationship of subjects to the symbolic contract which *is* the social contract: a difference, then, in the relationship to power, language and meaning.[74]

Sexual difference (like differences of race, class, culture, sexual orientation) is not determining, but translates into differing relationships to the distribution of power and the production of meaning. Kristeva calls on women "to emphasize the multiplicity of female expressions . . . so that from the intersection of these differences there might arise, more precisely, less commercially and more truthfully, the real *fundamental difference* between the two sexes."[75] Within the context of one of the most extensive analyses of the psychic processes that support totalizing symbolic structures, she theorizes a flexible discourse capable of transforming the symbolic order by exposing the operations that construct dominant identity and abjected difference. Such fantasized constructions oppress all women by maintaining the exclusion of real maternal and differentiated female experience from circulation in the cultural community. The set of distinctions Kristeva establishes between the maternally connoted semiotic register, symbolization of the maternal, and women intervenes in the conflation of women with woman. Her insistence on the provisionality of any thetic position prevents stabilizing the replacement of one identity with another. Reification does not change the system or imaginatively engage in the psychic alteration of either the political or personal unconscious.

This engagement constitutes poetic *practice* as Kristeva defines it, a process of positing and dissolving meaning and the unity of the subject.[76] Poetic practice encompasses the ethical when the subject, as "an excess: never one, always already divided," dissolves narcissistic fixations.[77] Subject to bodily drives and material conditions, the poetic subject does not renaturalize self-unity, but enacts heterogeneous contradiction, articulating a "system of representation that binds the text" with the semiotic and the sociosymbolic.[78] Poetic practice exemplifies as well as constitutes a dynamic pattern that schematizes the simultaneous acceptance and transgression of the material, the social, the Law. This definition is so self-contradictory, however, that even the sympathetic Oliver asks in frustration what kind of a revolution "breaks the Symbolic even while it is coopted by it?"[79] Such a capricious, equivocal revolutionary practice might be construed as "feminine," although women needn't, as we know, be included in that term.

To consider more specifically the (referentially aberrant) possibility that women poets articulate such a practice, I would like to turn now to de Lauretis's feminist assertion that the experience of femaleness engenders subjectivity. She has over the past decade or so developed one of the most sustained accounts of what she defines as the task left for feminist theory: to address women (not woman) and to theorize "how the experience of sexuality, in engendering one as female, does effect or construct what we may call a female subject."[80]

In the final chapter of *Alice Doesn't*, "Semiotics and Experience," de Lauretis argues an approach to the feminist conundrum of essentialism: the problem of the relation between subjective identity, text, and world. She criticizes Kristeva for her exclusive concern with the mechanisms of the unconscious that exceed the symbolic structures, a criticism that, as should by now be clear, is an oversimplification. By working closely through semiotic theory (Umberto Eco's and Charles Sanders Peirce's), however, de Lauretis does consider what Kristeva touches upon but does not elaborate: the subjective and social aspects of meaning production by women. Moreover, de Lauretis very specifically accounts for the relation of aesthetic practice to gendered experience. To do so, she postulates the relationship between the body, whose experience is determined by sexual difference, and the semiotic subject, which not only is produced by but produces signs. She then goes on to establish a conceptual structure in which to understand how an engendered subjectivity, a female subject, transforms the codes she employs.

De Lauretis culls the basis of her semiotic theory from Peirce. Observing that he "greatly complicates the [classical] picture in which a signifier would immediately correspond to a signified," she quotes a famous passage in which he defines a number of terms important to her own thinking:

> A sign, or representamen, is something which stands to somebody for something in some respect or capacity. It addresses somebody, that is, it creates in the mind of that person an equivalent sign, or perhaps a more developed sign. That sign which it creates I call the *interpretant* of the first sign. The sign stands for something, its *object.* It stands for that object, not in all respects, but in reference to a sort of idea, which I have sometimes called the *ground* of the representation.[81]

The passage is significant, notes de Lauretis, because it admits the context of enunciation and reception into its definition of how signs function. For Peirce, the *interpretant* is the equivalent sign that is created in the mind of a person addressed by a first sign, the *representamen.* The interpretant is the "ground" that "conditions" the representamen; the representamen creates the interpretant. The two signs are equivalent but not the same, the interpretant being "perhaps a more developed sign."

With this definition established, de Lauretis is able to draw a distinction between her feminist semiotic theory and Lacan's virtually endless signifying chain of desire. Like Kristeva and de Man, albeit very differently, she does this by theorizing a positionality of interpretation constructed through a dynamic oscillation. Following Peirce, de Lauretis recasts the semiotic process as "a series of ongoing mediations between 'outer world' and 'inner' or mental representations," whose meaning resides in a final interpretant. This final interpretant is actually a meaning effect produced by emotional and mental effort exerted on the inner world. The final interpretant makes sense of the emotional and mental effort that preceded it, producing "a *habit-change,*" at once a logical conclusion (a modification of thought) and a change in one's tendencies toward action (a modification of intention).[82] The process that results in the logical interpretant produces this modification, which de Lauretis understands as "a disposition, a readiness (for action), a set of expectations."[83]

In the following passage, she attempts to negotiate the tricky "terrain of subjectivity as conscious *and* unconscious":

> As we use or receive signs, we produce interpretants. Their significate effects [meanings] must pass through each of us, each body and each consciousness, before they may produce an effect or an action upon the world. *The individual's habit as a semiotic production is both the result and the condition of the social production of meaning.*[84]

The notion of the logical interpretant enables de Lauretis to assert a relation between an embodied subject (in whom a "modification" is carried out through logical interpretation of other signs), experience, and history. Experience, she elaborates, is "a *process* by which, for all social beings, subjectivity is constructed." The process places the subject in material, economic, and interpersonal relations that are perceived as subjective but that are actually social and historical.[85]

This definition is central to her argument. With the body "restored," as she puts it, de Lauretis can then contend that the semiotic subject is both affected by the social practice of signs and actively engaged in meaning production and self-representation. Her argument in *Alice Doesn't* is focused on the assertion that sexual difference determines both: the affect of social practice and the effect of meaning production. (Because of the experiential and historical specificity of each embodied subject, however, this focus can be readily broadened to include consideration of other differences, as de Lauretis herself has done in the decade since *Alice Doesn't* was published.) Through the notion of this interaction of affect and effect in the subject, she is able to account for how the aesthetic and micropolitical practices on the part of a gendered subject (for example, MacKinnon's notion of consciousness-raising) transform culturally shared meanings and signs. Changing ideas in relation to representation, in Peirce's sense of a sign's "ground," these practices intervene in ideological as well as perceptual codes. Through her active work with signs, as it pertains to this study, through a poetic *practice* in Kristeva's sense of the term, a female artist transforms the ground of the codes she uses and, modified by them, in turn modifies them and thus the reading as well as writing subject.

Adapting de Man, de Lauretis terms the discontinuity between grammar, rhetoric, and logic the "real contradiction" of female subjectivity, which she asserts is the subject of feminism.[86] But forgetting that de Man, like Kristeva, is writing of the way poetic language works, de Lauretis does not consider the specificity of poetry. Kristeva, on the other hand, does not extensively consider the politics of sexual difference. Hence the intertextuality of my study's theorization of gendered poetic subjectivity as well as its paradox (to assert a female subjectivity, that is, in order to ponder its undoing). A brief return to the passage from Barrett Browning's letter will serve to specify the implications of my combinatory approach.

The rhetorical question puts a feminist subtext into the play of meanings that intervenes upon the ideology of gender, which Barrett Browning unsettles by interrogating as well as apparently accepting the absence of women poets historically. She is *not* concerned to assert that women did, could, or will write great poetry (Barrett Browning, after all, equivocates about the absence of "grandmothers" and admits not at all the absence of "mothers" or "sisters"). In ventriloquizing the Romantic exaltation of poetry, at the same time as she questions women's absence, she produces two meaning-effects. The first is that, figuratively speaking, she creates a glorious victory for those women who do manage to write poetry (the same could be said of Woolf's more-famous lament about Judith Shakespeare). The second is that, in seeming modest while implying an extravagantly immodest claim (the "divine breath" has passed *her* lips), she gets to have it both ways, sort of.

Such equivocation, although a problematic figure ("as are all figures of a problematic," as Elizabeth Meese observes),[87] might be an (in)appropriate characterization of a particular feminist linguistic strategy employed by the women poets I discuss. Equivocation undoes the ideology that has upheld the poetic image of woman and kept women in their place in the general scheme of things, but it does so without replacing the rejected ideal with another. Assumed so astutely in complicating women's absence from a genre concerned more with voice and image than with much-vaunted inspiration, this subversive position certainly puts into question the exclusion it acknowledges, as Barrett Browning's passage indicates. But equivocation is undecidable, refusing to come down rhetorically on one side or the other (for women, for example, to be pinned down to the grammatical erasure they might mimetically reproduce).

As such, it draws together under the rubric of a poetic strategy of logic and structure, as well as of rhetoric, the insights culled from de Manian deconstruction, Kristevan psychoanalysis, and de Lauretian semiotics, all of which share an emphasis on a nonsynthesized, dialectical play between discursive modalities. The method stages, I suggest, an analogous oscillation. Equivocation is not ironically saying one thing to mean the opposite; rather, it sustains contradiction by maintaining a (non)commitment to both meanings. Nor does the strategy lend itself to an hysterical, if figurative, makeover.[88] Like the related modes of irony and hysteria, equivocation keeps meaning in circulation through its mutability and indirection.[89] But while the former arguably gesture toward a subject who seems not to be but is actually in the know, equivocation enacts heterogeneous contradiction. It keeps a privileged subjectivity, such as the poetic subjects of this study, provisional and nontotalizing—which for de Man is linguistic vertigo, for de Lauretis a feminist intervention upon the return of power to the male term, and for Kristeva an ethical imperative.

Like a semiotic masquerade of femininity, equivocation operates in rhetorical and grammatical structures to produce a distance between one's position and one's meaning that a female speaker is able to manipulate and render readable by and for other women. According to the *OED*, however, which represents the meaning of the word by and for men, *equivocation* denotes not only "ambiguity" but "prevarication," a surprising ethical judgment implicit in a word that etymologically simply denotes equal voices (*equi* + *vox*). It was with that sense of the equality of parallel voices that I first began to think about H.D.'s rhetorical strategy with Freud as emblematic of a more general feminist strategy. When I at last looked the word up, I was fascinated by the implications of lying and of betraying one's (overdetermined) word, as in an oath, by the act of equivocation. I had "forgotten" that connotation of the word. The etymology of prevarication (*prae* + *varicari*, to walk crookedly) suggests that the reason for the embedded judgment is based on the assumption of a truth-content in words from which one could stray. For a woman to speak equivocally is to employ ambiguity in order to lie to a man. As employed by H.D. or her poetic surrogate, Helen, for example, equivocation gives the lie to scheming woman, the logic of "truth" about "her" (the path from which women necessarily stray), dissociating the female speaker from that figure which poetry has traditionally set up to contain her. In de-scribing woman, women poets not only manufacture distances between themselves and conventional images of the feminine, but refuse to reinstate that ideal.

The poets on which this study focuses interrupt the uniformity of pattern and trope in dominant figurations of femininity. They question the schemes of coherence that the traditional lyric, in its desire to seem unified as well as visionary, seeks to defend itself from seeing. They posit dissimulating subjects (they lie in that they simulate truth) who constitute themselves in division and thereby refrain from reifying conventions of poetic subjectivity as well as of gender. Like the Sphinx, occupying precisely the symbolic blind spot represented by Oedipus's literal blindness (and, thus, no longer a *monstrous* sight), they are beyond the gaze of man, in response to whose inclusionary fictions they might also equivocally quip, "That's what you think." In the opening they generate beside themselves, they scheme themselves, creating an imaginative distance from the poetic tradition with which they differ and an ethical divestment of the privileged (totalizing) subject position it epitomizes.

2 *"I Did'nt Be—Myself"*

*E*mily Dickinson's life and works enact, to an extreme of degree, if not of kind,[1] the symbolic dynamic that structures the poetic tradition and larger cultural relations it represents. By withdrawing herself from the social scene, increasingly shunning the presence of others in person, as Gary Stonum recounts, at the same time as her correspondence expanded voluminously, Dickinson was able to control the distance between herself and the world outside her immediate family.[2] Stonum asserts a connection between the move from speaking to writing and her poetics of dissemination, a decentralization of authorial power and deferral of the writer's to the reader's authority. A substantial contribution to our understanding of the Dickinsonian sublime, and one on which this chapter will build, Stonum's study falls short in its failure to consider whether gender has any bearing on Dickinson's liberation of the mind's "spectral power" from the control of "attitude and accent" exerted by "corporeal friend" (*L* 330), her refusal of "bodily presence," and her subjectivity.

Joanne Feit Diehl and Cristanne Miller, among other feminists critics, have argued that, while eschewing identification with the feminism of her day, Dickinson was aware that power relations between the sexes were a defining feature of her life and thus of the construction of her poems.[3] Her strong admiration for Elizabeth

Barrett Browning and George Eliot in particular suggests that gender identification built her confidence in the "new poetic language" she created.[4] "Informed by syntactic equivocations and hermetic linguistic strategies," Diehl notes, Dickinson's poetic (and oedipal) response to the "father" of the American sublime, Emerson, was an internalization of the split between the Emersonian Me and Not Me.[5] The "transformation" this split marked enabled her to resist "the woman poet's provisional status within the romantic literary tradition."[6] To such observations Mary Loeffelholz has added a consideration of class, contending that it is specifically the middle-class woman poet's status within the Romantic tradition's underlying bourgeois political identity that is provisional (that other women had no status, provisional or otherwise, seems to be Loeffelholz's point). Women of this class, Loeffelholz observes, do not "participate immediately or coherently either in bourgeois relations to capital or in bourgeois ideologies of individualism and universality." But they are nonetheless implicated in literary as well as class relations, "since the sublime language of nature presupposes sexual difference as natural—while claiming at the same time to transcend that difference."[7]

As Carol Smith-Rosenberg tells us, middle-class white women in nineteenth-century Victorian America existed "as a unique caste within a male world; as active participants in the dominant male class structure; [and] as male-constructed symbols of class distinctions."[8] Economically disempowered and socially "demure," the Victorian woman was, by the 1840s of Emily Dickinson's youth, "the symbol and personification of male bourgeois hegemony."[9] To fulfill their symbolic function, girls of this class were socialized into an ambivalence that directly affected their relationship to language, to speech, and to the grammar and rhetoric of self-representation. Joanne Dobson situates Dickinson within the pervasive contemporary "ideal of feminine reticence." It was this ideal, for example, that Dickinson's feminist "preceptor," Thomas Wentworth Higginson, satirized in *Women and the Alphabet* (1881), as "the Invisible Lady ... who remained unseen, and had apparently no human organs except a brain and a tongue."[10] For some women of Dickinson's class, the struggle against male hegemony resulted in feminism; in marked contrast, Dickinson conformed, but, as Dobson admits, to an odd and incomparable extreme. She complied, we might say, with a vengeance, productive of various splits in relation to subjectivity and the Romantic sublime that this chapter will examine.

As Letter 330, quoted above, suggests, according to Stonum, Dickinson eschewed any authority *her* body might have exerted as source of utterance. But the control someone's presence might cause works both ways. Remaining invisible has the effect of splitting "presence" between withheld body and proffered voice. This split does not simply fulfill the bourgeois ideal; it also allows Dickinson to evade *any* body's control. As I shall argue in the first section to follow in this chapter, Dickinson eludes a controlling gaze determined by the sexual politics that help to structure a male-dominated hegemony.

The complex conjunction of vexed (feminine) presence, obscured (masculine) sight, and an engendered subject in Emily Dickinson's poetry suggests that she intervened in the Romantic connection between power, presence, and seeing (in effect, the dynamics of the male gaze). Her work posits strategies of self-dislocation and textual displacement as alternatives to the passive, objectified positions the feminine typically occupied in Romantic literature. The themes of the Romantics influenced her, but she challenged rather than adopted the notion of transcendence, and explored rather than reified Romantic constructions, Loeffelholz asserts.[11] Diehl suggests that because of Dickinson's skepticism, she eschewed the "compensatory gestures" that the male Romantics found in nature to allay "the potentially disintegrative danger . . . of a too intense imaginative isolation."[12] In the second section to follow, I shall extend Diehl's insights in order to examine how Dickinson was as often enabled as disabled by the self-difference that the Romantics imaginatively resolved in the face of the awesome and unrepresentable aspects of nature that characterize the poetry of the sublime.[13]

In the last sections of this chapter, I shall argue that Dickinson transforms her refusal to unify the "fracture within" (*L* 268) into a resonant tolerance for internal alterity, which she terms *Ecstasy*. Iconoclast as well as recluse, Dickinson critically (dis)engaged the feminine conventions of her day pertaining to her own class. That critique coalesces in her representations of the maternal. She sublimates the maternal, I contend, as a mode of writing that redefines the relation of poetic source to poetic word. She deprivileges the sense of the word's finality, positing in its stead an exchange of reader and writer through a semantically mobile and open text.

A PEACH BEFORE ITS TIME

For women, "normality" consists in never settling down, in remaining changeable and capricious.

—Sarah Kofman, *The Enigma of Woman*

It was so delicious to see you—a Peach before the time, it makes all seasons possible and Zones—a caprice.

—Emily Dickinson, *L* 438

What do you weave from all these threads, for I know you have'nt been idle the while I've been speaking to you, bring it nearer the window, and I will see, it's all wrong unless it has one gold thread in it, a long, big shining fibre which hides the others—and which will fade away into Heaven while you hold it, and from there come back to me.

—Emily Dickinson, *L* 35

In the early Letter 35 from which the third quotation is taken, written to a schoolgirl friend, Dickinson construes writing as a communal, signifying process that mediates between presence and absence, writer and reader. The spinner/writer sends out "threads" the weaver/reader "weaves." The text(ile) acquires significance by its passage through the other: the reader finds the "one gold thread" that was veiled for the writer, who cannot see it until the other brings it to (the) light.

But the passage does not represent (*pace* Stonum) simply a deferral on the writer's part to the reader's authority, for the writer's thread fades even as the reader holds it. "Heaven" mediates the return: the imperceptible the perceived, the unknowable the known, the unrepresentable the represented. We cannot know the medium through which the exchange passes. We only know (of) "Heaven" *in other words—Heaven, Afterlife, God.* Naming marks a rupture in the very process of naming. The weaver loses the thread of thought, which returns to the spinner.

The exchange is not about meaning and interpretive authority per se; rather, the process is everything, the exchange having made the letter meaningful and the text emptied of significance. The spinner's thread returns to her, but "meaning" has fallen away before the metaphor for ungraspable signification the text itself images. As the reader tries to hold the gold thread she perceives (to grasp it, stabilize it), any message she might construe is interrupted, the thread fading, meaning's metaphor reconstituting with the writer. The thread of Dickinson's thought weaves a complex fabric of vexed presence and obscured sight, unfinished reading, and the metaphorization of meaning mediated by an act of perception that itself can be signified only by metaphor.[14] The writer/reader relationship playfully represented in this passage is a dialectical exchange between equals, at once destructive and constitutive of the text.

It is significant that even when the dynamics of gender difference and asymmetrical power do not come into play, the writer and reader having more or less equivalent *authority*, Dickinson represents herself not as a unified or even "present" identity but as a consciousness split between two types of activities, two locations: the place from which she "speaks" (writes) and the place in which she "sees" (reads her words along with her reader). Such self-inscription is enabling as well as literally duplicitous, for it is the capacity to double herself, to be imaginatively "present" in two places at once, that allows her to (re)present herself. The passage suggests that, for Dickinson, "presence" in relation to sight (she can see but not be seen) is not idealized for its immediacy but constituted in division, a notion that the passage celebrates.

In contrast, the second epigraph, from letter 438, images seeing a friend as a sensual, punningly "fruitful" gift, a sort of visitation that causes the boundaries between seasons to disappear and geographical zones to seem mere "caprice." There is something sublime and, foregrounded by the confusion of taste and sight, oral (preoedipal) about the sensations Dickinson describes: all seems possible at the same time and in the same place. Presence in this passage seems a higher truth that causes divisions and separations to fall away. An imaginary plenitude has ripened in their place, a little, transitory haven (heaven) exceeding symbolic structures of linearity, chronology, and classification.

But the more one contemplates the passage, the more delineations of predication and syntax dissolve, and the sublime moment of numinous presence spills over into uncanny ambiguity. A "Peach before the time" is not only an unexpected pleasure, but also an unnatural event, both a delight and an aberration. The imagined coincidence of "all seasons . . . and Zones," if one takes the section between the dashes as parenthetical and nonrestrictive, is not only actually unimaginable but unnatural as well. But seasons and zones are not simply imposed, and therefore unnatural (or "false") divisions; they are also based on simple observation of cyclical and geographical (or natural) changes. In addition to such figural confusion of natural and unnatural, true and false, the passage's rhetorical validation of the higher truth of unified presence is made, ironically enough, through a divisive strategy: hierarchization. In this reading, figure and logic do not coincide but contradict each other: the unity professed rhetorically is undone grammatically. The passage itself is a "caprice."

But to read the passage otherwise is to suggest that Dickinson designates the visit a caprice, and at the rhetorical level this reading also frets the idealization of presence. Dickinson's dictionary defines *caprice* as "a shaking in fever, rigors, whim, freak, fancy."[15] Webster notes that the word combines the Latin for "head," *ca,* + *freak,* to denote a sudden bursting, breaking, starting. The literal head in the definition figuratively changes, as in "a sudden start of mind" or "change of opinion." Pursuing the linguistic trail, we find that Webster defines "freak" as "a sudden starting or change of place." In other words, "caprice" implies that the "head" changes not only its mind, but its place, that to change one's mind is a figure for losing one's head. We don't want to put too literal a face on this head, but such a change does suggest a state of alienation, as in the statement, "I'm not myself today." Presence in this reading is not a wholeness but a shaking loose of the self from the self: a division, a separation instituted in someone who does not, implicitly, know her own mind from herself.

Although she might not have had all this in her own head when she wrote her note to Samuel Bowles, Dickinson complicates in this passage at the level of both rhetoric and grammar the connection between seeing and presence. Even when she seems to idealize presence along classic metaphysical lines (presence = the oneness of body and voice), she undermines its unity. According to Dobson, such a split was the result of a culturally monitored restriction on female expression:

> For women's writing the significance of the decorum of "invisibility," which amounted to the barring of female subjectivity from the public sphere . . . resulted in a conspiracy of literary discourse that pitted the "feminine" . . . against the "female" . . . in such a way that the latter was all but eliminated from women's texts.[16]

Although, as Dobson suggests in the passage above, this division certainly resulted in discursive poses that suppressed women's experience in print, that suppression was not absolute; women surely encoded their protests of a culturally mandated decorum.[17]

Dickinson's case is not exemplary, in other words, but it is more complex, not least, as Dobson speculates, because she had no economic pressure to write work acceptable for publication. She poses as well, as Martha Nell Smith has convincingly argued:[18] Like her contemporaries, for example, "she" is split between an external decorum and an internal resistance or contradiction signified by "pose." But more evident in her work than that of her contemporaries is the internal split of a subject-in-process, to borrow Kristeva's term, which often structures her representation of the speaking subject. By juxtaposing the two passages from Dickinson's letters with the quotation from Kofman ("For women, 'normality' consists in never settling down, in remaining changeable and capricious"), I wish to suggest that Kofman offers a useful account of this doubly split subject. She postulates why a split female subject differs in degree, if not in kind, from a male subject.

In Letter 438, we recall, seeing Bowles does not lead to a specular, unified identity; rather, "presence" seems to consist in never settling down, in remaining changeable and capricious. That depiction is one stereotype for the feminine mind, and it coincides, in fact, with the theory of feminine sexuality for Freud, which Kofman ironically extends by taking his definition of what comprises "normal" feminine sexuality to its logical conclusion. In the following passage, she summarizes his account of the girl's developmental difference from the boy's:

> Man's sexuality develops smoothly, with no break or crisis, owing to its fixation on the initial love object: the mother. As for the girl, by analogy . . . it may be conjectured that her first love object is also her mother or a mother substitute . . . : [But] she has to undergo crises and accomplish a supplementary task—at the time of the Oedipus complex, the father becomes her love object. Furthermore, the girl does not remain fixated on her father as the boy does on the mother: if her development is normal, she is expected to pass from the paternal object to another, definitive object choice.[19]

As Kofman's reiteration of the process makes clear, to achieve normal sexual development, at least according to the androcentric cultural conventions that Freud's theory epitomizes as well as magisterially explicates, the girl has a more difficult passage than the boy. She must supplement in her sexuality the split both sexes experience in subjectivity.

To develop "normally," that is, the girl "has to undergo" a "break" or narcissistic "crisis," the difference between the castration threat (the boy's split) and the castration complex (for the girl, the *fact* of castration).[20] She must shake herself loose from her desire for the mother, changing her mind again and again. The girl becomes "capricious." Nor can she "settle" on the mother or her substitute as narcissistic object choice, the one who reflects the boy's unified image back to him. The boy's mother and her substitute will, as in the preoedipal stage, mirror him back to himself as a fantasized whole (in essence, the masquerade of femininity). The girl in Freud's scenario can only achieve "normality" by becoming the reflexive (m)other herself.

Kofman's witty literalization of Freud's description of what makes women feminine—caprice—on the other hand, implies that the girl can assume a position that is not only divided but potentially disruptive of androcentric convention, resisting what is in effect the dynamic of women's specularization. It is this operation that Dickinson's texts suggest she perceived and developed strategies to elude. That notion provides one approach to the "feminine caprices" of the speaking subjects in her work. Through the intervention upon a presence/sight integrity (that, for instance, of Emerson's Me expanded to encompass the Not Me), Dickinson represents a divided *female* subject who does not fantasize wholeness. Rather, she posits herself *by means of* such splitting, inscribing a creative disruption of the gender conventions in which she wrote, at the same time as she appears not simply to comply with the restrictive conditions of femininity for her class, but to capitalize on them.[21]

In the attempt to understand the history of women's literature, as Marie La Place cautions, "it is important to take into account that in a nineteenth-century context the assertion that women have a self . . . is . . . subversive."[22] As both Miller and Loeffelholz discuss, the fiction and poetry produced by Dickinson's female contemporaries were important influences on her, although her stylistic innovations often obscure the trace. These fictions are quintessentially American bourgeois ideology about transcending suffering and finding one's "true self." But Dickinson did not consistently reproduce those images of unified selfhood so much as she undermined and explored the operations that might lead to identity or any sense of a consolidated "self."[23]

In a letter written toward the end of her life, Dickinson explicitly connects the activity of seeing with anxiety at the discovery of sexual difference: "In all the circumference of Expression, those guileless words of Adam and Eve never were surpassed, 'I was afraid and hid Myself'" (*L* 946). In the Bible, Adam speaks these words; Dickinson's revision includes Eve as speaking subject and suppresses the original reason for Adam's fear (his transgression of God's authority). In Dickinson's version, fear of exposure is grammatically and rhetorically conjoined with the frustration of vision. And in that conjunction, we can begin to read a different kind and cause of fear. Fear is not posited in the subject whose eyes have been opened; instead, the subject who is open to (others') eyes has been posited in fear, causing that subject to "hide." Dickinson's revision of the passage from Genesis to include Eve associates the

advent of subjectivity in women with the anxiety produced by sexual identity as relegated to visual spectacle.

The disturbance of the connection between seeing and being in
Dickinson's work suggests her insights not only into the specularity
of identity but into the specularization of the figure of woman that
typically accompanies the inequality of power in gender politics[24]–
her *to-be-looked-at-ness*, as film theorist Laura Mulvey characterizes
this distinctly engendered operation. Applying Freud's theory of the
scopophiliac instinct to sexual difference, Mulvey, too, observes an
active/passive split along lines of gender: "The determining male
gaze projects its phantasy on to the female figure which is styled
accordingly."[25] Dickinson's revised genealogy of knowledge, as
characterized by the passage from Letter 946 quoted above, works
to obscure, even upset, positions of visual mastery and patriarchal
authority most often inhabited by male figures in her poetry.[26]

As a striking example, consider the response she elicited even
from the feminist (or, as she called him, her "Master teacher") Higginson, in the following passage:

> Sometimes I take out your letters & verses, dear friend, and
> when I feel their strange power, it is not strange that I find
> it hard to write. . . . I have the greatest desire to see you,
> always feeling that perhaps if I could once take you by the
> hand I might be something to you; but till then you only
> enshroud yourself in this fiery mist & I cannot reach you,
> but only rejoice in the rare sparkles of light. . . . I should like
> to hear from you very often, but feel always timid lest what
> I *write* should be badly aimed. . . . It would be so easy, I
> fear, to miss you. . . . I think if I could once see you & know
> that you are real, I might fare better. (*L* 330a; Higginson's
> emphasis)

The "strangeness" of Dickinson's letters and poems produces anxiety in Higginson, having the effect of stilling his pen and causing
him temporarily to lose his sense of identity (and identification)
with regards to her.[27] Since he is unable to represent her (since she
refuses to present herself), he has nothing at which to "aim" his letters, no proper addressee, no image of her that reassuringly reflects

him back to himself. Higginson's elevated language (she is shrouded in "fiery mist," he "cannot reach" her, but "rejoice[s] in the rare sparkles of light") and his sense of self-loss before her inaccessibility suggest that he is experiencing a crisis of representation, what Neil Hertz has analyzed as an anxious "moment of blockage," Kant's "checking of the vital powers," in the literature of the Romantic sublime. At such moments of self-loss, Hertz observes, "The world is neither legible nor visible in the familiar way."[28]

For Higginson, there is a "strange power" in Dickinson's poems and letters. Unable to "see" her, he also cannot "read" her, and it is that uncanny sense of being in the territory of the unfamiliar that is at the same time oddly recognizable ("dear friend") that causes the lines between not being able to see, read, and write to blur for Higginson. As Hertz explains it, typically at these moments the subject seeks some emblem to reestablish boundaries and the capacity to interpret differences, but such reassertions of unified masculine identity are at woman's expense.[29]

And indeed, Higginson attempts to seduce Dickinson into installing herself, bodying forth reassurance, by a "visitation": "I wonder if it would be possible to lure you [to Boston for a lecture he is giving]." If he could but "see" her, he could assure himself that she is "real" and that he is "something" to her. Significantly, he also wishes to control who looks at whom. After relating the time at which he is to deliver his paper, Higginson then suggests that she visit when he is not lecturing, for "my object is to see you, more than entertain you." He is uncomfortable, it would seem, with the activity of lecturing, at least with regards to Dickinson, precisely because he would be the spectacle rather than the spectator. Rather than reading to her (*lecture*), he wishes to read her (*lecteur*). She, not he, is to be the object of the gaze.

Although she might connect the act of seeing most spectacularly with love, life, and knowledge, as Cynthia Griffin Wolff has argued, Dickinson more often renders those connections tenuous and problematic. She seems to constitute Higginson as a master teacher, one presumed to know more than she—for example, as in "I would like to learn—Could you tell me how to grow[?]" (*L* 261) and "I think you called me 'Wayward.' Will you help me improve?"(*L* 271). Her use of rhetorical questions not only requests help from Higginson, however, but casts doubt on his capacity to render it, undermining the very position of mastery in which she has placed him. And of course, it is her rhetoric that both places and displaces him. As his letter attests, she both locates him in and dislocates him from the position of knowledge, most primarily about *her.* Paradoxically installing him in the locus of both knowledge and nonknowledge, she cannot be served up to him for readerly consumption.

Dickinson's refusal of Higginson's request for her portrait implies that her reasons for denying her reader's view of her defy a process that would render her a static image associated not only with death but with dishonor. She counters with a radical notion of honor, the refusal to *deface* what is changeable and unfixable in her *living* features: Father "has no Mold of me, but I noticed the Quick wore off those things, in a few days, and forestall the dishonor–You will think no caprice of me" (*L* 268).

The word portrait she offers instead does not disguise its partiality. Preserving "the Quick" better than a "Mold," Dickinson's self-portrait replaces a totalizing visual image with discursive, mutable fragments (a *tête morcèlé*, as it were), all hair and eyes:

> Could you believe me–without? I had no portrait, now, but am small, like the Wren, and my Hair is bold, like the Chestnut Bur–and my eyes, like the Sherry in the Glass, that the Guest leaves–Would this do just as well? (*L* 268)

Dickinson's features are available for Higginson's viewing only through discursive representation, and are in effect effaced by the very metaphors she employs. She depicts herself as both mundane (a wren, a chestnut bur) and strange (as the etymology of "guest" connotes). She puts off Higginson's wishful desire to see her by putting off her likeness into unlikeness (at once other images and images of otherness). The passage enacts the unfixability of living features, a linguistic activity she implicitly celebrates by suggesting that her refusal to provide a photograph is an honorable one. Jeanne Larsen observes that Dickinson refuses to "sacrifice her head," refuses, that is, to be silenced by the patriarchy.[30] In this exemplary exchange with "the patriarchy," Dickinson goes it one better: she gives Higginson a head, but frustrates his pleasure in it. The rhetorical question with which she opens her letter is a "caprice" after all. As with similar questions to Higginson, she implies contradictory meanings, at once requesting that he (literally) take her word for it, questioning his willingness to comply, and casting doubt on her reliability as speaking subject.

Dickinson's errant self-description in this letter serves as preface to the most famous passage of self-representation in her canon, a cautionary statement about her narrative reliability: "When I state myself, as the Representative of the Verse—it does not mean—me—but a supposed person."[31] This passage returns the reader to the letter's opening, where she has ostensibly already "stated herself." In the context of the initial self-portrait, the second, which at first seemed a frank admission, appears less transparent, and we are suddenly confronted with a possibly disingenuous and certainly divided subject: the subject who speaks and the subject who is spoken of. Which one utters this statement? Dickinson is presumably referring to the fact that she speaks in personae in her poems, but is she writing as "herself" in this instance or as "the Representative of the Verse"? On what ground has she left the reader—in this case the desirous Higginson—to stand?

Such disjunction of grammar, rhetoric, and logic, as well as complication of the speaking subject, is also evident in the love poems in which Dickinson figures masculine objects of affection. Poem 480, which epitomizes Dickinson's methodology, announces itself a part of the very young "tradition" of women's revisionary love poetry by opening with a variation on Barrett Browning's famous line from *Sonnets from the Portuguese*: "'Why do I love' You, Sir?" Through the replacement of "How" with "Why," Dickinson reorients the poem's focus from the measure of love to its logic. But the speaker refuses direct reflection of and for her lover:

> "Why do I love" You, Sir?
> Because—
> The Wind does not require the Grass
> To answer—Wherefore when He pass
>
> She cannot keep Her place.
>
> (*P* 480)

Instead of the causal explanation "Because" seems to announce (with the dash functioning as colon), the text breaks off into analogy, the first of three in a paratactic series that structures the poem's meaning. The poem contradicts analogy's normative function, however, suppressing the logical connections. As in the passage above, the import of each ensuing analogy is to deny the possibility of responding to the very question the analogies seem graphically placed to answer. The purpose of the analogies is to obfuscate rather than to clarify a response.[32]

The speaker disperses herself, moreover, into a metaphor that is a figure for metonymic displacement.[33] The "I" of the first stanza, in fact, is already displaced. Since "I" is in quotation marks, she can only be "present" through the repetition of another's words, a subject constituted in the desire of the other to know. She (or perhaps *s/he* is more appropriate) both divides and "cannot keep Her place." In other words, her place shifts. Once the speaker speaks directly of herself, she seems both multiple and sexually undecidable, like the many individual blades that make up the collective "Grass": she is "We." The speaker is specifically "located" in non-knowledge as well as multiplicity:

> Because He [the wind] knows—and
> Do not You—
> And We know not—
>
> (*P* 480)

How could the speaker tell what she claims she doesn't know? The speaker's love is the result, as the perfect rhymes of this stanza highlight, of visibility:

> The Sunrise—Sir—compelleth Me—
> Because He's Sunrise—and I see—
> Therefore—Then—
> I love Thee—
>
> (*P* 480)

The visual relation set up here reverses the positions of male spectator/female spectacle.

But the implication of force on the Sun's part, as well as help-lessness on the speaker's part to avert his action (almost literally a repetition compulsion), suggests that the symbolic power structure is unchanged. "Therefore—Then—" the speaker's evasive response to Sir's question is to displace not only herself but her meaning along the diachronic axis of the poem. Such displacement has the effect of deferring disclosure, the only means the speaker has of put-ting off Sir's determination to know. In never answering his ques-tion, the speaker places meaning, and Sir's desire to control it, beyond the poem's frame entirely (a movement that, according to Stonum, characterizes her poetics as a whole).

The poem similarly recasts the relationship of knowledge to sight. The poem seems to be written out of the eccentric "compul-sion" to censor its own center (sight),[34] for at the center of this poem is not vision but blindness and silence:

> The Lightning—never asked an Eye
> Wherefore it shut—when He was by—
> Because He knows it cannot speak—
> And reasons not contained—
> —Of Talk—
> There be—preferred by Daintier Folk
>
> (*P* 480)

The object of love, "Sir," has become the locus of knowledge, but of an illusional and tenuous sort. "Do not You [know?]" rhetorically implies that "Sir" does, in fact, know, but at the same time could mean that he doesn't or that the speaker doesn't know that "Sir" does (not) know. "Sir" is posited in the apparently masterful though undaintily contradictory place of, to be precise, not knowing that he knows what he cannot know (because "it cannot speak" and is not contained "Of Talk"). The speaker operates as a divide that separates speech from what cannot be spoken: what separates s/he from herself, Dickinson's often undecidable speaker. The poem is telling an unreadable and unwriteable story (a woman's real experience, we might say). Although the text describes romantic love as the result of a visual econ-omy, it resists at the point at which it seems most to invest in such specularization. The speaker who sees and loves (and therefore seems, temporarily at least, to know her own mind) cannot be reconciled, in the final analysis, with the speakers ("We") who do not know.

Poem 275 similarly plays with the notion of a shifting and displaced speaking subject who eludes the reader's visual appropriation both inside and outside the text on a number of levels. The poem seems at first a simple protestation of "Everlasting" devotion, the speaker asserting to the addressee that she has been falsely accused of withholding herself. She assures him that he has but to say "What more the Woman can," that she "may dower thee / With last Delight I own!":

> Doubt Me! My Dim Companion!
> Why God, would be content
> With but a fraction of the Life—
> Poured thee, without a stint—
> The whole of me—forever—
>
> (P275)

The poem continues by cataloging the "self" she has already given him: what he lacks

> cannot be my Spirit—
> For that was thine, before—
> I ceded all of Dust I knew—
>
> (P275)

But at the point where the speaker exhausts the list of the pleasures and parts she assures her lover are now in his possession and signify that she is "wholly" his, it becomes clear that those delights have a limit that language marks. Though earthbound, they are not, as it were, earthly:

> What Opulence the more
> Had I—a freckled Maiden
> Whose farthest of Degree,
> Was—that she might—
> Some distant Heaven,
> Dwell timidly, with thee!
>
> (P275)

The "Opulence" denied on earth is to be sublimated, but into a distinctly *unopulent* vision of heaven. The speaker's oddly timid "farthest of Degree" is postponed until some vague future time in some vaguely transcendent, but clearly far away and indescribable place ("*Some* distant Heaven"). The speaker's hyperbolic rhetorical gestures are confounded by the actual emptiness of her descriptions.

The projected and apparently desired change of place from earth in the present to heaven in the future signals not only a thematic but a semiotic break in the poem, suggested by the common etymological root of *freckled* and *freak* (as defined earlier, "a sudden starting or change of place") and delineated by the subject's splitting into "I" and "she."[35] "Freckled" not only contains, in its root, the suggestion of a break but implies "bold," "saucy," and "active" as well, thus connoting experience rather than innocence, an overexposure to the "Sun" that puts "blots" on more than one's complexion! The "freckled Maiden" might be unwed, but she is not "untouched," as "Intact" in the last stanza meant in Dickinson's day. But this implication is, of course, precisely the irony with which the speaker plays:

> Sift her, from Brow to Barefoot!
> Strain till your last Surmise—
> Drop, like a Tapestry, away,
> Before the Fire's Eyes—
> Winnow her finest fondness—
> But hallow just the snow
> Intact, in Everlasting flake—
> Oh, Caviler, for you!
>
> (*P 275*)

To separate her in order to know and to analyze her, as "Sift," "Strain," and "Winnow" connote, reveals to the lover not the whole woman but her dissection into pieces, a frustrating difference between her "self" and its parts. Such separations in the poem are figured, as "Dim" and "Some distant Heaven" indicate, as obscureness of vision, significantly enough. The speaker makes an association between the appropriative economies of visual and carnal possession, to which she subtly opposes her own, based on the capacity to "dower." This activity is ambiguous, however, for the phrase "I may dower thee" suggests both permission and deferred possibility. While the speaker assures her lover that he need only "Say quick," he says not a word within the framework of the poem. The gift (the "last Delight") remains suspended between the unexercised power and the permission to "dower."

Protesting perhaps too much, a subtly saucy tease on one plane, if not on the other, the speaker implies that only by maintaining an external separation on earth from her "Dim Companion" can she avoid the internal "separation," one that divides Maids from Madames and the "Maiden" from herself, that would render her forever unable to be either "wholly" his or wholly herself. Her lover can only wholly possess her by not "having" her; rather, he must "hallow" her, both venerating and leaving her, in a word that shares its etymology with "hallow," "whole" (read another way, *al[l]-one*). He has the whole, it would seem, but not the hole. But the external separation that is necessary to preserve the inside "Intact" already doubles an internal split, because, as we've seen, the speaking subject breaks into another, a division at the center of the poem as well as of the speaker. Keeping herself whole for him necessitates losing her body: the invisible "I," with all but her "last Delight" ceded away, displaced by her "freckled," suggestively bawdy, but *bodiless* other. In an ironic literalization of women's loss of autonomous identity in the institution of heterosexuality, the text indicates that the speaker can only be "more" with her lover when "she" is no longer "I" (that is, with/holding herself).

It is often impossible to grasp—literally to get one's hands on—the elusive female speakers in Dickinson's work. Dickinson and her poetic surrogates validate the very sublimation that they seem most to protest, as a duplicitously evasive and enabling strategy. Within the poetic frame, the splitting "self" renders location of her, as well as positions of mastery and specularization inhabited by masculine figures, difficult by obfuscating any unobstructed views of the speaking subject. A fundamental aspect of Dickinson's poetic project could be characterized as vexing such master plans as would relegate woman to anything so fixed as her status as sign in *man*'s service. But we might venture at this stage to explore further, particularly with regard to the dialectic between earthly and heavenly delights in the last poem, what the nature of Dickinson's stake in a divided speaking subject may have been, especially because the fault line occurs in a highly sexualized territory, and because that which gets sublimated is, as it happens, the female body.

DISAPPOINTING DAISIES

"Could you tell me what home is"
"I never had a mother. I suppose a mother is one to whom you hurry when you are troubled."
–Emily Dickinson, *L* 342b

I always ran Home to Awe when a child, if anything befell me. He was an awful Mother,
but I liked him better than none.
–Emily Dickinson, *L* 405

⇶

By way of beginning to address the issue with which I closed the previous section, the suggestion that Dickinson's divided subjectivity was disabling as well as liberating, I would like to look in this section more closely at Dickinson's problematic identification with the conventional feminine figure, as exemplified in her life by her own mother, and by the maternal figure represented in the series of Master letters. Barbara Mossberg and Betsy Erkkila both contend that Dickinson's hyperbolic, if inconsistent, comments about lacking a mother indicate a refusal "to conform to the nineteenth-century feminine ideal her mother represented," a refusal that led to an "identity conflict."[36] Miller observes that Dickinson was ambivalent about identifying with women because she associated femininity with powerlessness.[37]

The letters quoted above bespeak not only the lack of a mother as adequate role model, but the lack of a mother to whom Dickinson could run "if anything befell" her, if she were "troubled." In place of the mother she represents herself as (not) having, a mother powerless to help her, Dickinson substitutes a powerful mother, both awful, because she could not create a "home," and awe-full, the all-powerful (preoedipal) mother whom she can still inscribe as both "mother" and "He." Threatened by a "home" that did not contain a mother powerful enough to avert trouble, she describes herself as homeless. Representing her dilemma as a choice between the absolutes of "Awe" or "none," she repopulates "Home" with the sublime. She establishes an implicit *connection* between an absent or problematic mother and the sublime.

Mossberg's and Miller's comments suggest not simply refusal to conform on Dickinson's part (or conformity with a vengeance), but ambivalence indicated by rhetorical equivocation: being of two minds, both attracted to and repulsed by a silenced mother disenfranchised of all power and autonomy. She once wrote Higginson, for example, that "My Mother does not care for thought—and Father . . . buys me many Books—but begs me not to read them—because he fears they joggle the Mind" (*L* 261). Not to read is to become her mother, not to "care for thought." To read, however, is to risk joggling the (feminine) mind. To "joggle the mind" by reading (or writing, as Gilbert and Gubar have most notably argued) was anxiety-producing for women in Dickinson's day. In Dickinson's paradoxical representation, reading produces anxiety because it is to submit to the "Father" (he buys books for her), but it is also to defy him (he prohibits reading).[38] Reading constitutes precisely the kind of equivocal subject I have been theorizing, representing at once the attempt to please the "Father" and the transgressive effort to think like and to speak to one's own censor.

Dickinson intimated such a dilemma in her last "Master" letter: "Oh, did I offend it—[Did'nt it want me to tell it the truth]" (*L* 248).[39] Brackets indicate content that has been crossed out: in this passage, the "truth" is both withheld by not naming the referent of "truth" and already erased. A previously inscribed transgression, made of and in writing, is doubly expunged. In order to retain the approval of her Master, Dickinson must repress her own meaning. But to do this she must reject that part of herself that wants "to tell it the truth," a disabling self-censorship, as the hystericization of her language suggests:

> Daisy—Daisy—offend it—who bends her smaller life to his (it's) meeker (lower) every day—who only asks—a task—
> [who] something to do for love of it—(*L* 248)

If the Master letters can be taken as any indication of what "part" Dickinson repressed in order to assume the position of self-abnegation before an idealized love object, it is arguably herself as a desiring subject, figured initially in the letters as empowered mothering.

Although Dickinson opens the first letter with an admission of illness, she immediately doubles that position by asserting her lover's equally ill condition, ostensibly out of concern for him. But what at first appears as similarity is actually hierarchized into a structure of stronger/weaker: "I am ill, but grieving more that you are ill, I make my stronger hand work long eno' to tell you" (*L* 187). Being the "stronger" of the two seems to have very much to do with who controls knowledge and discourse, who gets to know and who gets told. In this passage, she "tells" him something (that she is "stronger"), but she does not tell him everything ("I did not tell you that today had been the Sabbath Day"). The Master has not been able to read her messages both literally (the letter isn't sent) and figuratively ("You ask me what my flowers said–then they were disobedient–I gave them messages").

By the second letter, "mothering" from a designatedly "stronger" place has given way to the figure of "Daisy" and "the little mother–with the big child" (*L* 233) (the "child" is her heart, which has outgrown her). Increasingly powerless, she has also become passive: "I waited a long time–Master–but I can wait more–." She had asked him for "Redemption" but says, "you gave me something else." The redemption-substitute has come in a manner and form over which she had no control. She has been alternatively redeemed for the Master, that is, through whose eyes she now sees herself: "Would Daisy disappoint you–no–she would'nt–Sir–." She longs for the reassuring presence of her lover's face before her: "it were comfort forever–just to look in your face, while you looked in mine–." The gaze she describes seems a mutual one between equals, but only if we forget the judgment she anticipates in her use of the word *disappoint.* Dickinson wishes to be the object of Master's desire, not the agent of her own look or desire; she wishes she could look at him looking at her *with approval,* the asymmetrical structure of specularization the passage reproduces.

As she represents herself in terms of Master's self-reflexive gaze, the status of the power she formerly held by "not telling" grows uncertain:

> [I did'nt tell you for a long time, but I knew you had altered me–I]
> You say I do not tell you all–Daisy confessed–
> and denied not

> [Will you tell me if you will?]
> I did'nt think to tell you, you did'nt come to me
>   'in white,' nor ever told me why,
>
> (L 233)

She oscillates in these passages between knowing/withholding information and not knowing/asking for information. It is unclear whether, for example, the confession that Master has changed her, under erasure in her letter, hasn't already taken place. She has already "confessed" and "denied not," after all, in language uncomfortably invoking the image of an inquisition. And while she seems only to confess to not "telling all," by the close of the letter the positions of Dickinson and her Master in the first letter have been reversed. The Master has not come in person or in writing, and hasn't "told" why.

Although "the love is the same," Dickinson herself has been "altered." By the last letter, she has sustained what are suggestively the narcissistic wounds that have decided her place: "I've got a Tomahawk in my side but that dont hurt me much. [If you] Her master stabs her more–" (*L* 248). By representing herself as wounded, she has entered a visual economy based on mutilation and loss that corresponds to the Freudian definition of feminine sexuality criticized by French feminists like Kofman and Irigaray.[40] Dickinson's characterization of her relation with the Master in the passages above sketches a violent scenario, depicting a speaker at odds with herself. She is wounded both by his refusal to look (she has the tomahawk in her side because of his rejection of her) and by the look itself (he "stabs her more"). But while she sees herself as mutilated, she also attempts to displace the violation, the subject splitting off from "I" to "she." This split provides no playful evasion through the embrace of her contradictory status, however, but only the replication of violence. Finding no alternative, she resigns herself to an inferior status: finally, having "confessed" all, she relinquishes, like her mother, "thought": she doesn't "think to tell."

In the last letter, no longer shifting between positions of empowerment and enigma, mothering and girlishness, knowing and not telling, Dickinson's "stronger hand" has been reassuringly restrained into the figures of Daisy and child ("your best little girl"), whom "nobody else will see" or, apparently, hear (she will be "still" when he wants her to be). A personalization as well as extreme literalization of the ideal of feminine reticence, this instance of sexual self-suppression is conventionally expressed in the language of self-abnegation. As such, it seems to confirm Kristeva's observation that women have trouble entering the symbolic order because, to do so, they must deny maternal identification—that is, abject themselves. Dickinson's writing the mother out of the Master letters in favor of writing in the girl is a retreat from representing herself as subjective to representing herself as objectified.[41]

The darkness at the heart of the Master letters is that Dickinson can find no alternative to the socially sanctioned feminine positions, no escape from the frames that bind her. She discards the most acceptable trope for female sexuality, mothering, only to repress herself as a potentially active lover as well, recuperating herself into a different, but equally conventional, identification of women with passivity. The letters' trajectory establishes not a stronger but weaker "self," and exemplifies Dickinson's problems in finding alternatives to identification with the feminine conventions of her day.

Abjecting the mother with whom she refuses to identify, Dickinson repeats her own mother's fate, for she has no object identification with which to replace the mother; she despairs at her failure to abnegate herself enough to establish herself as an appropriate object for another's desire, the only other position Western culture has symbolically offered women. She becomes the abject, which has no object, whom "nobody will see" because she is to be for Master's eyes only and he won't look. Finally un(re)presentable, Dickinson descends in the Master letters into a broken, melancholy language that is symptomatic of the narcissistic crisis within: what she represses in order to achieve Master's approval and what, one way or another, will come out, renders her increasingly incoherent.

According to Kristeva, however, there is another "moment on the journey" into signification. The same subject and speech bring into being both the abject and the sublime, for as Kristeva observes, "The abject is edged with the sublime [which also 'has no object']."[42] In contrast to abjection, sublimation offers the possibility of naming what precedes or lies outside the nominal, the objectal; it keeps the abject under control. The Master letters do not sublimate the maternal; they are permeated by self-abjection. But they do suggest a necessary disjunction between the abjected mother/ self, the divided subject, and the sublime. With this rupture in mind, we are now in a position to relate Dickinson's self-representation more specifically to her version of the Romantic sublime.

CEASELESS ROSEMARY

Men do not call the surgeon, to commend—the Bone, but to set it, Sir, and fracture within, is more critical.

−Emily Dickinson, *L* 268

We meet no Stranger but Ourself.

−Emily Dickinson, *L* 260

Starting from Kant's notion of the mathematical sublime (the "momentary checking of the vital powers"), Hertz examines literary/autobiographical moments in which the artist's typical representation of "the poised relationship of attentuated subject and divided object reveals [the subject's] inherent instability by breaking down and giving way to scenarios more or less violent, in which the aggressive reassertion of the subject's stability is bought at some other subject's expense." Such "moments of blockage" are rendered as utter self-loss, after which the self is then recuperated in exaltation, "a confirmation of the unitary status of the self."[43]

Hertz is fascinated by the violence that seems necessarily to accompany the reestablishment of the unitary self. But, Hertz asks, at the end of the line, "Who pays? and Why?" and goes on to suggest that it is precisely at these points of unreadability that questions of gender enter in: "When these dramas turn violent, women are frequently the victims of choice."[44] His explanation of why such gestures are at women's expense in relation to the sublime scenario bears closer examination. Reviewing Thomas Weiskel's analysis of the "negative sublime" as a preoedipal/oedipal sequence, Hertz suggests that an "end-of-the-line" moment occurs in Weiskel's own text. Weiskel postulates that in the traumatic phase of the negative sublime, there occurs a desire to be inundated and, at the same time, anxiety about being annihilated:

> to survive . . . the ego must go on the offensive and cease to
> be passive. This movement from passive to active is techni-
> cally a reaction formation, and the oedipal configuration . . .
> thus appears as itself a defense against the original wish. The
> wish to be inundated is reversed into a wish to possess.[45]

The oedipal structure is "superimposed upon an original ambivalence, a rapid alternation of attraction and repulsion,"[46] which suggests that Weiskel as well as the authors of the literature of the sublime, Hertz observes, have "an investment in moving from the
murkier regions of the preoedipal or maternal into the clearer light
of what Weiskel reads as a 'secondary oedipal system' . . . where
the position of Father, Mother, and Child are more firmly triangu-
lated—at considerable cost, but in a reassuring fashion."[47] The clarity of the oedipal is infinitely preferable to the seductive but chaotic
terrors of the preoedipal.

But such clarity is established at the expense of the mother, she
who has trouble, notes Kristeva, both acknowledging and being
acknowledged by the symbolic realm. She is abjected, a necessary
precondition of narcissism, for this abjection enables the child to
acquire both identity and language. According to Kristeva in *Powers
of Horror*, the abject is the "pseudo-object" of primal repression,
which is the most "archaic" separation from the mother. The child
experiences this separation as a blankness (*vide*), which Kristeva
connects to the bar or gap between signifier and signified in Saus-
surian linguistics. The *vide* is constitutive of the beginnings of the
symbolic function. It is what appears as the first separation between
what is not yet an *ego* (the child) and what is not yet an *object* (the
mother). Maintaining the separation between the mother and child,
the *vide* thus becomes the "third party, eventually the father," that
helps "the future subject" by contributing the "light" of the "symbolic." Importantly, as we have seen, the child already engages in
"strategies" that prefigure the logic of the symbolic order: "Even
before being *like* [i.e., identifying with the father], 'I' am not but do
separate, reject, ab-ject."[48] For Kristeva, were it not for a "solidarity"
or "complicity" between the not-yet subject and the not-yet father,
"chaos will take away all possibility of distinction, of a trace and of
symbolization, leading to the confusion of the limits of bodies, of

words, of the real and the symbolic."[49] Specifying the implications of her notions, Hertz suggests that "we should not be surprised that it is 'the mother' who is cast (and cast out)" in the symbolic role of that which is abjected in order to stabilize the subject: "assertions of unified identity typically entail 'gestures of misogyny.'"[50] Such assertions illustrate Kristeva's point that it is the conflation of women with the maternal function that has contributed to the oppression of women.

Hertz's analysis helps us further to bridge the gap between feminist concerns to address, rather than gloss over, such misogynistic gestures and Kristeva's theory of subjectivity. Just as the development of a female subject traces a more complex trajectory than that of a male subject, as discussed above, so the operations of abjection and sublimation might comprise more difficult undertakings for women than for men because of the symbolic function as "sacrifice" the feminine has played.[51] The Master letters, tracing a traumatic phase into which they increasingly descend, reverse the movement from passive to active that Weiskel describes as characteristic of resolution in the literature of the sublime.

If we turn to some Dickinson poems to which Hertz's notion of the end-of-the-line structures apply, what we find is a similar pattern staged: an attentuated self signals the sublime scenario; that attentuation, however, is not resolved but remains suspended in irresolvability. Such poems represent not only a dislocated, shifting, at times abjected self, but alienation. The divided self represented in such poems does not, or cannot, "put itself back together again" at the expense of a violence to an externalized feminine other, for in these instances, the violence accompanying specularity and unified subjectivity has no object but the feminine subject herself.

"Like Eyes that looked on Wastes" (P 458) illustrates what Hertz has described (discussing Wordsworth) as "an end-of-the-line structure of pure self-reflexivity: a poet presents a surrogate of himself, the 'I' who says 'I think,' discovering that the object of his reflection is necessarily split."[52] Dickinson's poem doubles that split, for the speaker is looking as if into a mirror that reflects back, as Wallace Stevens will put it in "The Snow Man," both "Nothing that is not there and the nothing that is":

> Like Eyes that looked on Wastes–
> Incredulous of Ought
> But Blank–and steady Wilderness–
> Diversified by Night–
>
> Just Infinites of Nought–
> As far as it could see
> So looked the face I looked upon–
> So looked itself–on Me–
>
> (*P* 438)

The dashes in the last line seem particularly eloquent here, graphically enacting both the separation of and the connection between "itself" and "Me." The "necessarily split" object of reflection, the face, is here both "other" and "Me"; the "I" cannot cover over that split in order to achieve even an illusory sense of unitary identity.

Hertz notes that questions of gender at such moments aid the author/surrogate in moving out of suspension and relocating the self on firm ground. But in Dickinson's poem, there is nothing to move the speaker out of specular suspension. Signifying nothing, the metonymic chain of synonyms ("Wastes," "Ought," "Blank," "Nought") does not advance meaning, although, eerily, "nothing" defers meaning indefinitely. Caught in a structure of similarities from which nothing can (not) escape, "nothing" multiplies–an abyss of nothing(s) ("Infinites of Nought"). Although "nothing" is repeated with a difference, in rhyme as well as synonym, that difference nevertheless is repeatedly turned into reflexive sameness. In such poems metonymy offers no liberating displacement or subversive indeterminacy; rather, it highlights a *mise en abîme* of the Same masquerading as difference. The paradox of a "steady Wilderness–/Diversified by Night" suggests that the only difference the poem allows is the difference between varying degrees of opacity, varying reflections of what is, in essence, nonreflective. The prosodic elements that turn the poem technically in upon itself underscore the poem's theme. With nothing in which to locate herself except the other's eyes, the speaker cannot unify herself at the expense of the other because "it" is "s/he."

The dynamics of power and self-assertion typically accompanying this structure are apparent, as suggested by the language of the overwhelming sublime ("Incredulous," "Infinites") and the power connoted by the words that characterize the relationship of the two figures ("Queen" and "reign"). But no self-consolidation can be mobilized except that imposed by Law: "The Misery a Compact." The self is "unified" by a contractual "agreement . . . between parties," as Dickinson's dictionary defines "compact." The figure of an introjected legal "Compact" marks the inescapable sense of internal alienation from which the self cannot be "absolved" without dissolving itself. The issue of gender identity comes in at the end of the poem, not in order that the feminine necessarily be sacrificed to the process of reestablishing a reassuringly unified self, but to reenforce the impossibility of resolution:

> Neither would be a Queen
> Without the Other—Therefore—
> We perish—tho' We reign—
>
> (*P* 458)

Enacting a similar dilemma, Poem 642, "Me from Myself—to banish," defines the solution as both violent and impossible:

> But since Myself—assault Me—
> How have I peace
> Except by subjugating
> Consciousness?
>
> And since We're mutual Monarch
> How this be
> Except by Abdication—
> Me—of Me?
>
> (*P* 642)

Because it cannot be externalized, violence in such poems is specifically destructive rather than reconstitutive of the self.

In "One need not be a Chamber—to be Haunted" (*P* 670), the irresolution of an internalized division is similarly sustained, the reader left suspended in the poem's own indecision. What interests me about this poem is the way it combines the dynamics of the end-of-the line structure—the self threateningly overwhelmed—with the language of what Mary Ann Doane has described as "the paranoid subgroup" in literature and film, the Gothic. Instead of sexuality, she points out, the genre offers masochistic fantasy. Doane locates this Gothic subgenre within an analysis of representations of femininity: "the space which the woman is culturally assigned, the home, through its fragmentation into places that are seen and unseen, becomes the site of terror and victimization—the look turned violently against itself."[53]

In Dickinson's poem, the image of the house and the unseen (uncanny) Gothic threat have been figured as internal, causing the self "one's a'self [to] encounter":

One need not be a Chamber—to be Haunted—
One need not be a House—
The Brain has Corridors—surpassing
Material Place—

Far safer, of a Midnight Meeting
External Ghost
Than it's interior Confronting—
That Cooler Host.

Far safer, through an Abbey gallop,
The Stones a'chase—
Than Unarmed, one's a'self encounter—
In lonesome Place—

Ourself behind ourself, concealed—
Should startle most—
Assassin hid in our Apartment
Be Horror's least.

The Body—borrows a Revolver—
He bolts the Door—
O'erlooking a superior spectre—
Or More—

(*P* 670)

The metonymic chain signifying haunted internality ("Chamber," "House," "Corridors," "lonesome Place," "Apartment") creates an image of the self itself, of course, as the mysterious Gothic house. The poem *embodies* the dynamic of a look turned against itself.

The problem set up in the first stanza and sustained until the last is an internalized menace that prevents the self from keeping inside and outside separate, which is precisely the nature of the preoedipal Weiskel has discussed as characteristic of the negative sublime. That impasse seems resolved in the last stanza, where the self threatening itself, the internal danger, has negotiated a passage to externalization: the self is finally able to bolt the door against itself. But with body now armed, and gendered, against a threat to which "He" can "bolt the Door," the newly established distinction in fact blurs. The unseen becomes a "seen" that mirrors, and further confuses, the difference between this self and its menacing other.

The gendered "body" that emerges at the end of this poem seems to signal, like the poetic conventions of the sublime, an attempt to identify and thereby control differences, but the move does not solve the self's crisis so much as it renders the poem's resolution ambiguous. The initial "One" (though never really *one*) is haunted by the discovery of "Ourself behind ourself, concealed" (the "fracture within"). In the poem's conclusion, "He" arms himself, attempting to fix a previously indeterminate gender identity and to control the look: he is "O'erlooking." But "O'erlooking" is open to two mutually exclusive meanings: looking over (seeing or overseeing, suggestive of control) and overlooking (failing to see, suggestive of repression). The look in the penultimate line is, moreover, returned, mirroring the body's attempt to oversee difference, for the etymology of "spectre" (L. *specere*) implies looking as well as being looked at. If we fix the other that is also the self (constituted as/in the other), we theoretically gain the capacity to remain in the plenitude of imaginary identification that offers us the possibility of wholeness. But such reflexivity in these poems by Dickinson does not achieve wholeness. The poems remain suspended between difference and identity, reassurance and threat.

Though the capacity to unify may be illusory for male poets, it is more often sustained in their poetry, for the difference within can be effectively externalized as feminine. That resolution is not one

Dickinson takes, as the poems discussed above illustrate. If internal difference nevertheless seems undesirable, then the attempt to hold the alienated self in one's mutual, self-mirroring gaze in Poem 670 may be construed as the attempt to stabilize an identity threatened by splits and fractures. But at the same time, gendering the body as "He" in the last stanza suggests a desire to delineate a difference that must be closely guarded if it is not to be pulled back into an imaginary confusion of identification.

Poem 670 turns on this paradoxical axis and concludes in con-tradictory excess, not synthesis. The illusion on which self-unity is founded is at *issue* in the poem, foregrounded by the self's mascu-line gender, but hardly resolved. As the perfect rhymes of the final stanza suggest, the self *thinks* "He" has reconstituted himself safely, made himself impermeable to what the specter represents. The "Revolver" the self "borrows" in order to defend himself highlights the potential violence of the process. The poem represents as well the self-delusion such defenses require: thinking himself safe, "He" overlooks (fails to recognize) an internal, unassimilable difference by which "He" is still haunted.

The poem indicates that the desire to return, to reclaim one's lost identity, to uncover the secret Home holds—all elements of Gothic fascination and autobiographical motive—is a frightful jour-ney for women, but not because of "the fear of femaleness itself," as Claire Kahane characterizes the Gothic.[54] Rather, discovering Home's secret implies revealing that the enemy that is "Ourself behind ourself" is the split feminine self who has, if we take the poem at its word, internalized masculinity, by definition as fear of femaleness. To wit, the speaker in Poem 670 is herself the uncanny locus in which "His" drama unfolds. The confrontation with the oedipal mother, as Doane implies, is with received misogynistic *representations* of femininity (castrated, disempowered). In contrast to the Master letters, Dickinson's poems of attentuated selfhood record a failure fully to sublimate (control) a phallogocentric femi-nine presence, which spills out of the poetic frame, as suggested by that which exceeds the visual register of Poem 670's "superior spec-tre": the ominous "Or More" of the last line.

If sublimation via visual representation produces a sense of mastery over an overwhelming presence figured as feminine, then

Dickinson complicates its consolations. Poem 675's central image, "Essential Oils," more affirmatively exceeds the resolution of the sublime scenario. The puns that have caused this poem to be read as metapoetic are, at the same time, significantly tinged with a violently expelled and vulvomorphic sexuality (what Jane Gallop, following Michèlle Montrelay, has called the *odor di femina*).[55] This "essence" can only be covertly "expressed," at once evoked and disguised, by the poem's metaphysical import:[56]

> Essential Oils–are wrung–
> The Attar from the Rose
> Be not expressed by Suns–alone–
> It is the gift of Screws–
>
> The General Rose–decay–
> But this–in Lady's Drawer
> Make Summer–When the Lady lie
> In Ceaseless Rosemary–

> (*P675*)

Miller notes that "screw" had the same colloquial use in the nineteenth century that it does today, and that "Drawer" puns on "drawers."[57] The sachet, then, is meant to mask the woman's trace on even *this* "this" (on freshly laundered drawers, for example?). The pun on "Suns," coupled with the hyphenated isolation of "alone," connotes an activity that "sons" alone (only) don't express (daughters can write, too), and that "sons" don't express alone (that is, they express it through a dialectical process: in a word, intercourse; masturbation won't do it): "Essential Oils" are the "gift" of many wrung "Screws."

An evergreen used to scent corpses in the nineteenth century as well as to spice food, rosemary disguises unacceptably intense smells. Its name doubles the by-now thoroughly sexualized "Rose" and joins to it "Mary," Christianity's mother who "expressed" the essential Word made Flesh from her own flesh, after which she was, according to patristic doctrine, restored to her original immaculate state.[58] But what if the Lady "lies" about the indeterminate "this" in her "Drawer(s)" that made "Summer"? Like Rose-Mary, essence is "wrung" from her body, causing her to (re)produce words, after which she does her laundry, smells nice again. She purifies herself, disguises through sublimation the odiferous union of expressed essences as if it were the smell of decay. She manages sublimation, makes sense and masks scents, but it costs her her life. The overwhelming scents in this poem exceed the metaphysical economy overtly celebrated by the text, and are associated quite literally with female corpses that litter the literary corpus. Still, uncannily, macabrely, "the Lady" persists in smelling!

That odor, of course, is from what we might see (or what we can't see but can certainly smell) as keeping the expulsion of femininity in Dickinson's poems, upon which the unification of the self depends, incomplete. Dickinson does not provide us with the sublime's structural climax to self-loss, the self-reclamation and reassuring return to the oedipal territory that characterizes the resolving trajectory, but with that loss's impasse to satisfactory closure for women. Her poems sustain their focus on the "Wastes" (the *vides*) that both inspire and frustrate representation, the speaker's gaze "Incredulous of Ought / But Blank—and steady Wilderness—": that which can only be designated but not grasped in language, and like Kristeva's semiotic *chora*, connoted as nourishing (*Essential* Oils). Sublimation doesn't fully manage to repress (indeed, it *expresses*, as Poem 675 insists) what emits or emotes from this space, causing an implicitly female anxiety—but also exhilaration—associated with the bio-logic of the mother's/our own bodies. A trace. A whiff. Another scent(s) of place.

ECSTATIC CONTRACTS

In the territory of the sublime, at the limits of identity, observes Kristeva, all subjects put up an image of the mother, a "fantasied" but necessary protection against self-loss.[59] The poems discussed above are structured by ambivalence in relation to that figure, but they do not, as we have seen, move out of that murky terrain to regain the self. They oscillate between anxiety and exhilaration, but settle on neither. The anxiety is not resolved, the exhilarating return to clarity never completed. Like the male Romantics, at the threshold of identity, Dickinson too figures the feminine, but unlike them, since for her that figure functions in part as surrogate self, she does not fully exorcise it from the text.

We might at this point reconsider the possibility that the structure of a doubly split subject is emblematic of Dickinson's work. It provides an intersection where the sublime's attenuated subject, unable or refusing to externalize the split as an abjected feminine image, conjoins with the more positive figure of the ebullient, letter-writing Dickinson. Stonum asserts that one of the distinctions of Dickinson's literary project is that the economy she affirms is "entirely linguistic or discursive—that is to say, poetic."[60] Her disseminatory poems defer (to), as well as differ from, their meaning(s) to readers as a way of eschewing mastery. I would like in this section to complicate the issue by suggesting that she doesn't eschew control so much as she redefines it as a trope for a particular writing *practice.* Her discourse is marked by an ambivalence sublimated in what I shall characterize as Dickinson's "mothering" poetics.

Dickinson's art does not dispense with, but (re)charges the formal conventions of her day. As Miller observes, her language use, in comparison with her female contemporaries, is not unique in its designs. But, unlike the work of those contemporaries, the regularity of Dickinson's prosody contrasts with her disruptive punctuation, inverted and elliptical syntax, metrical irregularity, off-rhyme, and ungrammaticality.[61] She retains her contemporaries' thematic emphasis on love, at times quite conventionally (for example: "If I can stop one Heart from breaking" [*P* 919]). There is, however, a version in her thinking of this common theme that extends it specifically to a writing whose relationship to the Law is distinctly revised.

In Poem 247, she calls this version an "*Extatic* contract"—in a legal sense, an agreement among parties (that is, intersubjective); in a poetic sense, writing's affirmation of a double as well as divided subject (that is, etymologically, being beside oneself: ek-static). "Take all away from me," she writes, "but leave me Ecstasy, / And I am richer then than all my Fellow Men" (*P* 1640 and *L* 960), and she continues: "And what *is* Ecstasy but Affection and what is Affection but the Germ of the little Note?" (*L* 960, Dickinson's emphasis). In the former passage, Dickinson describes a passive yet oddly privileged process of deprivation. Although she represents herself as having no control of ownership, her being left in the end with nothing but ecstasy is cast in terms of an economic standard by which she excels.[62] In the latter passage, the self-dislocation implied by ecstasy is the emotional economy ("Affection") that germinates writing (the note she has sent). She evinces an *aspiration* to self-difference whose meaning transfers through corporeal ecstasy, proffered affection, and on to ek-static writing, the significance of which resides in its destination. Dickinson transforms her thematically conventional retention of "love" into a more radical poetic economy built on an ek-static subjectivity. Mobilized by a recognition of internal alterity, this subject writes to exceed herself, dowering affection translated by/into/as words: "This loved Philology" (*P* 1651).

Dickinson's reconceptualization of love generates the shift from a specular to a discursive economy, which allows her not only to resist objectification, but to reject the sadistic resolution of the sublime's crisis. She does not, however, oppose this convention with a "feminine" alternative, masochism or self-abnegating renunciation,[63] but with the refusal to settle on either version. Dickinson's work sustains an indeterminacy that equivocates at the levels of grammar, rhetoric, and logic. To take but one example, the demonstrative pronoun *this* has no referent but nevertheless demonstrates a delightful and macabre survival of both the Rose's and the Lady's "decay." Such an economy is based on a mutually constitutive exchange, to recall the discussion of the early letter that opened this chapter (*L* 35), between one context and another, between written word and its reader, and thus transferring to the future.[64] The Lady's "this" is both left to the reader to make of it what she can, and continues to make what the Lady did in the first place, "Summer," making the reader reproduce the original (the "gold thread" returns) as well as produce her own "this." This "this" retains its original integrity even as the ambiguity of expression leaves "it" open to shifting interpretations through time.

This "this–in Lady's Drawer," sign for both absence and presence, enacts the linguistic sublimation of ambivalence about the maternal itself. Split between abjection and identification, refusing to settle on the mother as an object of either operation, Dickinson transfers the process to poetic activity. She avows a writing practice that creates a text able to mean differently down through the ages without sacrificing itself (by analogy, maternal love without self-loss), and disavows the practice if the word remains so attached to its authorial origins that meaning is forever legislated, subjugating any reader's power. Such sublimation suggests that Dickinson's poetic economy might be informed by what I term an ethics of "maternal" care,[65] one whose value depends on the nature of the "mother's" trace—whether, for instance, it dowers or despairs. The mother (word) that gives with conditions, takes; the (mother) word that gives without conditions, dowers us.[66]

The implications of Dickinson's discursive ethics become clearer if we look at how she uses the word *care*. It crops up in the same early letter, which includes a description of her refusal to participate in the mass religious conversions that overtook the Connecticut Valley of her youth, when she alone of all her family had not been "called":

> Christ is calling everyone here, all my companions have answered, even my darling Vinnie believes she loves, and trusts him, and I am standing alone in rebellion, and growing very careless. (*L* 35)

The primary meaning of *careless* is, of course, "having no care" and "unthinking" / "heedless," as Dickinson's dictionary defines it, and as she herself seems to suggest. But her use of the word connotes *care-less* as well, that is, *love-less*. Such a sense does not necessarily suggest the concomitant *motherless*, but her dictionary glosses the definition with a conventionally misogynistic image: the example of carelessness is that of "a *careless* mother; a mother *careless of* or *about* her children, is an unnatural parent."

For Dickinson, "A Word dropped careless on a Page" (*P* 1261) doesn't germinate a care-full, dialectical exchange between text and reader, original and transformed meaning, through time, but breeds "Infection in the sentence."[67] Such carelessness doesn't deny meaning: the source of the contamination is the signifying medium itself, "Word." But carelessness also arouses ("stimulates") the eye's consumption (in both senses of the word) of a single sense, "Infection":

> We may inhale Despair
> At distances of Centuries
> From the Malaria—
>
>   (*P* 1261)

Inspiring sickness through its bondage to literality, the care-less word has no meaning other than the repetition of its own love-less origin. This process reproduces a constant signification tied to a body whose desire to control, induced by despair, survives even as that "Wrinkled Maker" lies "folded in perpetual seam," rendering the Maker's presence a ghastly present (both a perpetual "seem" and an unseemly gift).

While the Maker's gender isn't overtly designated, we might set up a metonymic chain suggestive of fecundity tainted with the mother (word's) contaminating corpus. Beginning with the implications of *careless* uncovered by a trip to Dickinson's dictionary, we could continue on through the eroticized connotations of *stimulate*, to a word that conflates infection and reproduction, *breeds* (a conflation Margaret Dickie notes as well),[68] to catch finally an unmistakable whiff of the *odor di femina*: "Malaria," that is, "bad air" (of "sickness," a euphemism in Dickinson's day, according to Wolff, for pregnancy).[69] This excess is one of feminine suffering caused by the internalization of dominant fictions of femininity. The textual trace of pain runs as uncomfortably close to the surface as a mother who, paradoxically sickeningly present in her dutiful sacrifice of self, threatens to infect the reader every time she reads the seemly "lie," poetic inspiration or virtuous renunciation, meant to disguise self-denial. The self-abnegating writer, actually careless because she is dead, nevertheless exerts control, because her word is bound to represent, and thereby perpetuate, her body's experience of a despair that locks word to body in perpetuity. No exchange, no passage out of the letter (that is, the literal), is possible here. Only the return of displaced despair stimulating the whole morbid "infection" all over again.

In contrast, we have the literary foremother of "I think I was enchanted"(*P* 593), Elizabeth Barrett Browning. As a female *artist* she represented for her poetic daughter the actualization of a language that transports the speaker/reader out of herself (identification with conventional femininity), offering her a creative alternative to orthodox conversion. As Hertz comments about such "moments of blockage" as the one in which the speaker of Poem 593 is located, the literature of the sublime draws on the language of religious conversion: "that is, from a literature that describes major experiential transformation, the mind not merely challenged and thereby invigorated but thoroughly 'turned around'."[70] After having "read that Foreign Lady," the speaker is "enchanted," her consciousness altered, as the etymology of the word suggests, by (lyric) song. The world seems transformed:

> The Dark—felt beautiful—
>
> And whether it was noon at night—
> Or only Heaven—at Noon—
> For very Lunacy of Light
> I had not power to tell—
>
> The Bees—became as Butterflies—
> The Butterflies—as Swans—
> Approached—and spurned the narrow Grass—
> And just the meanest Tunes
>
> That Nature murmured to herself
> To keep herself in Cheer—
> I took for Giants—practising
> Titanic Opera—
>
> The Days—to Mighty Metres stept—
> The Homeliest—adorned
> As if unto a Jubilee
> 'Twere suddenly confirmed—
>
> (P 593)

The speaker cannot "tell" whether it is the world or her perception that has changed, as suggested by words denoting both sensibility ("I felt," "I took for") and metamorphosis ("as Butterflies," "as Swans," "as if a Jubilee") rather than empirical knowledge. The poem details a different kind of epistemological "confirmation" than either science or orthodox religion provides.

Since "Conversion of the Mind / Like Sanctifying in the Soul– / Is Witnessed–not explained–," the speaker most obviously bears witness to, rather than explains, what she insists is both indefinable and unrepresentable ("I could not have defined the change," "I had not power to tell"). Through the formal union of sound and sense, the text gestures toward a sublime feminine realm, which poetic language equivocally marks. Thematically, for example, "meanest Tunes" transform into "Titanic Opera," but metrically, mean and "Mighty Metres" are undifferentiated in the poem. The import resides, ironically, in the very discourse it exceeds. But should the transformed self be "poisoned" by sanity, threatening to revert again to a "sombre Girl," the antidote nevertheless lies in the magical poetry the dead literary mother has left behind as her legacy:

> 'Twas a Divine Insanity–
> The Danger to be Sane
> Should I again experience–
> 'Tis Antidote to turn–
>
> To Tomes of solid Witchcraft
> Magicians be asleep–
> But Magic–hath an Element
> Like Deity–to keep–
>
> (*P* 593)

The speaker is threatened not so much by division of, but reversion to, an unaltered self.

Even though she represents her state of pure sensual perception as divinely postlogical, however, the text puts her credibility in question: she is "insane." Thus, because she can neither refute nor counter, because she cannot reason but only see, her version is in essence a con/version. It is not only another story that resists conventional resolutions to her state (the incorporation into the self of alterity), but a criminal tale, fully contaminated by an unreliable and, we might recall, capricious femininity. Having been deprived of her reason (having metaphorically lost her head), the speaker has also been given her head, through her heretical reading of that "Foreign Lady." As poetic "Antidote," the foremother's word has the power to heal her literary daughter from the poisonous sanity of a patristic doctrine that has, implicitly, been sanitized of feminine influences (or effluences) nominalized as witchcraft.[71] The speaker finds a subversive genealogy in "Tomes of solid Witchcraft," trace of an occulted female-identified activity.[72] Dickinson's poem imaginatively achieves the transformation of ambivalence about the maternal (text) into affirmation of its magical and godlike capacity to "keep." The poem both transfers its power to its readers and itself retains an original potency to which we can turn and return. By ingesting its magic, the speaker/reader is restored and can then herself engage in the creative capacity to (dis)figure: to wit, to write herself.

As implied earlier, however, the speaker's identification with this idealized version of poetic "mothering" is inflected by her incredibility. Like the poetic text itself, the speaker is different from, as well as nourished by, that which she experiences. The poem complicates its representation of a female reader's relationship to a female writer's body of work, undermining through the speaker's unreliability, as well as valorizing through the speaker's vision, the reality of this heretical feminine power. Doubling the divide between mother writer and daughter reader, poetic language is situated precisely between them, the medium of exchange through which not only maternal identification is (de)privileged, but reproduced through a mind-altering embrace of difference. The ecstatic internal state is catalyzed by reading a literally foreign, as well as external, other (the "Foreign Lady"). Like the bifurcation of the maternal figure into "good" and "bad" mothering, the tension between conservative prosody and transformative semantic possibility characterizes the "extatic contract" of Dickinson's oeuvre.

In a letter Dickinson wrote late in her life to Judge Lord, her suitor, the issues that I have been exploring in this chapter conjoin with "Witchcraft," an overdetermined word that she used to describe the maternal antidote to paternal poison in Poem 593. She wryly redeems the term from its pejorative New England specificity, resemanticizing it by conflating it with a version of love that is

at once bawdy and ascetic, located in both deprivation and nour-
ishment:

> It may surprise you I speak of God–I know him but a little,
> but Cupid taught Jehovah to many an untutored Mind–
> Witchcraft is wiser than we–(*L* 562)

In this passage, Dickinson disrupts and reverses the orthodox
Christian view that it is God who teaches love, at the same time as
she playfully confuses Cupid with Witchcraft.

Earlier in the letter, she had noted conventionally that love
"makes a difference with all," changing her experience and perception of the world. The metonymic chain of associations she set up
to illustrate this difference began ordinarily enough, with "the whis-
tle of a Boy passing late at Night" and "the Low [?] of a Bird." But
the series ends startlingly: "[sheet cut away] Satan." Whatever she
wrote modifying "Satan," graphically unreadable and unknowable,
is also implicitly unspeakable: the letter seems suddenly heretical.
Redefining the Christian doctrine of (brotherly) love, Dickinson
sets up Cupid and Witchcraft as heterogeneously/dialogically interchangeable in an association that invokes a dangerous, distinctly
unchristian heritage. What seems reassuringly redeemed for love is
not only a satanic (that is, Romantic) eruption, but also a vertiginous play of and with the discursive trace of an expunged feminine
activity infamous for (among other things) the capacity of its prac-
tioners to leave their human bodies and to shift shapes during
ecstatic trances.

Finally, Dickinson irreverently characterizes the Bible at the
same time as she specifically questions the universality of its words:
"the Bible says very roguishly, that the 'wayfaring Man, though a
Fool–need not err therein'; need the 'wayfaring' Woman?" By separating woman out from man, this ironic question foregrounds the
oppressive and universalizing uses to which patristic language has
been put, and questions the proposition that when we say "Man"
we mean women as well. Dickinson's question plays off the etymological similarity between "wayfaring" (traveling) and "erring"
(straying, wandering), subverting self-location, as we saw in the letters to Higginson. With no *body* to love, Lord is told to appeal to the

Word, in an image that wittily carnalizes that most prominent member of the patriarchal canon: "Ask," Dickinson writes him, "your throbbing Scripture." This comment immediately precedes and ironically informs the coming to God (and we might surmise that the play between *God* and *Lord* was not lost on Dickinson) that love—a restored and reclaimed "witchcraft"—has taught her.

As Dickinson says in this letter's opening, "Dont you know you are happiest while I withhold and not confer—dont you know that 'No' is the wildest word we consign to Language?" Her renunciation of physical union bodies forth a split feminine subject unassociated with masochism and unconfined by specularization. Unattached to determinate meaning, this subject gives up her place as controlling center without vacating it. She divests her position of assumptions of (or pretentions to) poetic power, but does not sacrifice her agency as speaking subject (as did, for example, the Master letters). In so doing, she figures a power that gives without loss. Dickinson withholds herself in an affirmatively negative gesture that sexualizes her text, denying and evoking the body's absence upon which she, too, insists, miming poetic tradition at the same time as the erotic and spacious excess of her words humorously revise its gender conventions. As the "wildest word," *no* is a negative that inscribes an unconstrained, unsubmissive female desire consigned to, given over to the care of, language.[73] Dickinson has shifted the terms of love and poetry. Writing out of love, caring for Lord (rather than replacing him) with her words, she has an ecstatic contract with her pen. Like an irrepressibly shape-changing witch on her broomstick, she capriciously differs from and withholds herself. "Equivocal to the end," as Adrienne Rich puts it (*ARP*, 30), Dickinson gives and keeps her word.

3   *Less Is Moore*

MARIANNE MOORE'S
POETIC SUBJECT

*M*arianne Moore typifies, like Emily Dickinson before her, a radical conservatism. Betsy Erkkila characterizes her as a "modernist anomaly," a New Woman who observed a Victorian standard of decorum in her life, an avant-garde poet whose writing practice is informed by an earlier feminism's ethos of service.[1] Through her modernist poetics of multiple discourses, Moore revises images of hegemonic femininity and deprivileges poetry (or rather, Poetry), replacing traditional thematic and formal conventions, engendering differences.[2] As Rachel Blau DuPlessis observes, in a phrase that might apply to Dickinson as well, "She is her own standard."[3] Moore extends Dickinson's singularly divided romantic subjectivity into a modern subject-in-process at once constituted by and dispersed into poetic language.[4]

One aspect of Dickinson's poetic methodology that Moore appreciated, commenting on it in her 1933 review of the publication of an expanded edition of *Letters of Emily Dickinson* (ed. Mabel Loomis Todd), was "its daring associations of the prismatically true" (*CP*, 292). The phrase typifies Moore's own ideal of poetic organization through original ("daring") combinations of statements from a spectrum of truth(s).[5] Her project is characterized by the endeavor to change the dominant social order by altering its conventional representations through a poetic practice that entails a reassociating

73

activity. In contrast to the male modernists, Moore's is a poetics that may have longed to enact the direct treatment of a thing, but in fact more often worked from the world "already represented," as Bonnie Costello comments: "The poet's function [for Moore] is not to say something, so much as to creatively order and reimagine our sayings."[6] Such a "creative" reordering implies agency. Moore's methodology is influenced by the feminist perspective she brings to her own "daring associations of the prismatically true."[7]

Like Dickinson, Moore was conscious of the dynamics of the gaze, but rather than disappear, she performs "herself" as an "independent woman."[8] Moore's feminist modernism enables her to symbolize hegemonic masculinity, not as all-powerful, an entity that threatens one even from within, but as one perspective among others. The subject positions from which the Moore poems under discussion speak about the feminine can be characterized as equivocally inhabiting,[9] and exposing, a masculinist position, as I shall argue in this chapter. This chapter will consider the relationship in Moore's work of self-representation, subject position(s), and a feminist poetic methodology.

UNDOING FEMINOLATRY

Sobered by obstruction, with forces knit by the injustices of convention, Carey Thomas avowed what in life she contradicted: "Secrecy and guile are the only refuge of a down-trodden sex." The victim of gossip because she had discussed a scholastic matter with a German student on what her landlady termed "the betrothal sofa," she thence behaved as she had in the Cornell "elegant garden of young men," "not only with decorum but with marked decorum" and said years after, "Bryn Mawr need not be the less guarded because it is good."
 —Marianne Moore, "M. Carey Thomas of Bryn Mawr"

According to Marianne Moore, Carey Thomas's early experience of gender discrimination produced a contradiction between life and speech, self-representation and self, fundamental to her *modus operandi* as a woman in her culture. The young Thomas was seen as improper because she was conducting herself as if she were a man, as if the signs of gender she surely had on *were not there*. She was acting as if they were not there *in the wrong place*, "the betrothal sofa," where she should not have been except in a prescribed relationship to the man. Intoxicated by the coincidence of seeming and being, Thomas was unseemly. The consequence was that she was sobered up by becoming the "victim of gossip" that had been intended, as Moore's passage makes clear, to put the errant woman in her place.

Thomas was victimized, in effect, for not participating in the masquerade of feminine sexuality. Refusing to display herself as a conventional object of desire, she made a spectacle of herself. Refusing to be objectified, she was reduced to the object of gossip. Her self-presentation was misrepresentation. A neutral decorum is universal only insofar as the boundaries of propriety are not exceeded, after which a woman must re-mark herself "feminine." Behaving with "decorum" but not with "marked decorum" is, for a woman, to behave as a man.

I have been implying, of course, that the decorum for which Moore herself was so validated was also a *marked* decorum. As Carolyn Burke comments, "For the women writers of [the modernist] generation, stating the self was rarely a straight-forward undertaking." Elsewhere she contends that their awareness of gender issues "differently inflected" how and what they wrote, producing a cultural critique different in kind from the male modernists.[10] Along the same lines, DuPlessis describes the woman writer as a "marked marker": ideology, culture, representation will always inflect what she (re)marks, or notices, as well as what she herself marks, or writes.[11] In the passage quoted as epigraph to this section, for example, Moore marks Thomas's problem as the integrity of seeming and being, for which she suffered a victimization that left its mark on her future thinking around the issue of "appropriate" female conduct. In Moore's description of Thomas's later, barely successful negotiation of the academy, her public conduct has changed:

> Any who have thought of Carey Thomas as ipso facto Bryn Mawr, will find it difficult to realize what handicap "the shrine of womanhood" once constituted, and that a woman who was virtual administrator and dean of a college was made president officially by a majority of but one vote; then only after years of "wary foresight in holding back and driving forward at the right moments," was grudgingly elected to the board of trustees. (*CP*, 417)

Thomas's maneuvers are now marked by canny double moves alternating between strategic self-silencing and articulation that revise her earlier straightforwardness. Remarking that one's gender profoundly affects one's performance, Moore learned the lesson by rote. The contradictions, linguistic strategies, and masquerades that mark her self-portraits and poetry, which themselves are marks of the effects of gender, "can be made legible in feminist readings," DuPlessis suggests.[12]

Of the legibility such readings afford us, one example, that of Moore's "trademark" costume, shall suffice to illustrate. In the late 1940s, Costello recounts, Moore "walked into a milliner's shop and asked to be fitted as Washington Crossing the Delaware. The tricorn hat and cape [with a skirt] soon became the trademark of this deliberate American."[13] Costello reads what is in effect Moore's transvestism, which Costello discreetly overlooks, as indication of her stylistic cultivation of everything American. In an otherwise even-toned scholarly study, John M. Slatin is disturbed by Moore's cross-dressing, which, like Costello, he hastens to read as sign for her poetic style (although in his version Moore comes out the worse for wear). Discussing a photograph of the costumed Moore before the Brooklyn Bridge, taken in 1958 and shown in 1980 at the Rosenbach Collection in an exhibit entitled "In *Her Own* Image" (emphasis added),[14] Slatin (in 1986) describes how this portrait of the artist shows "a caricature, partly self-created and self-sustaining, . . . and like the *Complete Poems* of 1967, . . . sadly incomplete," unfortunately "shading into eccentricity."[15] Moore's crime is her longevity as well as her loss of the literary right stuff: the "living relic" creaking around Slatin's version of Moore's portrait could not have written the "aggressive," "rigorous" poems of her early career.[16] In search of a truer, more authentic Moore than the "kindly old lady" who doesn't know when to leave well enough alone, Slatin (who, as master reader, does know) has determined that Moore's masquerade is charade.

Although Slatin and Costello are right to transfer a reading of Moore's costume to her poetics, I suggest that we consider for a moment, rather than gloss over, the incongruities of Moore's dress. Molesworth tells us that Moore was very influenced in her thinking about the semiotics of fashion by Frank Parsons's *The Psychology of*

Dress.[17] Parsons uses the terms *clothes* and *costumes* synonymously, to go beyond, as he puts it, the sense of function or aesthetics in which fashion is usually understood. He argues that because clothes are an important material expression of an age's ideas (architecture being another), and fashion has historically been dictated hierarchically down through the classes, costuming has political implications. A centrally dictated style constitutes, in effect, an exercise of political control.[18] If one follows fashion, one participates in the reproduction of hegemonic power. It follows for Parsons, writing in the years ensuing not only World War I but the Russian revolution, that in a democracy ("Utopian individualism"), the democratization (or "proletariatization") of fashion allows for what American culture ideologizes: individual expression.[19]

Moore may not have adopted Parsons's polemical analysis of the history of Western fashion whole cloth, but his notions do suggest that Moore's assumption of overdetermined signs of not only revolutionary and nationalistic, but of masculine, authority indicates that her costume might be far more complicated than inadvertent self-parody.[20] It might also be, for example, an "ironic manipulation of the semiotics of performance and production," to borrow Nancy K. Miller's characterization of Lucy's performance of masculinity in *Villette.*[21] Sandra Gilbert suggests that Moore's early "female female" impersonation enabled her to adopt "an equivocally empowering" approach to the position of "fetishized femininity" in which she had been placed by critics, and from which she ironically questioned cultural conventions.[22] Moore's later costume plays with boundaries between hierarchized categories. Her appearance before the Brooklyn Bridge conjures up baseball (the Dodgers) as well as bards (Whitman and Hart Crane), flamboyant (and defiantly aging) New Women as well as idealized representations of (dead) Founding Fathers. As Gilbert asserts, Moore's playful dress signals "her 'old maid's' freedom from heterosexualized femininity."[23] Moore's performative dissociation from the masquerade of femininity (from woman defined as erotic object of the male gaze), as well as her "charade of masculinity" (the phrase is Stephen Heath's), refuses to reproduce conventions of either position.

Her late-life self-portraits indicate that she performed a similar operation of decontextualization in her writing, what I am calling a "masquerade" (though not in the Lacanian sense of the term). She plays with authorial identity. Establishing a "plural authority" of authorship,[24] the note on the notes in *The Complete Poems* seems an apology for the notes she nevertheless includes, as well as for her "hybrid method of composition."[25] Moore does not consider objections to her methodology, however, but recontextualizes them by wittily shifting their terms:

> A willingness to satisfy contradictory objections to one's manner of writing might turn one's work into the donkey that finally found itself being carried by its masters, since some readers suggest that quotation-marks are disruptive of pleasant progress; others, that notes to what should be complete are a pedantry or evidence of an insufficiently realized task. But since in anything I have written, there have been lines in which the chief interest is borrowed, and I have not yet been able to outgrow this hybrid method of composition, acknowledgements seem only honest. (*P*, 262)

As the disruption of the sense of completeness and "pleasant progress" implies, contemporary critics objected to Moore's use of quotation marks because they both remind readers of the text's constructedness and point beyond the poetic frame (the poem is not a self-contained, organic unit). But the "willingness to satisfy" such objections would place her, Moore notes, in an unnatural–even as(s)inine–position. She raises the issue of honesty instead, suggesting that perhaps "those who are annoyed by provisos . . . could be persuaded to take probity on faith and disregard the notes" (*P*, 262). In old age, as even Slatin admits, Moore was still capable of irony: Moore's notes, *not* her probity, are at issue.

Apparently eschewing "guile and secrecy," Moore is neither guileless nor straightforward, keeping back the fact that her acknowledgments, like the *Complete Poems*, are incomplete, as Lynn Keller substantiates, at the same time as she claims to be owning up to "borrowed" interest.[26] Moore typically "misquotes" the authors, moreover, whose words she represents as replacing her own.[27] She exceeds the supplement, sending the reader beyond the notes already outside the poetic framework, in a reading project that not only slyly reproduces Moore's own objectionable creative method, but further defers the complete knowledge of the texts' author(s) and the sense of the poems' completion. She disrupts the logic of the objections to incompleteness, demonstrating that the sense of "completeness" is artificial, not natural. Moore recomposes the processes by which we know, inscribing a more tenuous, active relationship of reading subject and written text to knowledge that may never be complete. I propose to consider her methodology a masquerade, redefined, like Moore's costume, as the active process of taking things out of their original contexts and putting them in new ones. This process constructs a new lyric subjectivity as well as questions discrete epistemological categories that, among other things, order gender identity.[28]

According to Costello, Moore equivocates about the relationship of her poetic material to her signature style, syllabics. The uniqueness of Moore's formal principle is that, unlike conventional metrics, "Syllabic measure works independently of statement, allowing statement its own order while establishing a new order in which words are liberated from syntax."[29] Slatin observes that whereas in conventional verse prosodic elements aid the understanding of syntactic and semantic relationships, "there is no such identifiable base" in Moore's work.[30] Freeing words from syntactic and semantic relation means, in one sense, liberating them from the purposeful function of poetic utterance. Moore's signature syllabic form is, in other words, a nonsignifying feature of the text against the grain of which meaning must be read.

At which point the form spills over into a meaningful feature, as when, in "In the Days of Prismatic Colour," for example, poetic meter parodied as a monstrous complexity associated with Eve is characterized as being "as it al-//ways has been—at the antipodes from the init-/ial great truths" (*P*, 41). Form seems in such lines (however coincidentally) to support and enact content. Although Moore's patterns bear no "discernible logic," Slatin comments, "once the form of the original stanza has been repeated—once form has become pattern—pattern *becomes* a logic," albeit an "inexplicable" one.[31] But how logical can an inexplicable logic be? Given the passage's import, the rhetoric of judgment against complexity and by extension, woman, the material does *not* support the method. Moore's equivocal disjunction of form and content, sustaining the regulated pattern against which the judgment of feminine verbal chaos presses, interrogates the misogynistic statement the poem is often understood as evincing (if gender is considered at all).

In "The Paper Nautilus," a poem that specifically associates the maternal with (good) form, the distinction between the signifying poetic statement and the nonsignifying formal pattern is similarly fluid. What is striking about the poem is the way the maternal figure of the poetic statement is identified so fully with her constructing activity that the finished product—literally the egg, figuratively the poem—eventually replaces her both textually and metapoetically. When her function is fulfilled, she disappears with her progeny. In addition to the conventional maternal ideal the poem purveys, the mother as reliable locus of love, the maternal role is dissociated from the mother herself. Since the maternal is graphically portrayed as an untenable identity for women, it cannot be redeemed as an unproblematic figure for the female poet.[32]

What seems at first a seamless integrity of content and form dissolves with the mother's uncanny disappearance. The paper nautilus "constructs her thin glass shell" solely for a functional purpose, to protect the eggs. This "watchful" maker/mother hardly "eats until the eggs are hatched," and doesn't stop until

> the intensively
> watched eggs coming from
> the shell free it when they are freed,—
> leaving its wasp-nest flaws
> of white on white, and close-
>
> laid Ionic chiton-folds
> like the lines in the mane of
> a Parthenon horse,
> round which the arms had
> wound themselves as if they knew love
> is the only fortress
> strong enough to trust to.

(P, 121–22)

The rhetorical closure, the assured knowledge of the strength of mother love which this final passage urges, is put in question by the subjunctive "as if," as well as by odd line breaks the syllabic form determines. The knowledge is strangely, grammatically predicated: it is the "arms," which can be understood in at least two ways,[33] that seem to but may only appear as if they know love (the line break forcing us to pause at this reading before pushing on to complete the "real" meaning). The poetic statement represents the mother as protective. The syllabic form highlights the status of maternal love as uncertain, and the mother herself, through another line break, as monstrous: "a devil-/fish" (*P*, 121).

To be sure, as feminist critics have noted, the maternal is thematically distinguished from bureaucratic greed ("authorities . . . / shaped by mercenaries"), as well as from writers succumbing to seductive bourgeois comforts ("teatime fame"). But the idealized images of the maternal are rendered equivocal by their interaction with the poem's formal features. The rhymes—as when the eggs, "hindered to succeed," are finally "freed"—semantically highlight liberation but technically bind the words. Once again we are pressed to read the poem's rhetoric against the formal grain, which disrupts with equivocation the text's conventional logic about the feminine and its maternal function and divides the poem's apparently singular voice. Through the dissociation of the mother-poet figure from her maternal/creative role, Moore leaves us both with an ambivalent validation of mother-artist for her conventionally maternal attributes and with a "shell" (though a beautiful one): the hollow ideology that not only constructs the institution, "motherhood," into which so many women have been assimilated historically, but the female "poetess" as representative of an empty, or emptied, formalism.

Moore's is a poetry that announces itself as *Observations*, the title of her first major collection, but her method of observation is inseparable from her eclectic reading habits. As feminist theory has postulated more recently,[34] reading entails for women a critical rereading not only of the canon, but of the woman it reifies. "Feminolatry," Moore suggests in her review of Pound's *Cantos*, is *old-fashioned* (*CP*, 272), and in her poems that most obviously train their attention on gender issues, she subverts it by exposing idealizing portraits of the decorously feminine or nurturingly maternal as cultural constructions.[35] Such stereotypes are undermined by Moore's typical deployment of categories to redefine them in her work, as Cristanne Miller observes of the black male maternal figure in "The Hero."[36]

In its conflation of feminine figure and poetic text, "A Carriage from Sweden" recalls the critical reconfiguration of the mother's aesthetic status in "The Paper Nautilus." The "beautiful she" and "this put-away/museum-piece," of which she "reminds" the speaker, are poetically associated:

> pine fair hair, steady gannet-clear
>   eyes and the pine-needled-path deer-
>   swift step; that is Sweden, land of the
>   free and the soil for a spruce-tree—
>
> vertical though a seedling—all
>   needles: from a green trunk, green shelf
>   on shelf fanning out by itself.
>
> (P, 131–32)

The equanimity of the syllabic form's distribution of line breaks and syntactic units not only graphically highlights, but lexically enacts, the thematic blurring of these two beautifully made objects.[37]

A meditation on metaphor as well as artistic craft, the poem literalizes its disruption of the normative hierarchy between tenor and vehicle (both, the poem underscores, are "man-made"). "A Carriage from Sweden" effectively confuses the two terms: Swedish woman and carriage are interchangeable. The woman may be a sign for the carriage, or vice versa, but the conflation of the lost craft's perfection with as telling an image of "the shrine of womanhood" as occurs anywhere in Moore's canon undoes the romantic ideal that frames the poem. Within the poetic frame, carriage and woman remain metonymically suspended en route to an undesignated location: the beautiful "she" is picked up by the carriage but never, we might say, put down.

As "The Paper Nautilus" and "A Carriage from Sweden" suggest, Moore's images of the feminine are elusive and shifting at the times they seem most reified. Her "hybrid method of composition" creates a Bakhtinian heteroglossia of competing ideologies and multiple discourses (even when there are no graphic marks of difference, like quotations marks), locating woman as an ideal in one language but disrupting it in another.[38] When "feminine" qualities are overtly examined, Moore portrays femininity as a site of a unitary, specularized identity, which keeps paradoxically slipping away. The epistemological systems for which it serves as both reflection and foundation are exposed as romances constructed at woman's expense. "Roses Only," for example, installs itself in the poetic tradition of the courtly love poem.[39] Moore's depiction of the spectacle of femininity, which the rose symbolizes, turns the tables on the homologizing reasons for the poetics of praise: it validates the rose for her (phallic) thorns, not her beauty. Though thorns "are not proof against a worm, the elements, or mildew," they can protect the rose from "the predatory hand" that might "prove" her "too violently." In Moore's irreverent revision of romantic convention, thorns offer protection from the appropriative logic of memorial assimilation and metaphoric substitution that underwrites heterosexual poetic tradition.

The text is also a complex depiction of dynamics that silence female speaking subjects. Throughout the poem we are offered the speaker's interpretation of the rose, for example, rather than the rose's about herself. Not altogether mindless (as the speaker admits the rose "must have brains"), it is nevertheless "idle" for her to attempt "to confute presumptions resulting from observations," which in the text's closing compel the rose's audience to comment that "your thorns are the best part of you." Others' observations define and determine her.

Though the rose be "brilliant," in other words, she is dumb, for as an address to the rose, the poem relegates her to ignorance as well as to silence. This vision of the rose is construed by a speaker who, as knowledge conflates with sight ("in view," "observations," "audience"), is also in the position of the male gaze. Dickinson typically frustrates the power of this position; in contrast, Moore's

transvestite poetic subject assumes that place. The rose becomes a
problematic sign, like Moore herself, for femininity:

> . . . you, a symbol of the
> unit, stiff and sharp,
> conscious of surpassing by dint of native superiority and
> liking for everything
> self-dependent, anything an
>
> ambitious civilisation might produce . . .
>
> (lines 4–9)

Traditionally a double symbol of female genitals and the tran-
science of beauty, the revised rose of this suggestive passage is a
rose . . . is a phallus. Unitary, self-referential, superior because self-
sufficient, the rose reflects, it would seem, the male term. Without
her thorns, in fact, the rose is improperly unknowable—a "what-is-
this, a mere/ /peculiarity" (lines 18–19). Not a unit, the rose is composed of multiple *parts,* which the speaker constantly overlooks in
order to value the "best part."

The movement of the poem's closing is to recognize and then
suppress the recognition of the rose as enigmatic, perpetually
"Guarding the/ infinitesimal pieces of [her] mind" (lines 22–23)
from her audience and appearing to oscillate between masculinity
and femininity. This epistemological opacity compels the rose's
viewer to remark with the masculine the site of an independence
from it, reinstalling the rose as proper object of reflection on the
speaker's part. "Roses Only" reflects not the possibilities for equitable heterosexual relations, but the reasons for their absence, the
assimilating desire that the apparently heterogeneous covers over,
as exemplified by romantic discourse. The poem sets up a disparity
between what the speaker sees and what the speaker says about the
rose. Moore's own view of male-dominated culture is evident in the
speaker's machinations: the speaker resolves the question of the
rose's identity in her stead.

The text enacts how the repression of difference is constituent
of identity, an operation that creates a sort of calm eye within language's stormy heterogeneity. A consummate resolution may

apparently be arrived at (Moore's last lines are typically epigrammatic, or "hyperdetermined," as Taffy Martin terms it),[40] but the multiple levels on which her poems operate disrupt the closure, just as her style fractures the poem's finish. Jeanne Heuving suggests that Moore may have been "far less motivated by needs for self-protection than by unwillingness to reinscribe existing gender determinations,"[41] as "The Paper Nautilus," "A Carriage from Sweden," and "Roses Only" confirm.

"People's Surroundings" is another case in point. Through the literally unruly structure of this free-verse list poem, Moore presses the conventional function of the feminine figure in poetry toward an unconventional, multiple significance. The "acacia-like lady" who, unlike the rose, has no obvious physical protection against "the touch of a hand" (*P,* 56), appears at first as an expendable link in the metonymic chain of flowers and colors that spill through the poem and signify Bluebeard's personal domain, from which she can only "escape" through death. Endlessly substitutable (Bluebeard is infamous, of course, for murduring his wives), she disappears "like an obedient chameleon," submissive to the point of annihilation. She is victim of a self-reflexive aesthetic order in which male presence elevated to the status of myth (significantly, he is named) erases the female (she is one of the "flowers" in his garden). The acacia-lady represents the consequences of embodying the decorously feminine and the principle of stylistic accomodation: she is dispersed into the surroundings she originally ornamented.

If we pause not on "obedient," but on "chameleon," however, which images in the poem's context the acacia-lady's capacity for self-differing mutability, another possibility opens up. To disappear "like" a chameleon is to give the semblance of disappearance: a chameleon has the ability to change its color in order to blend (in effect, to disappear) into its environment while actually still there. She is not simply analogous to Keats's "chameleon poet," of which she reminds readers, for she functions as an ambiguous figure of both sacrifice and adaptive survival. Her uncertain elimination underscores the uncanny disengenderment of the surroundings that have been identified as Bluebeard's. The "hand" that touches, the "mind of this establishment," and "the eye [that] knows what to skip," all synecdoches for dominance and control, are not more securely attached to an authorizing masculine presence at the center of things because of the erasure of the feminine. Rather, they are exceeded by the technique of the list itself, which detaches those details from their original contextual association with masculinity. As in "Roses Only," Moore complicates the connection between knowledge and sight. Rhetorically connecting knowledge and blindness (the epistemological system on which gender hierarchy is based, as Irigaray has shown us), Moore's poem suggests that the Emersonian eye inside the poem is invested in not seeing the woman it knows is still there—what the readerly eye outside the poem doesn't know that it sees.

Moore's speakers' claims to knowledge about woman are contradicted by a text's dialogism, as the last poem I shall discuss along this line of thinking, "Sojourn in the Whale," demonstrates. One of Moore's few poems of "feminine complaint," as Heuving states,[42] the poem is also written with the recent Easter Uprising of 1916 in mind, and as DuPlessis suggests, evinces a compensatory "cultural feminism."[43] We are clearly invited to make the analogy between Ireland's position in relation to Britain and the position of women in relation to men.[44] Developing out of the constrictions imperialism has placed on Ireland, her wisdom is characterized by men as knowing when to submit and by the speaker as ironic equivocation:

> You have been compelled by hags to spin
>   gold thread from straw and have heard men say:
> "There is a feminine temperament in direct contrast to ours,
>
> which makes her do these things. Circumscribed by a
>   heritage of blindness and native
>   incompetence, she will become wise and will be forced
>   to give in.
> Compelled by experience, she will turn back;
>
> water seeks its own level":
>   and you have smiled. "Water in motion is far
>   from level." You have seen it, when obstacles happened to bar
> the path, rise automatically.

(*P,* 90)

Since Ireland's circumscription is the result of externally imposed deprivations, the passage questions the men's version of Ireland's "heritage," distinguishing between their assumptions and Ireland's experience. The men, not Ireland herself, think that the "feminine temperament" *seeks* the subordinate level to which it has been historically "compelled."

Moore troubles these waters, of course, for assumptions are not synonymous with assured knowledge in her work, as we have seen. The poem implicitly asks who defines blindness and wisdom. As means of both access to Ireland and its best defense, moreover, the sea is a subtly ironic figure of "water in motion," which might rise to engulf "obstacles" (like ships), leveling all hierarchical differences established by colonizing forces. The poem's syllabic structure enacts this theme formally.

There is not only a disjunction of knowledges in the poem, then, but also an interrogation of the epistemology that establishes hierarchical structures. The men cannot imagine that their definition of experience is different from Ireland's, who has "lived and lived on every kind of shortage" and been "compelled" to spin gold from straw (*P*, 90). Ireland's compulsion for heroic romance, illogic, and miracle does not reiterate the men's compulsion for reason and dominance ("compelled" is repeated, but agency and import shift). Presented consistently in quotation, the men's voices are immersed in as well as interrupt the speaker's own discourse about Ireland. Ireland's voice, also occurring in quotation, is thus on equal (poetic) footing with the men's voices. The Irish hags, uncannily exceeding normative or naturalized boundaries, foreground a difference between the conventional views of woman the men voice and Ireland's duplicitous speech. Hags compel Ireland to spin gold from straw, signifying another artistic economy aligned both with the miraculous and with the unnatural (as aging women, hags both are repulsive to men and are forceful beings).

The language romance unsettles is history, associated with "a heritage of blindness," one manifestation of which is a masculine misrecognition of the feminine as monstrous. Like "Roses Only," "Sojourn in the Whale" depicts the absence of sympathetic heterosexual relations, the complacent misreading of feminine temperament by men, as well as the relation of the disempowered to the powerful. In portraying a disinherited but unruly Ireland, whose experience corresponds to women's oppression, the text connects feminine subversion with a fluidity that counters the restrictions placed on it and cannot be permanently contained by the interpretations imposed on it.[45]

The complexities of the text's subjectivity also illustrates the transvestite position I am suggesting that Moore adopts, which here is precisely equivocal. At the same time as the speaker observes the feminine capacity to transgress oppressive circumstances, in speaking so often for Ireland, the speaker repeats the appropriation of voice that the text represents as a masculine gesture. As apostrophe, however, the poem establishes an addressee, but does not grammatically indicate an addressor, whose place seems empty, like that of woman's in the conventions of literature and philosophy.[46] The speaker in Moore's poem occupies this position—at once woman's linguistic place and barred to women—in place of women. Although dissociated from the feminine, if the speaker is nevertheless "feminine," as critics usually understand "her" to be, she linguistically masquerades in the masculine position. Through such miming, the speaker exposes the exploitation of the feminine in the symbolic order.

On multiple levels, Moore's poems question the assumptions on which hegemonic men base their knowledge about women. But as heterogeneous discursive complexes (romance and history, fable and fact, observation and hearsay) all questioning each other's authority, these texts, like their speakers, are also contradictory. They represent *woman* in the position of the repressed, the silenced and spoken for, that is an impossible one for a woman to speak from. Their correctives are often expressed in a romantic discourse that, despite its capacity to undercut with irony history's representation of imperialistic expansionism as heroic, is itself incredible. These speakers trace a canny movement that recalls Carey Thomas's revised public strategies. Like the powerful undertow the feminist undercurrent of "Sojourn in the Whale" creates beneath the poem's urbane surface, Moore's drift in the poems discussed above seems to be the countering (in)directions, the equivocations, a female subject takes within dominant conventions and discourse.

A (DE)*MATER*IALIZING METHOD

We might ask at this point what the metapoetic questions of repetition, representation, and reproduction have to do with themes of social and cultural oppression?[47] Moore's technical strategies bear directly on the politics as well as the poetics of her work, since, as Diehl has observed, Moore associates the dangers of power with matters of style.[48] "People's Surroundings," for example, begins as an examination of how style makes the (predatory) man. In the poems discussed above, Moore unsettles a previous reading of woman as the ground on which a secure masculine identity establishes itself, suggesting that such repression distorts perception. Like Dickinson, she will draw a connection between sight (of woman) and knowledge (of masculine self) in Western epistemology. She criticizes such "feminolatry," the tendency in our literary heritage to figure woman as paradoxical threat to, and assurance of, the stability of, monological discourse and hierarchical thinking.

What other poems by Moore suggest is that division already inhabits androcentric culture, as Kristeva has theorized more recently. To examine this split, she mobilizes in a number of poems the mythic trope also central to canonical American literary consciousness—the Fall. And just as that narrative, exemplifying for the West the fall from the integrity of word and thing, Adam's and Eve's fall from innocence into knowledge, castigates Eve, so Moore perceives that woman, and alterity in general, has symbolized the separation from Truth, which is the fallen condition. In the Fall series to which I shall now turn, Moore treats "truth," like representational strategies, as an issue to be explored from a gendered perspective.

"Virginia Britannia" examines the ideologically motivated processes of artistic reproduction and the heritage of colonization at the root of America's dominant national identity.[49] The poem depicts the first colonists' attempts to establish English "dominion" and "identity" in what was to them "virgin" territory. Moore characterizes the activity of reproduction in dominant American culture's history as the mimetic desire to replicate its European origins and suppress the aboriginal, demonstrating its connection to racism as well as misogyny. She represents that desire as a controlling gesture, a will to power, which is a grand—that is, a tragic—illusion.

The colonists attempted to reproduce England in an "un-English" land. They were careful to import only what would replicate England: "the white wall-rose," the "all-green box-sculptured grounds," and the "walls of [English] yews" (*P*, 107, 108). Nevertheless the "almost" of the "almost English green" surrounding these transplants (*P*, 107) signifies the failure to suppress the proliferating fecundity of a land ironically named by the colonists for the state, and the queen who represented it, of being still untouched by (Western) man.

As the text makes clear, since there was no originally pristine territory, the colonists' preoccupation with reproducing their origins necessitated the assimilation of indigenous heterogeneity. Captain Smith's motto, "invincible digestion," literalizes the incorporation of difference that the process of hierarchization symbolizes (he was "patient with/ his inferiors" [*P*, 107]). But as an indigestible (and feminized) otherness, the natives "painted" as Turks were finally "no/ odder than we were" (*P*, 107), signs of the power differential the poem thematizes critically and equalizes grammatically (colonists and natives being equals parts of the grammatical unit). Undoing the hierarchizing process metaphor establishes, Moore's poetic parallels highlight the rhetorical yoking of like parts that sustain and tolerate difference:

> . . . Odd Pamunkey
> princess, birdclaw-ear-ringed; with a pet raccoon
> from the Mattaponi (what a bear!). Feminine
> odd Indian young lady! Odd thin-
> gauze-and-taffeta-dressed English one! Terrapin
> meat and crested spoon
> feed the mistress of French plum-and-turquoise-piped
> chaise-longue;
> (*P*, 109)

And as its names suggests, the mockingbird, that "terse Virginian" the text celebrates (a figure for Moore's poetic subjectivity itself), produces not an exact replica but a parodic reflection, which the poem underscores grammatically.

In importing Africans as slaves (*P*, 109), the colonists introduced the race whose presence would forever haunt any assumption of homogeneity of people or language. The efforts to "imprison" multiplicity result, in the "Black/idiom," in "'advancin' back-/wards in a circle'" (*P*, 109). Moore criticizes the appropriative "arrogance" that characterized these colonists, as Slatin and Cristanne Miller variously argue, the heritage they bequeathed of imprisoning and subjugating men of other races and women of all races (as, for example, witches, invoked in the grammatical joining of "witch-cross door and 'strong sweet prison'" [*P*, 109]). She suggests that the founding fathers did not introduce freedom but reproduced the tyranny from which they fled (or so the origin tale goes). This self-aggrandizing activity is at once represented and frustrated by language (colonizing "Indian-/named Virginian/streams in counties named for English lords" [*P*, 109–10]), which Moore's inclusion of Black dialect graphically enacts.

That notion is associated as well with the hegemonic masculine fear of cultural identity collapsing before unwieldy nature and the desire for permanence, as J. Hillis Miller characterizes one aspect of the Romantic project,[50] which the poem overtly revises in its Wordsworthian final stanza:

> The live oak's darkening filigree
> of undulating boughs, the etched
> solidity of a cypress indivisible
>> from the now aged English hackberry,
>> become with lost identity,
>> part of the ground, as sunset flames increasingly
> against the leaf-chiseled
>> blackening ridge of green; while clouds expanding above
>> the town's assertiveness, dwarf it, dwarf arrogance
>>> that can misunderstand
>>> importance; and
> are to the child an intimation of what glory is.
>
> (*P*, 111)

Shifting from historical to aesthetic connotations, descriptive words like "etched," "filigree," and "chiseled" depict the natural world of contemporary Virginia as a (de)constructive recreation. The first settlers' efforts in the new world to "colonize"–both to reproduce England and, as the poem moves through history, to forge a separate identity–are displaced by the poem's increasingly clear aestheticization. The language of romantic figuration unsettles the constructions of historical identity, suggesting that they are defensive and self-deceiving. Just as the discrete boundaries between oak, cypress, and "now aged English hackberry" have blurred with time and get further "lost" in sunset's shadows, so the homogeneous integrity of the poem's collective speaker, "we," dissolves into the universalized voice, underscoring the arbitrary nature of delineations fixed by the process of nationalizing identity itself.

Exploring the nature of "our" historical identity and indicating the unoriginal quality at the root of being original, Moore examines the politics of imitation and ironizes America's oft-repeated literary return to the Edenic myth. With their "tobacco-crop / records on church walls; a Devil's Woodyard / and the one-brick- / / thick serpentine wall built by / Jefferson," the founding fathers are imaged not as Adamic. Rather, like the new republic's first symbol, the rattlesnake, they are implicitly the real serpents introducing the intolerance of (linguistic, racial, gender) difference into the garden, not a one of "us," to "our" shame, "a synonym for mercy" (*P,* 110). Finally, since "we" too are "odd," the attempt to put off difference onto the other is always already doomed. Imitation opens to division that already inhabits "us," and like language itself, "we" slip into difference by the act of deference to an original, idealized identity, the completion of whose reproduction is deferred and finally frustrated by the very process of reconstruction.

"In the Days of Prismatic Colors," as suggested earlier, as well as "Marriage," and "An Octopus," associate the topos of the Fall with misogyny and an occulted matrophobia, as Adrienne Rich will call it in *Of Woman Born* (although, as Sabine Sielke reminds us, the spheres of marriage and motherhood are overtly separated in Moore's work).[51] In ways we have been analyzing, all three poems represent the speaker as aligning the feminine with a threatening and divisive force. Taken together ("Marriage" and "An Octopus" were in fact originally parts of the same notes for a longer poem),[52] these texts present an extensive deconstruction of patristic and popular Western images of woman, as well as of modernist male nostalgia for an unmediated (objective) relationship between words and things. Moore's method in these poems, as elsewhere, is to inhabit–masquerade in–speaking positions that reproduce conventional symbols of woman, in order to expose their illogic. Moore dissociates these images from the poems' speakers, as well as from the feminine figures themselves, mobilizing this move at both rhetorical and grammatical levels.

In "In the Days of Prismatic Colors," to review briefly, Eve is throughout the poem implicitly connected with the introduction of complexity and sophistication (etymologically, the misuse of language) into the world. This connection enacts a tension between content and form, the syllabic structure at once "freeing" the poem from traditional formal features and attempting to restrain the very linguistic chaos the speaker excoriates. For Adam, the world before Eve was straightforward; even "obliqueness was a variation / of the perpendicular" (*P,* 41). After her arrival, however, complexity contaminates Paradise, not because it is inherently "a crime," as the speaker insists, but because it enables Eve to obscure Truth:

> . . . Complexity,
> moreover, that has been committed to darkness, instead of
>
> granting itself to be the pestilence that it is, moves all
>   a-
>   bout as if to bewilder us with the dismal
> fallacy that insistence
>   is the measure of achievement and that all
> truth must be dark.
>
> (*P,* 41)

After Eve's arrival, obliqueness (indirection) and complexity (multiplicity) bewilder Adam because they no longer line up with the perpendicular–erect, upright, *masculine*–but are criminally "slant." Like complexity,

> . . . sophistication is as it al-
>
> ways has been—at the antipodes from the init-
>   ial great truths. "Part of it was crawling, part of it
> was about to crawl, the rest
>   was torpid in its lair." In the short-legged, fit-
> ful advance, the gurgling and all the minutiae—we have the
>   classic
>
> multitude of feet. To what purpose! Truth is no Apollo
>   Belvedere, no formal thing. The wave may go over it if it likes.
> Know that it will be there when it says,
>   "I shall be there when the wave has gone by."
>   (*P*, 41–42)

In such passages, where word breaks coincide with line breaks through the form's arbitrary distribution of syllables, hyphenation replicates the splitting and complexity Moore explores thematically, lexically foregrounding the narrative fall into division.

As the original namer, whose words were one with the things he named, Adam represents the right use of language. To him, it is the serpentine, oblique, and now not only contaminating but monstrous nature of Eve's rhetorical issue that gives fitful birth to a classic tradition at variance with originary Truth. Monstrous and lurching, poetic tradition, as the passage above suggests, obfuscates rather than reveals truth, aligned with Eve's criminal complexity. In the dialectic the speaker sets up in this closing passage, withstanding the wave bespeaks a Truth that endures not only formal constraints, but a dousing of woman's rhetorical fluidity.

But the foundation of this opposition doesn't withstand the vicissitudes of Moore's own text. While "Truth's" final statement seems to provide a univocal closure, it is already subject to division. The resolution is a repeated, not an originary truth, at one remove both by virtue of the quotation marks and by the fact that this is not a postlapsarian point of view. The originary state that preceded refinement is unrecuperable and always already carried "to the point of murkiness" by the introduction of any discourse one employs to retrieve it. The poem questions the speaker's nostalgia for such a mystified past. Even in the prelapsarian world, obliqueness was a *variation* of the perpendicular, although that difference was suppressed in order to (mis)recognize similarity. It was, implicitly, never "plain to see" when complexity originated. In Moore's emendation of the Bible, Adam's objection to Eve is no longer on the grounds of moral inferiority, but because of her incorrect use of language, her refusal to reflect his own naming back to him, which he perceives as monstrous.

Moore's awareness of a pattern of demonization of the feminine, which she implies in her portraits of Irish hags and mystifying Eves, emerges in the explorations in "Marriage" and "An Octopus" of women's relationship to androcentric culture. Central to both is Moore's characterization of femininity as threat to masculine identity or, to put it another way, what woman represents for man. Both "Marriage" and "An Octopus" occupy speaking positions from which to examine the cultural features that have historically rendered femininity unspeakable and woman's place one of erasure and contradiction.[53] Both poems dissociate women from conventional, misogynistic images and reassociate them with other possible representations through multiple discourses and free verse structures.[54]

As its title indicates, "Marriage" analyzes the institution that symbolizes for Moore the hierarchization of the sexes and the concomitant attempt to contain women in marriage and motherhood. Questioning society's notions of what constitutes civilization, "What," the poem asks at one point, "can one do for them– / these savages" (*P,* 68)? Love in this enterprise has several versions, none of which is synonymous: it is "the fight to be affectionate," a "truth" known only "by the tooth of disputation," "a fine art," "an experiment," "a duty," a "recreation" (*P,* 66). Impossible to represent univocally, as the proliferation of quotations in the poem enacts, marriage has an undecidable relationship to love, and its participants an oppositional relation to union, as a number of critics have remarked of this very "disputatious" poem.[55]

If through its image of the Union's famous orator, Daniel Webster, the poem's resolution imposes closure by shifting to political history,[56] that shift highlights the relation between the politics of gender and other forms of subjugation with which Moore's work is often concerned. Marriage conflates with the edifice of the republic, another contentious union constructed by rhetoric and ideology, whose idealized surface disguises the political oppositions whose "unity" is soldered by force:

> "'Liberty and union
> now and forever';
>
> The Book on the writing-table;
> The hand in the breast-pocket."
>
> (*P*, 70)

The figure of Webster in this passage is an image of male power wielded through oratory, words, and the forced syntactic yoking of opposites.[57] The tone in which Webster's words are quoted is cynical, the repetition ironizing the glorified illusion sustained by rhetoric.[58] Like Webster's version of the new republic, the conventional "Book" on marriage is prescriptive. In Moore's stark selection of detail, however, the book is on the writing table, a factor that attenuates the permanence of what the statue symbolizes by gesturing toward process. The sinister, disembodied hand we have seen elsewhere in Moore's poetry as synecdoche for a predatory sexual politics is here, in the poem's final image, literally unsightly.

In her depictions of Eve's multiple voices and the initial speaker's unstable status, Moore figures alternatives to both Webster's archaic verbal force and Adam's solipsism. These feminine figures are aligned with the poem's fragmented structure itself (as Sielke observes of Eve).[59] Eve's androgynous looks, multiple consciousness, and autonomy impress the speaker:

> I have seen her
> when she was so handsome
> she gave me a start,
> able to write simultaneously
> in three languages—
> English, German and French—
> and talk in the meantime";
> equally positive in demanding a commotion
> and in stipulating quiet:
> "*I* should like to be alone"[.]
>
> (*P*, 62)[60]

Her amazing linguistic capacity is disturbing to Adam. The "strange experience of beauty" is "too much," a poisonous "wave of consciousness" that "tears one to pieces" (*P*, 63). In the face of what is disorienting and self-contradictory about Eve, even Adam's physical integrity is threatened.

The poem's speaking (and reading) subject, who shares Eve's linguistic facility and for whom Eve is thus a figure, declares that marriage has required "all one's criminal ingenuity / to avoid!" (*P*, 62). She eludes "Marriage" as well as marriage. In a series of refractions through quotations and mercurial subject positions, this speaker disperses into the third-person neutral "one" and the collective "we Occidentals," who are characterized as "self lost" (*P*, 67). "I" never resurfaces except in quotations.[61] The speaker's evasive subjectivity not only exemplifies the feminine ingenuity needed to maintain autonomy from prescribed unions, but its method recalls Carey Thomas's negotiation of the academy.[62] Seeming to offer an objective picture of gender relations, the speaker dissolves in the play with and mime of the boundaries erected in public discourse by the institutionalization of this archaic practice into which so many women have disappeared along with their names.

As paradoxical sign for a movement that is both disappearance and proliferation, the initial "I," like Eve, poses a contrast to Adam's experience of "a solemn joy / in seeing that he has become an idol" (*P*, 64). Perceiving "what it was not / intended that he should," Adam gets locked in a narcissistic jouissance in which he is his own object of desire:

> he loves himself so much,
> he can permit himself
> no rival in that love.
>
> (*P*, 68)

Adam will suffer no competing claim for his love. Through the text's revision of Milton's Eve, the juxtaposition of male narcissism with female narcissism—

> "She loves herself so much,
> she cannot see herself enough—["]
>
> (*P*, 68)

becomes a criticism of women's status in marriage. This "model of petrine fidelity" can see enough of her husband *but not of herself.* As the etymology of *petrine* connotes, she is petrified in marriage into "a statuette," "the logical last touch / to an expansive splendor" (*P,* 68), the decorous *objet d'art* shaped by an economy of masculine reflexivity.

The authority the wife has to counter the misogynistic logic of petrine doctrine is, like the Wife of Bath's, "experience" (*though noon auctoritee*), which "attests / that men have power / and sometimes one is made to feel it" (*P,* 67).[63] As in "Sojourn in the Whale," women's experience differs from men's. The "irony preserved / in 'the Ahasuerus *tête-à-tête* banquet'" (*P,* 67) is, as the allusion to the exchange of the overtly disobedient Vashti for the apparently compliant Esther suggests, that the woman who seems most controllable is the least. At once submissive and rebellious (that is, precisely, equivocal), the petrine wife is "that orator reminding you, / 'I am yours to command'"—a far more opaque discursive position than Webster's (*P,* 69).

Adam's response to such interpretive opacity is to portray Eve as "poison," an uncontrollable linguistic fluidity (which the speaker herself celebrates) that has the power to contaminate One, and as such, a divinized and dangerously autonomous power:

> who "darkeneth her countenance
> as a bear doth,"
> the spiked hand
> that has affection for one
> and proves it to the bone,
> impatient to assure you
> that impatience is the mark of independence,
> not of bondage.
>
> (*P,* 66)

The passage playfully literalizes, but also seriously extends, the implications of the old cliché about the woman, desperate to get married, who gets her "claws" in a man. As untouchable virgin and huntress, this independent Diana-wife proffers an affection that permanently marks one. Introducing Adam to knowledge of mortality as well as sexual difference,

> ["] . . . 'a wife is a coffin,'
> that severe object
> with the pleasing geometry
> stipulating space not people,
> refusing to be buried
> and uniquely disappointing,
> revengefully wrought in the attitude
> of an adoring child
> to a distinguished parent."
>
> (*P*, 67–68)

Like a coffin refusing to be buried, a wife is a weird purveyor of contradictory appearances for the husband: pleasing, terrifying, demanding, disappointing, revengeful, and adoring. Mercurial, she cannot be reconciled with him or redeemed for him.

The unnatural coffin in this passage also indicates how the male speaker uncannily disfigures the woman into a few detached body parts, a *corps morcèlé*, the product of repressed fear:[64]

> He says, "These mummies
> must be handled carefully—
> 'the crumbs from a lion's meal,
> a couple of shins and the bit of an ear'[."]
>
> (*P*, 67)

"Mummy," of course, can be read in two ways: either as a preserved, corporeal husk from a vanished culture or as the repressed preoedipal Mother. But either reading indicates the man's attempt to recuperate the unfamiliar back into the familiar: for the dead to appear living or for a woman's autonomous power to be permanently domesticated. Characterizing the untenable position into which wives are placed, objectified as ornaments and petrified into marital and maternal stasis, the poem elaborates why the institution and the language by which it is upheld work to keep "Mummy" fossilized in her domestic roles.

Moore's (dis)solution is to remove the debate about woman's biological inferiority to rhetoric.[65] The juxtaposition of "the fact of woman" ("not the sound of the flute / but very poison") with Carey Thomas's feminist observation ("Men are monopolists / . . . unfit to be the guardians / of another person's happiness") counters the figure of woman as contamination with the figure of man as tyrant. Equivocating on which version is reliable, Moore's poetics enact a linguistic democracy meant to remind the Republic of the real nature of democratic plurality, an inclusive, nonhierarchizing enterprise that, if realized, would assuredly revolutionize it.[66] Eve's rhetorical issue, returning to haunt Adam in this poem, is, by now not surprisingly, monstrously menacing ("'something feline, / something colubrine' . . . / a crouching mythological monster" [*P*, 63]), for in this world of signs, the "Book" can be rewritten by women.

In "Marriage" Moore scrutinizes the cultural constructions that have ensured male dominance through the coinciding maternalization and infantilization of women produced in bourgeois marriages. "An Octopus" examines the various economic and aesthetic structures employed to consume the natural world, which is, in the paradox that characterizes the sublime, already a representation and unrepresentable. The themes of political and sexual subjugation fully conjoin in "An Octopus" with Moore's extensive analysis of the metatextual issues she raises in "Virginia Britannia" and her transformation of the lyric "I" into a multiply positioned subject-in-process. As the poem unfolds, authorial concerns of stylistic "assimilation" are analogous to man's historical repression of the feminine as well as to his ambivalence about the maternal.

Moore first establishes nature's relationship to a male-dominated world and discourse. Like native Virginia, the pristine natural world of Mount Tacoma is home to "the original American menagerie of styles," a heterogeneity (the details of which proliferate in the poem) which men attempt to "conquer" through the imposition of an order provided by a homogeneous style (*P*, 74). Such endeavors are connected in this poem, as elsewhere in Moore's work, with the history of the West's colonization of unruly difference through imitation and reproduction, the attempt to regulate regions condemned for their "sacrosanct remoteness" (*P*, 75).

The poem depicts such linguistic recuperation as the subject of a male-authored debate about representation and interpretation. The wilderness, now a "game preserve," is the site in which conflicting activities largely associated with the spectacle of appropriate and excessive masculinity can be played out. Like prophets in this postlapsarian paradise, the proper authorities ("odd oracles of cool official sarcasm") have "prohibited" the trappings of masculine violence and despoilment that have accompanied the economic exploitation of the forest (the "guns, nets, seines, traps and explosives, / hired vehicles, gambling and intoxicants" [*P,* 75]).

Such preservation of the wilderness reforms it into a more appropriate masculine economy, implied by the erotic rectitude of the language inscribing the forest as a locus of desire–its "beauty" stimulating "invigorating pleasures" as well as "moral vigor" (*P,* 75). This perspective, however, implicitly overwrites unruly detail, like the Greeks to which it alludes, who liked "smoothness" and distrusted "what could not be clearly seen" (*P,* 75). Although more attentive than the Greeks to what was behind deceptively smooth surfaces, Henry James winds up "'damned by the public for decorum'; / not decorum but restraint" (*P,* 76). Although an ambiguous figure,[67] for he grammatically parallels the mountain, which is similarly "damned for its sacrosanct remoteness," James's sin seems to be a "Neatness of finish" that undermines the recognition of the very multiplicity that his restraint was meant to observe.[68] Moore's use of the word *decorum* implies that neither the Greeks nor James could adapt "their intelligence" to the *un*cultivated–the wilderness as truly home to untamed diversity (*P,* 73–74).

This homologic, male-authorized economy is countered by disconcerting self-reflection in the text. In a passage that alludes to both the Declaration of Independence and Genesis, two founding patriarchal texts, the speaker declares:

> It is self-evident
> that it is frightful to have everything afraid of one;
> that one must do as one is told
> and eat rice, prunes, dates, raisins, hardtack, and tomatoes
> if one would "conquer the main peak of Mount Tacoma[."]
>
> (*P,* 75)

While it is Eve, after all, who is best known for first eating what she was told not to eat,[69] the speaker's relationship to knowledge as well as to our literary and historical heritage is an uncomfortable recognition not only of authorial but of related ethical issues raised by the desire for mastery.[70] Although, like Dickinson, Moore does not precisely eschew mastery, poetic power entails for her the acknowledgment that not only is one frightening, but that swallowing what one's told to in order to conquer the mountain is in itself "frightful."

An earlier moment of self-reflection is also uncomfortable, but with differences that engender the poem's metatextual concerns. Invoking Eve in *Paradise Lost*, "The Goat's Mirror" is a pool that "prejudices you in favor of itself / before you have had time to see the others" (*P*, 72).[71] But Moore's scene does not represent a feminine "you" caught in the impropriety of narcissistic self-gazing; rather, it frustrates the expectations of correspondence "of look and identification, power and knowledge" that returns power to the masculine.[72] The reflection of self, which evokes the smoothness prized by the Greeks, does not return the "you" to herself, but mirrors another scene altogether, the shifting tumult of the wilderness elsewhere:

> this is the property . . .
> . . . .
> of "thoughtful beavers
> making drains which seem the work of careful men with shovels,"
> and of the bears inspecting unexpectedly
> ant-hills and berry-bushes.
> . . . .
>
> their den is somewhere else, concealed in the confusion
> of "blue forests thrown together with marble and jasper and agate
> as if whole quarries had been dynamited."
> And farther up, in stag-at-bay position
> as a scintillating fragment of these terrible stalagmites,
> stands the goat,
> its eye fixed on the waterfall which never seems to fall . . .
> . . . .
>
> A special antelope
> acclimated to "grottoes from which issue penetrating draughts
> which make you wonder why you came,"

it stands its ground
on cliffs the color of the clouds, of petrified white vapor—
black feet, eyes, nose, and horns, engraved on dazzling ice-fields,
the ermine body on the crystal peak;
the sun kindling its shoulders to maximum heat like acetylene,
                                        dyeing them white—
upon this antique pedestal,
"a mountain with those graceful lines which prove it a volcano,"
its top a complete cone like Fujiyama's
till an explosion blew it off.

                                        (*P,* 72–73)

As such words as *composed, engraved, graceful lines,* and *antique pedestal* make clear, what is reflected on the water's smooth surface is not an unmediated catalog of natural details but a highly stylized composition.

The aesthetic reproduction suggests the illusion of coherent vision as well as of permanence and resemblance: the details seem exhaustive but are selected fragments, and the whole reflection images the tenuousness of any claims to permanence of a surface smoothed of complexities. Like "gusts of a storm / obliterating the shadows of the fir-trees" (*P,* 72) reflected on the water a moment before, or the "graceful lines" of a dormant volcano, the composition is unstable. The scene undermines the fixity that it seems to establish, and contradicts the later "assertion" that the forest is "essentially humane," for the only human element is present through mistaken perception: beavers' dams seem the work of men, but are not. Despite what it seems, and in spite of man's efforts to appropriate it, the wilderness is a no-man's land of tumultuous and shifting surfaces.

If the scene in fact invokes Eve's self-gaze, then she is both conventionally aligned with nature and depicted as seeing the (in)decorously deceptive surface women are supposed to reflect and for which woman has been castigated in patristic tradition. But the fact that she does not, precisely speaking, see her own image raises the possibility that the notion of woman as deceptive, as an at once coerced and unreliable reflection of man, differs from women themselves. We are not seeing anything behind that surface but the reflection of another scene. That view figures the gaze of the other as problematic and the otherness of a feminine gaze as the site in which conflicting readings of femininity itself are played out. A woman sees herself reflected both as nothing other than other (the essential gender stereotype that conflates woman and nature) and as a decentering of interpretive perception.

But another dynamic may be at work in this scene. The "we" speaker (as distinct from the unrecognizing "you") may well be watching a moment in which an autonomous difference is made visible. Observing "you" gazing into a reflection that should mirror "you" back but doesn't, "we" is arguably a collective feminine gaze watching as a sense of otherness dawns in the man. That unattached alterity is certainly uncanny: the "penetrating draughts," like Eve's rhetorical issue, "make you wonder why you came." Punning on "draughts," Moore's poem inscribes a scene of writing in which "we" (women) produce "drafts" of what "we" see. Such moments alter the dynamics of the masquerade, for mirrored back is not man to himself, but disconcerting feminine reflections, in all senses of the word.[73]

The speaker echoes the pun on incompletion, admitting to being devoid of "such power [to name] as Adam had." She is in the ambiguous position both of postlapsarian Adam and of Eve (who never had the power to name). "Is 'tree' the word for these things / 'flat on the ground like vines'?" (*P*, 76), she asks just prior to the text's closing. Since the mountain is "Distinguished by a beauty / of which 'the visitor dare never fully speak at home/for fear of being stoned as an impostor'" (*P*, 73), the speaker's credibility is called into question. Has the speaker dared to speak fully, thus risking the charge of imposture? And is the speaker then an impostor for saying things that are inappropriate or unbelievable? Or has the speaker given a necessarily partial account because the subject cannot be completely represented, or is, in a word, unspeakable?

If femininity is, to masculinist thinking, the unspeakable enigma *par excellence*, then it might well be the implicit subtext of this poem, as Diehl cogently argues.[74] Traditionally an image associated with sublimity, Costello reminds us, the "octopus" is unnameable because it is inconceivable ("of *unimagined* delicacy").[75] The glacier lies "Deceptively reserved and flat," "killing prey with the concentric

crushing rigor of the python," its pallor "ghostly" and "changing,"
its "maneuvers 'creepy to behold'" (*P,* 71). Moore's speaker in such
passages tries to describe something that refuses linguistic fixity,
remarking the connotations conventionally indicative of femininity.
But as a gothic, Medusa-like image (hovering forward "spider fashion," "its arms seeming to approach from all directions"), the glacier
functions as well as a figure for the phallic mother.[76] Passages in earlier drafts excised from subsequent drafts suggest Moore's own sense
of threat from maternal destructiveness, her profound ambivalence,
like Dickinson's, toward her mother, as critics like Diehl have noted.
I would suggest in addition, however, that the personal context in
the final draft of "An Octopus" might have been deleted precisely
in order that the poem more fully participate in the broader cultural
critique of misogyny and matrophobia that I have tried to demonstrate is central to Moore's Fall series. Moore transposes personal
and conventional maternal figurations in "An Octopus," effecting a
poetic elaboration of what is ambivalent for man about maternal
power as well as feminine alterity, encapsulated in the traditional
symbolism of the sublime.

The capacity of the marked one (woman) to become a marker
(writer), DuPlessis asserts, sometimes entails "a critical transposition of a culturally hegemonic source."[77] Recalling the complex
maternal poet-figure in "The Paper Nautilus," Moore's transposition in "An Octopus" evokes femininity, maternity, and traditionally feminine arts ("misleadingly like lace") linked with "the original
American menagerie of styles," to which man has responded with
repression in the psychoanalytical as well as in the political sense of
the term. Etymologically, *menagerie* is associated with the domain of
the feminine: the home (*ménage*) of the mother. Diehl suggests that
in its at-once nurturing and threatening qualities, the glacier is an
"almost uncanny presence."[78] I want to pursue her implication for
a moment, because it refers us to the glacier's association with
Freud's notion of the uncanny in his essay of the same title:

> It often happens that neurotic men declare that they feel
> there is something uncanny about the female genital
> organs. This *unheimlich* place, however, is the entrance to
> the former *Heim* [home] of all human beings, to the place

where each one of us lived once upon a time and in the beginning. . . . [T]he *unheimlich* is what was once *heimisch,* familiar; the prefix *'un'* ['un–'] is the token of repression.[79]

Shoshona Felman elaborates that such womb nostalgia is "a nostalgia for femininity as snug and canny, *heimlich,* i.e., according to Freud's definition, 'belonging to the *house* or to the *family,*' tame, companionable to man."[80] Her observations extend Freud's analysis of neurotic men to a normative masculine economy of desire. Such an extension applies to Moore's text as well. Her representation is also uncanny. The repetition of "creepy," for example, which occurs in both the literal and the figurative sense, connotes the return to the infantile bodily sensations of being around the all-powerful mother, as well as, in the final image of the glacier's "claw cut by the avalanche" that stops both knowledge and representation, the "discovery" of the mother's castration.

Underscoring problems of imaging an occulted, unseen, or fantasized event, this poem repeatedly stages a "run-in" with the limits of representation, when the figural replaces the literal. Simultaneously lure to, and veiled from, the gaze, the glacier sustains the "wound" at the end that both marks it as a site of femininity and refuses, in its "relentless" accumulation of "facts," reduction to the cut (*P,* 76). Severing the glacier's claw, the avalanche camouflages it "in a curtain of powdered snow launched like a waterfall"(*P,* 76). The avalanche images another deceptively smooth surface behind which we know is the glacier, invisibly present like the chameleon-like acacia lady, but from which we cannot tell what has happened. The final scene reinstalls an image both of desire and undecidability. As de Lauretis observes of such textual instances, the wound becomes a cipher for irreducible difference: "that which is elided, left out, not represented or representable."[81]

In place of the unrepresentable, maternal castration, "An Octopus" images in its unruly accumulation of detail women's artistic production undoing as well as coexisting with male textual strategies of control. Like Penelope's unravelling tricks, the figure of the road at the poem's center, "doubling back and forth until where snow begins, it ends" (*P,* 74), reinforces the sense of "double-crossing" feminine creations. Threading the reader hither and thither, deceiving us "into thinking that [we] have progressed" (*P,* 71), the text–like the road and the poetic subjectivity it symbolizes–ends with the image of an epistemological blank (avalanche or maternal fetish). This "neat" closure seems to participate in the very "Neatness of finish" for which the public lost sympathy with James. But the "neat" return to an at once fetishized and de*mater*ialized glacial claw splits the poem between its tidy formal resolution and the figurative gap into which the glacier's logical significance has fallen. It reiterates the glacial mystery (the "enigma of women") that cannot be contained by political, psychic, or aesthetic pretensions to "completeness," any more than it can be explained by charges of "incompleteness."

A REMARKABLE WOMAN

Moore's works will often seem metatextual reflections that have "universal" application. Her apparently gender-neutral speakers shift and dance in the spaces between multiple quotations, juxtaposed in structures peculiar to her work. As Burke puts it, if hers "is a variety of the collage poetics that has been linked with Poundian logopoeia and with modernist poetry in general, it is surely an idiosyncratic, separatist version of this practice."[82] Although her poems appear to repeat and reproduce the stereotypical feminine, Moore engenders the metatextual issues she explores in her work, (dis)figuring feminine otherness as (ir)resolution and insoluble differences. In the gaps her juxtapositions of fragments create, her female figures are defamiliarized as well as dematerialized, dissociated from conventional bodies of images, reassociated in new linguistic and poetic contexts. This method bears the marks not of a feminine, nor of a female, but of a feminist operation.

Moore doesn't simply imitate to expose the patterns of repression. She redefines notions of imitation, repetition, and their relationship to originality. Like the speaking subjects in many of her poems, her self portraits masquerade as both masculine and feminine. That transvestite position, as I have called it, frees her to raise questions about women's proper relationship to the imposing male figures (like Washington, Webster, and James) that function as synecdoches for a male-dominated past–history and tradition as primarily hegemonic male-authored versions. In considering her relationship to that tradition, she is concerned to recognize both her debt to and her difference from it. She describes in the *Reader*'s foreword, for example, how she determines the quality of a literary "specimen" by whether it has had too much "help from past thinkers": "Is it subservient sing-song or has it 'muscles'?" she asks. Subservience to a past master produces monotonous and slavish nonsense, the completeness of finish, to invoke the objections to her work discussed earlier, that "would weigh as a leg-iron" (*MMR*, xiii). She inscribes another genealogy of artistic origin (the Irish hags, the lace-like glacier) that is quietly but insistently figured in her work.

She owns authorial presence by disowning it, representing herself as having at the very least an eccentric relationship to writing, as epitomized by the opening passage of the *Reader*'s foreword, which provides as complex a description of her authoring activities as Moore ever wrote:

> Published: it is enough. The magazine was discontinued. The edition was small. One paragraph needs restating. Newspaper cuts on the fold or disintegrates. When was it published and where? "The title was 'Words and . . . ' something else. Could you say what it was?" I have forgotten. Happened upon years later, it seems to have been "Words and Modes of Expression." What became of "Tedium and Integrity," the unfinished manuscript of which there was no duplicate? A housekeeper is needed to assort the untidiness. For whom? A curioso or just for the author? In that case "as safe at the publisher's as if chained to shelves of Bodley," Lamb said, smiling. (*MMR*, xiii)

Although Moore's portrait of publishing is also curious, I would like to consider here her still more curious representation of the author, who may simply be the ultimate destination of an unfinished manuscript that has been lost in an "untidiness" only a housekeeper, not an author and still less *the* author, is needed "to assort." Like "A Note on the Notes" (*P*, 262), an authorizing presence is attentuated. Moore both delineates herself as a published writer and dispels that identity by separating the representation of authorial activity from the signification of the self, which shifts. Not only is the "I" of the passage kept distinct from "the author," but the hierarchy that distinguishes author and intended audience is disassembled.

While Moore almost impossibly complicates this self-portrait (of the artist as dotty old lady), the inscription of the written product as lost, "curious," and "unfinished" invokes the fate of women's writing historically. In addition, that Moore does not explicitly represent herself or the author as a privileged producer of texts opens up a space in which the speaking subject, the indeterminate "I," and a conventional feminine figure can both be posited. The housekeeper's activities have curious alliances with Moore's explanation of that "objectionable" poetic strategy, her use of quotations: "When a thing has been said so well that it could not be said better, why paraphrase it? Hence my writing is, if not a cabinet of fossils, a kind of collection of flies in amber" (*MMR,* xv). Moore domesticates the literary activity of quoting by denying it status (it is not a science) and by implying that it is more like a hobby (the collector as amateur scientist). And according to Moore, it is a housekeeper who "assorts"–both classifies and harmonizes. It is she in the passage who keeps things both distinct from and in company with each other. She is the organizing not authoritative presence, the only one who seems to know (where things go). As one who sorts (others') things out, the housekeeper is reinscribed as one who associates things to create a new harmonious order. This recontextualizing activity redefines the notion of repetition (housework, most women know, is *never* done), Moore's use of quotation and its relation to "originality."

One last example from Moore's portraits of Carey Thomas offers a related clue to the methodological model she provided Moore. In the following passage, Moore makes specific distinctions between the male and female discursive modes of leading morning chapel:

> When I was in college, . . . feminism was not taken for granted; it was a cause. It was ardently implemented and fortified by Miss Thomas. . . . We felt it a serious deprivation to miss morning chapel exercises. . . . Dr. Barton

would read from the Bible in firm, even tones, and Miss
Thomas would comment on political, literary, or campus
matters. Our zeal to be present, you may have surmised,
was not devoutness. It was attributed to President Thomas's
unpredictable originality.[83]

Both rhetorical activities involve highly selective repetition. Dr.
Barton's sermon, however, delivered in the "firm, even" tones of
inherited authority, reiterates orthodox thought. In contrast, President Thomas repeats but does not replicate; her delivery is extem-
poraneous and nonauthoritarian. The young women listen eagerly
as this new reality unfolds unpredictably, making connections
between disparate and differently valued things—between gospel
and gossip, we might say.

Significantly, the girls' zeal is aroused not by religious devotion
but by Thomas's feminism. Passion is reserved and fervor inspired
by what Moore depicts as an assortment of elements recomposed
from a feminist perspective that produces new, and in fact original,
combinations. Her description suggests that she was not only
reconceptualizing originality as unpredictable combination, the
product of multiple associated discourses, not singular patristic
Truth. She was also representing another discursive and aesthetic
economy.

That "other economy" is not necessarily a comfortable one.
Moore herself was, as noted earlier, always evasive about her quoting ("why paraphrase what for maximum impact should be quoted
verbatim? I borrowed, at all events" [*CP*, 512]). There is something
"peculiar" about inhabiting "speech not her own," as Hugh Kenner
puts it,[84] that Moore evidently pondered (the housekeeper images,
after all, the subservience of economically underprivileged women
confined to houses not their own to do domestic labor for more
privileged women). Although her work is not a "cabinet" full of des-
sicated "fossils" from extinct species, languages, or literary fashions,
it does preserve "flies" she collects. The image readily signifies the
ekphrasis Moore surely had in mind. But in recalling the effects
both of mummification and glacial ice on its "prey," the image is
also unsavory, tainted by a weird necrophiliac fascination. Wrest-
ing words from context "kills" them, and preserving them in poetic

amber in order that they (appear) "live" effaces as well as commemorates difference—all aspects of figurative language that Moore's own poetic project foregrounds by the very visibility of its unpredictable juxtapositions.

Moore uses quotation not as a scientist interested in reconstructing the empirical whole, nor solely as a poetic bricoleur of sorts, as Margaret Holley aptly describes her methodology.[85] She uses the technique also as a *meddler* with (living) wholes, an Evean unnamer (Eve, after all, seeks knowledge and finds mortality). Her "hybrid method" produces not a different sort of poem (in the tradition if not the style of Western poetry), but a hybrid: a cross between two species, "something heterogeneous in origin or composition" that crosses the lines (of decorum) between genres and genuses. Thus "What I write . . . could only be called poetry because there is no other category in which to put it" (*MMR*, 258): "Verse: prose: a specimen" (*MMR*, xiii). Moore's *specimen* (sharing the same root as Dickinson's *spectre*, L. *specere*: to look at) denotes something meant to typify, to mirror a scientific truth back. Moore employs a technical term to subvert the categorization of her work, including it in a metonymic chain, joined and separated by colons, that travesties established gender as well as generic boundaries.

And if the "poetic" products of Moore's reading and seeing are hybrid specimens, what are they reflecting back? Wouldn't they, like the unseemly portrait of an old maid who donned a tricorne hat and a great cape to have her picture taken one sunny afternoon in Brooklyn, be unsettling reflections of hegemonic culture because of some quirky eccentricity to the portraits, some unsettling sense that something is wrong, out of place (the woman is dressed as a man dressed as a woman)? The answer is, as so often with Moore, yes and no. She is equivocal, putting into discourse what the language of dominant standards works to efface, the (feminine) other's knowledge.[86] She resists figurations of femininity, maternity, author-ity in her work that are comfortable not only to her male readers, whose critical objections to Moore's methods were discussed earlier, but to her female readers, who might wish her less equivocally affirmative.

I would like to turn to a reading of one last poem, "Sea Unicorns and Land Unicorns," which draws together the metatextual and methodological, as well as thematic, issues I have analyzed in

Moore's work. This poem exemplifies a recontextualizing activity that schematically harmonizes elements, a notion the poem reflects thematically as the representation of an alternative artistic economy of vision that has been trivialized in male-dominated culture (as it turns out, the notion of costume with which this chapter began). As phallic signifier, the unicorn contrasts with its double *manqué*:

> to be distinguished from those born without a horn,
> in use like Saint Jerome's tame lion, as domestics[.]
>   (*P*, 78)

The poem recounts the familiar tale of how this "strange animal" is tameable only by "this strange enemy," a virgin who reflects, as the grammatic parallel highlights, the unicorn itself.

But Moore's representational recasting of the unicorn suggests another reading as well, or rather, a reading of otherness. It is "strange" after all (the word insistently recurs in the poem), that the text denotes what are traditionally "feminine" as well as "masculine" traits in likening the virgin to the unicorn. Moore's version of the unicorn oscillates between snippets of the written record (indicated by quotation marks and implicitly male authored) and direct description. The quotations fasten upon the unicorn's untameability (the impossibility of domesticating him) and the virgin's phallic attributes: she is "as straight and slender as the crest, / or antlet of the one-beam'd beast" (*P*, 79). The portion not in quotations—handed down, like the subtle insistence of women's suppressed voices, "by word of mouth," gossip and hearsay—describes lady and unicorn as "inoffensive" and "gentle" as well as "wild" (literally beyond man's ken). By now we should not be surprised that the unicorn is characterized by coinciding signs of masculinity and femininity, both epistemologically enigmatic, "a puzzle to the hunters" (*P*, 78), and monstrously and marvelously bestial, "etched like an equine monster of an old celestial map" (*P*, 79). An ambivalent signifier, inspiring contradictory responses of desire and apprehension ("agreeable terror"), the unicorn can only be depicted, like Moore herself, oxymoronically.

As with other poems we have examined, this text establishes a tension between what the speaker knows (or rather, repeats from reading history and romance) and has seen (or rather, recognizes via representation: "I have not seen it [the unicorn] except in pictures"). The "record of it all" is based equally on verbal and oral repetition: "Upon the printed page, / also by word of mouth" (*P,* 79). Since there is no actual and originating presence preceding representation, Moore's text sustains (like H.D.'s prologue in *Helen in Egypt,* as we shall see in the next chapter) differing and coexisting versions, none of which is authentic because the unicorn is only known *from* representation. All accounts are equally true and fictive. It is the written record that depicts the unicorn as monstrously enigmatic, because unappropriability makes him inappropriately undecidable.

Another version is (re)markably female-"authored." Holley points out that the text's closing lines refer us to an anonymous poem printed in *Punch* in 1923,[87] but they also refer us back to Queen Elizabeth's fabulous dress. Not only does the closing subvert the assurance of an authorized text (and the speaker's voice, too, has dispersed into multiple discourses), but it restores a sense of the creation of the dressmaker (whose identity history has left unrecorded) as contiguous with the written accounts. Like the unicorn "engrossed by what appears of this strange enemy" (*P,* 79), male-authored works can be construed as at once engrossed by (absorbed with/in) and engrossed with (punning etymologically, en-larged by) traditional modes of feminine artistic expression. What the poem upsets is, to borrow Barbara Johnson's characterization of Zora Neale Hurston's subversion of monological discourse, the "unequivocal domination of one mode of signifying over another."[88] Inscribed as a figure in (and of) women's "embroideries" (*P,* 77),

> beside a cloud or dress of Virgin-Mary blue,
> improved "all over slightly with snakes of Venice gold,
> and silver, and some O's,"
>
> (*P,* 79)

the unicorn images traditionally female as well as male aesthetic practices.

As such, it signifies a "strange" story. Each occurrence of the word is in the context of spatial proximity and aesthetic balance,

suggesting that contiguity symbolizes the harmonization of opposing elements. Early on in the poem, for example, the unicorn is figured as simply one part of "this fourfold combination of strange ani-
mals, / upon embroideries / enwrought with 'polished garlands' of
agreeing difference" (*P,* 77). The import of these embroideries
seems not so much about opposing personalities, but about representing such personalities in a rhetorical and grammatical relation
of "agreeing difference":

> . . . combined in such a way
> that when they do agree, their unanimity is great,
> "in politics, in trade, law, sport, religion,
> china-collecting, tennis, and church going."
>
> (*P,* 77)

Within the material space and figural vision of tapestry and poem
alike, unicorn and virgin, lion and unicorn are matched "in reciprocity" (*P,* 78). The first virgin, Queen Elizabeth, invokes the political history behind this "strange fraternity" of arch enemies: the history of Britain's imperialism (the lion is Britain's emblem; the
unicorn, that of England's "rebellious child," Scotland). By bringing
the normatively mutually exclusive into syntactic relation, these
embroideries   topple   conventional   hierarchies—between,   for
instance, politics and china collecting, trade and tennis.

In other words, in Moore's poetic representation these women
were embroidering considerably more than thread![89] Through the
linguistic possibilities that such figural relationships as metonym and
oxymoron ("agreeing difference," "agreeable terror") have wrought,
as well as the thematic symbolism of the unicorn laying "its 'mild
wild head'" upon the virgin's lap, the poem envisions a fearless,
mutual tolerance. The schematic construction of a space in which
arms can be laid down because mutual respect results in mutual protection bespeaks a very strange story. The tale told by such embroideries, and such embroideries upon the stuff of politics, is implicitly
the "unmatched device" of women's historic resistance to reflecting
("matching") back the hegemonic world view in their art.

Such a critical project is by its very nature feminist, not feminine, a crucial distinction to make in conjunction with Moore's

equivocal authorial and poetic subjectivities and encoded politics. "Sea Unicorns and Land Unicorns" exemplifies a process that characterizes Moore's project, bearing the traces of a feminist methodology and ethics, the rereading and rewriting of inherited "master narratives" like the Fall.[90] Moore troubles such "truths," demonstrating that it is possible to work in a discursive arena, in the symbolic order, toward altering the language, images, and ideas that support male-dominated culture.

Like the authorial voice she modeled after Carey Thomas and the public costume she modeled after Washington, her poetic subjects eschew conventionally feminine identifications (for example, with any traditional notion of the maternal, whose figuration is reconstrued). Her speakers masquerade in positions constructed from the combination of contradictory signs, frustrating the cultural suppression and regulation of differences. Her texts worry—indeed fray—the orthodox views she quite literally *scraps*, the reassorted fragments she stitches into new harmonious and original fabrications to create new ways of knowing, new "truths," and new identities. Unravelling her own status as poet, and poetry as embroidered discourse, she pieces together a varied poetics that participates in the occulted heritage of aesthetic representations women have offered to counter the politics of imperialism and the assimilation of perspectival differences. Needling her way through the linguistic alternatives she fashions, she offers a remarkable vision, one that was not less revolutionary, we might say (reading Moore through her Washingtonian threads), for being in such (in)decorously poetic garb.

4 *Equi / Vocations*

H.D.'S DEMASCULINIZATION OF
THE SUBJECT IN *HELEN IN EGYPT*

I don't swallow everything he says whole, we argue about it.
                              —H.D., letter to Bryher, 19 November 1934

⇢⟫

*I*n H.D.'s playful fantasy, written during her second set of analytic sessions with Freud, she quite literally incorporates his
statements, but something stops her from swallowing them
"whole." She must, figuratively speaking, dismember his thinking
to take "it" in. Do the parts she swallows add up to the original
whole? Did she get it (all)? Or has she neglected a part?[1] Susan
Stanford Friedman argues that H.D. incorporates into her poetics
the psychoanalytic model she learned from Freud of reading/inter-
preting memories and dreams as well as cultural myths, and Claire
Buck asserts that the "central insight which H.D. takes from psychoanalysis is that the self is a text to be read."[2] As H.D. punningly puts
it in "The Master," a poem written at the time of her analysis,[3]

> I caught the dream
> and rose dreaming,
> and we wrought philosophy on the dream content,
> I was content[.]
>
>   (*CP*, 451)

117

Casual allusions to ritual ingestion aside, the passage quoted above from H.D.'s letter does indicate that, much as she revered her "papa" Professor, she also portrayed herself as a resisting consumer, who, in the process of swallowing Freud's words, changed them.[4] I will be suggesting in these pages that in *Helen in Egypt*, a text that critically questions the theoretical grounds for Freud's definition of femininity, what Sarah Kofman has called his *idée fixe*, women's "Penis envy,"[5] H.D. also recasts Freud on normative masculinity. Like the previous chapters on Dickinson and Moore, this chapter will focus on women's critical readings of dominant heterosexual constructs. But whereas, in the works of Dickinson and Moore, masculinity remains for the evasive poetic subject largely a symbolic force, *Helen in Egypt* represents a specificity of dominant and alternative masculinities in relation to Helen.

H.D.'s later work modifies Freud's theory in light of her own reading practice. Her poetics has also been changed by her experience of World War II. Like *Trilogy*, which was written with apocalyptic vision during the London blitz, *Helen in Egypt* contemplates war and peace. But what was represented as ideally clear in the earlier poem, distilled in the alchemical linguistic crucible of a warring world, the woman's knowledge of/as Truth, is at issue in the later, postwar poem. As Buck observes, *Helen in Egypt* "confronts the reader with both the poet's and the reader's ignorance" about Helen's knowledge and her status as locus of truth:[6]

> I said, I was instructed in the writ;
> but I had only heard of it[.]
>
> (*HE*, 22)

Like the text itself, which is composed of alternating prose and poetic passages, Helen is constituted in division (both doubled and duplicitous) and cut off from knowledge about herself (the unconscious). She seeks that knowledge through the tradition of male-authored representations of her (the canon), and discovers the absence of herself defined as subject from the registers of language and culture.[7] She confronts the ways in which a woman gets reconstructed as a rhetorical figure that can then be (mis)read, an interpretive activity that covers over gender asymmetry.

Helen in Egypt thus does not free "woman" or "man" from the phallic term.[8] Rather, H.D. dramatizes a revised Freudian scenario, remarkably coinciding in some ways, but differing significantly as well, with Lacan's contemporaneous rereading of Freud. She insists that readers inside and outside the text examine how relation to the symbolic phallus constructs gender difference (in the masculine imaginary conflation of phallus/penis, women can "be" the phallus that men "have"), and how the threat of its fantasized "loss" destabilizes masculinity. Although both Helen and Achilles are "wounded" (and both cross-dress), their responses to the recognition of symbolic castration markedly differ.

This difference is central to H.D.'s analysis of war and masculinity, since for her, as for Freud, as Friedman has thoroughly established, individual fantasy correlates to collective fantasy (myth). Achilles' violent attack on Helen, the recognition scene the text repeatedly reviews and reinterprets, exposes how woman functions as sign, as well as uncovers the homological balances of power that warfare, at the cultural level, and castration anxiety, at the individual level, play out. *Helen in Egypt* is an especially important work because it is a woman's epic-length analysis of the forces, the psychic conditions, that contributed to making the world wars through which H.D.'s generation lived, the crucibles in which H.D.'s feminism was forged, and in which, in combination with her study of mysticism and of Freudian theory, her poetry was alchemized.[9] The poem dramatizes the connection between the violent psychodynamic of gender difference that structures social relations and war.[10]

In *Helen in Egypt,* H.D., like Dickinson and Moore, not only analyzes what the maternal represents in the social order, but also attempts imaginatively to restore and transform that order through a more flexible, resonant poetic language. Diane Chisholm cogently demonstrates how H.D. champions a "hieroglyphic poetry as cultural cure," a poetics of dream processes, irreducible symbols, and narrative innovation that restores the repressed (eros and woman) as antidote to civilization's driven pessimism.[11] Throughout the poem Helen is portrayed as studying one "text" or another (mystical hieroglyphs, her memories, or those of Achilles) whose equivocal status, at once fact and invention (*HE,* 69), is never resolved.

The reading project within the poetic frame—"to relate the graven line / to a fact, graven in memory" (*HE*, 66)—is a figure not only for H.D.'s own process, at the metapoetic level. But recalling Dickinson's and Moore's relation to their readers, H.D.'s readers outside the poetic frame are also enjoined to reproduce *Helen in Egypt's* methodology through the analytic act that constitutes the reading of this poem: "*We all know the story of Helen of Troy but few of us have followed her to Egypt,*" the poem opens (*HE*, 1).[12] *Helen in Egypt* represents H.D.'s sustained attempt to confront the limits of our capacity to read, inscribe, and transform through poetic language the masculinist psyche that subsumes women into its symbolic constructions.[13]

AN UNORIGINAL WOMAN

The Greeks and Trojans alike fought for an illusion.

—*Helen in Egypt*

Like Pound's *Cantos*, to which H.D. compared *Helen in Egypt*, the fascist hero represented by Achilles figures prominently.[14] But H.D. represents him more as an epistemological conundrum than as a "subject rhyme" (the term is Kenner's) for an approved version of what masculinity is or should be: he is not unproblematically validated, for example, over erotic Paris or maternal Theseus. H.D. suggests that the "enigma of man" for women (to adapt Freud) is the warrior. Helen asks if a woman could ever "know what the heroes felt, / what spurred them to war and battle, / what fire charged them with fever?" (*HE*, 293), or understand "man's passion and birthright" (*HE*, 294). Man is, at least in *part*, "the riddle of the written stone" (*HE*, 31) that Helen studies in Egypt.[15] Observing women's exclusion from men's matters, whether wars or heroic epics, she perceives that

> his fortress and his tower
> and his throne
> were built for man, alone;

> no echo or soft whisper
> in those halls,
> no iridescent sheen,
>
> no iris-flower,
> no sweep of strings,
> no answering laughter,
>
> but the trumpet's call[.]
>
>   (*HE*, 30–31)

This passage illustrates a technique characteristic of the poetics of H.D., who employs metonym and synecdoche to invoke the spheres with which these images are associated, rather than a metaphor that would replace them (for H.D., metaphor represents a masculinist drive to mastery, as I shall presently discuss). Here the juxtaposition of metonyms highlights the contradiction of grammatically parallel but asymmetrically exclusive worlds of men and women. Woman's "echo" is not original, but nor is it mimetic (in Irigaray's sense of the term). It neither repeats nor revises man's "trumpet's call," but invokes another sound, which challenges "the trumpet-note" altogether: "a rhythm as yet un-heard," we are later told (*HE*, 229).

Helen's observations lead not to insight into an imbalance between masculine and feminine that could, potentially, be restored, however, but to disorientation. In "Pallinode," the first of the three sectioned parts of the poem, Helen doubts

> *her power to lure Achilles from this [war], or the power of women in general. There is no good in this postulate. She will get nowhere. She knows this.* (*HE*, 30)

What Helen knows, this passage indicates, is not the erotic power of women to draw men from war, but that she will "get nowhere." She contemplates the problem of masculinity and violence, and, we're told at one point, "*understands, though we do not know exactly what it is that she understands*" (*HE*, 191). Nonetheless, in the end she seems still to have gotten "nowhere," spending almost the whole third part, "Eidolon," in a trance trying to fathom what I shall term Achilles' "crisis of gender."

The narrative originally resolved, to be sure, with the confident invocation of the timeless moment within time, in which "the secret"–"the dart of Love / is the dart of Death"–was spelled out as "no secret" (*HE,* 303–4).[16] On the second typed manuscript draft of "Eidolon," after what is now the penultimate section of the poem, H.D. wrote, "The End–I am sure this is: but I am going over the whole now."[17] Some time later she appended a coda, also entitled *Eidolon,* which exceeds the final revelation to end on the following enigmatic note:

> *But what could Paris know of the sea*
> *its beat and long reverberation,*
> *its booming and delicate echo,*
> . . . .
> *the wind, the shoal, the broken shale,*
> *the infinite loneliness*
> *when one is never alone?*
>
> *only Achilles could break his heart*
> *and the world for a token,*
> *a memory forgotten.*
>
> (*HE,* 304)

Like an echo, the coda repeats the words of the text proper but changes their meaning through the very process of repetition. The rhetorical questions, to recall de Man's point discussed in chapter 1, render ambiguous the conclusive mysticism of the original resolution. *Eidolon* resemanticizes "Eidolon," contradicting the finality of insights that, like the perfect end rhymes in the closing stanza above, seem perfectly to resolve the poem but in essence clarify nothing. By ending the poem after The End, H.D. effectively raises the issue of the status of masculine identity after "the end": after revelations, in a post-apocalyptic world in which "Troy" has fallen; everyone, including the apparent victors, has lost ("he [Achilles] had lost / and they had lost– / the war-Lords of Greece" [*HE,* 19]); and nothing, no assured vision in this very visionary poem, has replaced what the war destroyed for both sides.[18]

Such obscuring of vision is in H.D.'s text first and foremost a figure for men's misinterpretation of, and in fact blindness to, women, in which the poem is specifically located, as are the constructions of gender that support heterosexual relations as well as war. The "illusion" the Greeks and Trojans fought for was Helen of Troy, who was, we are told at the beginning of the poem, "*a phantom, substituted for the real Helen*" (*HE,* 1). Differing male identities ("Greeks" and "Trojans"), which in the course of the war over "a phantom" produce "heroes"—*man's men,* as it were—are shown to be themselves distinguishable only through their often mobile alignment with a position: for example, whose side they're on. They are, that is, symbolic productions. Since nothing is clearly outside the framework of fantasy in the text,[19] H.D. suggests that what constitutes this "normative masculinity" is a dominant fiction, as Kaja Silverman remarks in another context,[20] no more or less "real" than the "phantom," Helen.

In "Pallinode," where Achilles and Helen meet in Egypt, he tells her about "*the adamant rule of the inner circle of the warrior caste*" that placed him in the world of male hegemony through Oedipal and homosocial bonds:

> The Command was bequest from the past,
> from father to son,
> the Command bound past to the present
>
> and the present to aeons to come,
> the Command was my father, my brother,
> my lover, my God[.]

> (*HE,* 61)

What disrupts this homogeneous chain of command through time seems at first the intrusion of differences. Achilles disagreed with the rest of the Command—Agamemnon, Menelaus, and Odysseus—over Odysseus's "plan / of the iron-horse" (*HE,* 52), for which, he tells Helen, he was ignominiously "shot like an underling" (*HE,* 60). He characterizes the problem as a misreading of an original oracular message, and wonders whether, not being able to "see" the correct way to read, "the Command read backward?" (*HE*, 54). He tries to correct their misreading by changing the "text" of the oracle altogether and deciphering Helen as she walks daily on the ramparts.

But this move confronts him with sexual difference, his reconnoiter (etymologically, a recognition) with a Helen who returns as well as receives his gaze. Her glance "transfixes" him (*HE*, 54), and because he is watching her and not the battle when his sandle comes loose, causes his own immediate demise and eventually the dispersal of the Command's power. Achilles at first recognizes Helen as other than himself, one on whom he cannot necessarily impose a meaning. This moment of insight is followed by his transfiguration from Immortal into "new Mortal": he dies out of the canonical poetic "commands" that immortalized him. In a process that results in another mystification of difference, Achilles conflates Helen with divinity:

> it was not the Command that betrayed,
> it was Another;
> She is stronger than God, they say[.]
>
> (*HE*, 61)

His visual revelation, based as it is on rumor and hearsay, has the effect of rhetorical "blindness."

Aptly enough, the poem begins with an earlier masculine blindness. The apocryphal fragments by Stesichorus and Euripides that inspired H.D.'s version, which form an alternative to the canonical analogues of Helen, originate in blindness, as the opening passage from "Pallinode" recounts:

> *Stesichorus of Sicily in his* Pallinode, *was the first to tell us* [of *Helen in Egypt*]. *Some centuries later, Euripides repeats the story. Stesichorus was said to have been struck blind because of his invective against Helen, but later was restored to sight, when he reinstated her in his* Pallinode. *Euripides, notably in* The Trojan Women, *reviles her, but he also is "restored to sight." The later, little understood* Helen in Egypt, *is again a* Pallinode, *a defence, explanation or apology.* (*HE*, 1)

In this passage, H.D. draws connections between authorial blindness, repetition, rhetoric, and the figure of woman. Did blindness accompany "truth," sight being restored as a reward for insight, or did it precede "truth," sight being restored in order to acquire insight? The passage obscures the chronology of the events that led to literature and the source of the literary event, giving us no actual referent for either of the pallinodes, thereby confusing the passage's origin in "truth" and the passage's true origin. Narrative as the corrective of a mis-take that had no originally correct "take" (but only a mistaken one) repeatedly engenders rhetoric (the need for "*a defence, explanation or apology*"). Blindness that was both punishment for and cause of the original misinterpretation becomes, through the process of repetition, a metaphor for interpretive blindness, or a figure for itself.[21]

In *Helen in Egypt*, H.D. questions the relation that representations of Helen in male-authored versions have had to Truth. She implies that Helen (like Moore's unicorn) is the gynetic sign that posits another, making the proliferation of texts possible, an original dividedness in and divisiveness over the subject of poetry. H.D. exposes how repetition both enacts and repeats a previous difference as the source, and at the source, of a text that has no source outside textuality. As Elizabeth Hirsh observes, H.D. "*multiplies Helens . . . in such a way that there can no longer be any question of which represents 'the original' or authoritative one.*"[22] Her opening performs a leveling between previously canonical and apocryphal versions of Helen, situating them all in rhetoric, opening a gap, by unsettling the distinctions between the "real" and the "phantom," into which she has placed her own *Helen*.[23]

The Greeks and the Trojans alike fought not only for an illusion but for an *allusion* as well, a place in the proliferating retellings of the fall of a Troy that never fell except in the telling (fantasy). Helen asks:

> Was it Apollo's snare
> so that poets forever,
> should be caught in the maze of the Walls
>
> of a Troy that never fell?

> (*HE*, 232)

Lyric's status in relation to truth, as well as to the ensnaring powers of the dramatic and epic poetry in which the canonical story of Helen is found, is an ambiguous one, as this passage implies. Poetry's "snare," H.D. suggests, may lie in the illusions that the dominant version constructs, whose fictive origins the tale seduces us into believing are true. Both would-be writers and readers purporting to read the cipher of the free-floating signifier, Helen, on the ramparts, the warriors fight to reappropriate her body as text (rather than as flesh, in H.D.'s astute perception), thereby inscribing themselves into "the scrolls of history, / un-sung as yet by the poets" (*HE*, 50). As in the heroic ideal, act ensures the actor's linguistic survival, the warriors are immortalized through the song: one body (corpse) being exchanged for another (corpus), flesh is made word and word is made history.[24]

However much the reflexivity of the passage above calls into question the status of H.D.'s own lyric text (her ironic equivocation is typical), Helen's portrait stands in stark contrast to that of the warriors, for she is outside the stake in the meaning they attribute to her. She observes that the war over ostensible differences can only be fought by forgetting gender difference:

> so they fought, forgetting women,
> hero to hero, sworn brother and lover,
> and cursing Helen through eternity.
>
> (*HE*, 4)

Like the art of poetry, war is made at women's expense, by subsuming all women under the rubric of one "phantom," onto which violence can be displaced and cause of loss projected. Although Helen as the image that at once symbolizes and glosses over difference is not replaced into the system but displaced into Egypt, her displacement is described in psychoanalytical as well as rhetorical terms (as Chisholm notes as well): *transposition* (to be moved from one place to another, etymologically akin to *transfer* and *translation*); *translation* (the Latin for the Greek "metaphor"); and *substitution* (etymologically, "to replace from below"). Such terms suggest that Helen's removal to Egypt transposes the psychological and sociocultural issues highlighted by the Trojan War, as symbolic of all wars.[25]

Empirical and figural violations, implicated with rhetorical as well as literal blindness in H.D.'s text, are bound up with the operations of projection and fantasy that characterize the appropriative male gaze.[26] As Irigaray elaborates the issue here, "The gaze is at stake" because the gazer gets to see without being seen, without "being seen seeing," or without anyone questioning who controls the gaze and the interpretation of what is seen.[27] H.D.'s depiction of the war that produces the poetic tale that eternally reviles Helen also reveals that "she" is a male-authored construction.

Implicit in Helen's phrase, "hero to hero," is the homological symmetry, literally a poetic repetition compulsion, that erases gender difference. War is a male affair, or, to put it another way, *homicidal*. The only difference between the two sides might just lie in where Helen *is laid*, the dynamics of improper vs. proper possession having caused an inequality in otherwise identical parties. The illusion for which "the Greeks and the Trojans alike" fought is finally that there was any difference between them, for "alike" functions ambiguously in the line, suggesting both identity and collectivity. H.D.'s astute insight is that war does not disrupt but renders visible the structures of gender asymmetry by which male dominance is maintained, coercing the makeover of any differences into its own homologous image.

War and the stories we tell about war articulate the patriarchy through its images of validated masculinity, mystify how the suppression, or naturalization, of gender difference (and other differences such as race and class elided into gender) structures war, and thereby conflate masculinity with patriarchy. But as Susan Jeffords has argued about representations of the Vietnam War, masculinity is the unacknowledged "mechanism for the installation of patriarchal structure."[28] One of the most radical aspects of H.D.'s poem is its refusal to restabilize Helen's and Achilles' gender identities so that they are once again clearly assigned to the masculine or feminine—that is, to borrow Jeffords's term, to re*masculinize* the text. The connections between genealogies of worldly and textual power are unraveled. Before the poem's time frame, Achilles has lost for good the sense of stable masculine identity his status in the patriarchy gave him. Such stability is a luxury Helen in any event never expe-

rienced: surviving her encounter with Achilles in Egypt depends, as
it turns out, on her capacity to differ from herself, to masquerade.

Achilles' "death" into "mortality" (symbolic castration) is
underscored by Helen's transition from distant, speechless cipher
in Troy to speaking subject in Egypt. Having lost his place in the
"book," Achilles no longer knows where or who he is:

> where are we? who are you?
> where is this desolate coast?
> who am I? am I a ghost.
>
> > (*HE*, 16)

Trying to prevent Achilles' recognition of her, she masks herself,
blackening her face "*like the prophetic* femme noire *of antiquity*" (*HE*,
15) and figuratively doubling herself: "'I am a woman of pleasure,' / I spoke ironically into the night" (*HE*, 12). Like all duplicitous speech, irony contains two mutually exclusive significations,
between which it oscillates: Helen both is and is not a woman of
"pleasure," both is and puts on a good act of being the prophetic
femme noire.

In short, her ploy works. Recalling Moore's public and poetic
costuming, H.D.'s representation of the masquerade frustrates its
normative, androcentric motive. Helen's refusal to reflect Achilles
back to himself as *Achilles* unhinges him, revealing the lack that a
sense of unified identity established by the genealogy of warriors
and of canonical texts had veiled. Confronted by Helen's unsettling
shiftiness, which renders her not only unrecognizable but uncanny,
he attempts to identify her as either monstrous or divine (if she is
not "woman," after all, what else could she be?):

> are you Hecate? are you a witch?
>
> a vulture, a hieroglyph,
> the sign or the name of a goddess?
> what sort of goddess is this?
>
> > (*HE*, 16)

As this passage illustrates, Achilles tries to gain power over Helen,
and, concomitantly, reestablish coherence, by locating her in lan-

guage. But in this process of identification, Helen becomes nothing more or less than a series of confusing and contradictory metaphors. Of conventions of romance as well as metaphor, Homans has argued that

> underwriting both the plot of male desire and the plot of metaphor is a hierarchical power structure implicit in both, a hierarchy that permits one term—whether the romantic (male) subject or one term of a metaphor—to claim the authority to define the other—whether the feminine object of romantic desire or the second term of a metaphor.[29]

Homans suggests that women employ metonymy to revise this metaphoric appropriation of the feminine, a strategy H.D.'s poem, like Moore's "A Carriage from Sweden," confirms. In her (sub)version of the conventions of romance as well as of metaphoric structure, the figuration to which Achilles' attempt to define Helen gives rise neither represses the ambiguity of her identity nor mitigates his ambivalence about her. Rather, both are put into play through metonymy: the chain of arguably hysterical substitutions the passage above rehearses.

Only when Achilles succeeds in placing her, suppressing the ambiguity under the rubric of a single identity, "Helena, cursed of Greece" (*HE,* 16), does Helen become for him one with the sign of all he has lost:

> you stole the chosen, the flower
> of all-time, of all-history,
> my children, my legions;
>
> for you were the ships burnt[.]
>
>   (*HE,* 17)

Achilles' consolidation of Helen, literally in a word (*Helena*), is potentially the activity to reestablish his own identity through her reflection of his former status. The word causes him instead, however, to remember simultaneously the sign for both identity and its loss. Thus, Achilles experiences recollection as a further displacement of himself. This metonymic move characterizes a significant difference between the canonical versions and H.D.'s own complex revisionary poetic agenda.

The instability of Helen's subjectivity in this scene precipitates Achilles' violent attempt to restabilize her as a sexually appropriable object for the disintegrating patriarchal order he represents. Finally at a loss for words, he tries first to strangle and then to rape Helen, confusing the two acts. Of precisely such a dynamic in mythic as well as in cinematic narrative structures, de Lauretis observes that when the terms of a double or divided desire on the part of the woman are enacted, the text must display that desire as duplicitous, impossible, or contradictory, and finally resolve the contradiction "by either the massive destruction or the territorialization" of the woman.[30] Helen learns in this scene that the coincidence of the signs *Helen* and *Helena, cursed of Greece* puts her in mortal danger.

When she refers to the notion of self-difference, she signifies Helena as a ghostly other inhabiting patriarchal consciousness itself, a (mirroring) double having no real substance:

> she whom you cursed
> was but the phantom and the shadow thrown
> of a reflection[.]
>
> (*HE*, 5)

Helen's self-inscription splits her into the subject and object of her own discourse—the one evasive and self-differing; the other the specularized object of the male gaze, a shadowy figure defined by her capacity to reflect.

Always being made other than herself (even by herself, albeit for very different reasons), Helen is unknowable (even to herself, as Buck points out).[31] The attempts to figure her out often end with a precise literalization of that phrase, in metaphors that try to define and confine her identity, as we have seen. Achilles' characterizations of her are all versions of a "Helena" the text is careful to distinguish from "Helen." In the second part, *Leuké,* the "white isle" to which Helen travels to seek Theseus's aid in the process of reconstructing her past and reintegrating her "selves" (*HE,* 170), he, too, translates her into metaphor:

> you are neither there nor here,
>
> but wavering
> like a Psyche
> with half-dried wings.
>
> (*HE*, 166)

Nowhere and unnameable, "like a butterfly, 'a Psyche,'" (*HE*, 165), she disappears into multiple tropes for self-transformation (an identity that refuses to be stabilized, for man), and the ineffable soul (an identity that is, by definition, indefinable, but again, *to man*).

Such figuration of Helen evokes (swamped as she is by "masculine narratives," as Hirsh observes)[32] the appropriative violence of interpretation itself.[33] Like the warriors they commanded, Achilles, Theseus, and Paris are represented as interested in mastering Helen as text, replacing her with a "phantom" double, subject to their control. Imposing their metaphors on her in order to translate her requires, of course, her exclusion from the linguistic terms of her reformation—in other words, her silence. Caught once again in a series of masculine projections, she finds herself finally on Leuké in no position *but* to reflect, both contained by and "entranced" container of their discourse.

A MAN'S MAN

If man operates under the threat of castration, if masculinity is culturally ordered by the castration complex, it might be said that the backlash, the return, on women of this castration anxiety is its displacement as decapitation . . . of woman, as loss of her head.
                                        —Hélène Cixous, "Castration or Decapitation?"

When we write of a woman, everything is out of place . . . the accent never falls where it does with a man.
                                        —Virginia Woolf, *Orlando*

The narrative events of *Helen in Egypt* that represent gender violence, including that of interpretive mastery, dramatize how dominant fictions depend on woman supplanting women. H.D. locates

Helen in relation to physical violence against, as well as narrative violation of, women, indicating the coincidence of–and the symbolic indifference between–men's acts of killing, fucking, and telling tales about women.[34] For hegemonic masculinity, repetition leads not to the ludic play of differences but to indifference. The phrase, "there was always another and another and another" (see *HE,* 167, 187, 218), is spoken by both Theseus and Paris, who observe and participate in the reduction of separate women to the Same. On Leuké, for instance, Theseus asks Helen whether they should match past lovers "like knuckle-players / with bones or stones for counters" (*HE,* 162). But he can no longer tell the women apart:

> . . . Ariadne, Phaedra, Hippolyta?
> or was it Helen on the way to Egypt,
> or was it Helen returning,
>
> or was it Helen on the sea-road,
> nearing Troy? was it one of these
> or all three? reflections . . .
>
> (*HE,* 163)

As Theseus's confusion between them indicates, women are only nominally differentiated. They have become tantalizing, metonymic reflections of remembered virility, "a certain sheen of cloth, / a certain ankle, / a strap over a shoulder" (*HE,* 164), but in themselves indistinguishable. Theseus's litany suddenly becomes "another story" (*HE,* 172), but, significantly, told with the same words. Paris reiterates that there was always "another and another and another" (*HE,* 218), referring to all the women "sacrificed in one way or another" to the Trojan War (*HE,* 173). Grammatically and semantically undifferentiated, the proper names of the women function as the women themselves do in the symbolic order: these women are the same (woman).

In Egypt Helen at first refuses this knowledge, stating in a passage that specifically associates sexual and scopic aggression that she doesn't want to know what Achilles' relationship to women had been:

whether he flouted his power,

while women fell, as the scythe
of his visored glance swept them over;
whether he laughed as they fell;

whether he found, here and there,
a girl for a change in pleasure,
when weary after the fray[.]

(*HE*, 33–34)

But as she re-members herself, realizing that her spirit was "miraculously" snatched "with its body" to Egypt (*HE*, 198), she stops refusing knowledge about Achilles, and must therefore acknowledge that she has been a victim of his aggression: "so my throat knew that day, / / his fingers' remorseless steel" (*HE*, 199). Remembering involves confronting the possibility of losing herself into a *mise en abîme* not only of linguistic repetition but of women's mutilated bodies as well. Eventually she identifies her own throat as "another / white throat [promised] to a goddess" (*HE*, 244). In the act of differentiating herself from Helena (her image), Helen discovers her indifference from other (images of) women in the dominant scopic economy. Woman poses, as Irigaray observes of this enculturated dynamic, "a negative image that provides male sexuality with an unfailingly phallic self-representation."[35] As H.D.'s resonant lines underscore, that image functions alike in love and war,[36] sacrificed to masculinist designs, expendable because in effect endlessly substitutable, a battle "spoil."[37]

As suggested earlier about H.D.'s use of metonymy to unravel hierarchies of metaphoric as well as of romantic plot structures, however, her text spoils the continuity of this *mise en abîme* of women, as it similarly intervenes in the smooth flow of patriarchal genealogy. Resisting masculine identifications that either "would re-create Troy / with Helen, not Hecuba for mother" (*HE*, 224), or cast her as the predatory "Grecian harlot," Helen confronts her potential disembodiment (her conflation with a male-authored image). This confrontation has the countereffect of empowering her as an embodied, and in the metaphysical economy with which this poem takes issue, as a female, subject. The fight she puts up takes the form of an invocation of the Name of the Mother (to adapt Lacan), *Thetis*, and represents the poetic capacity to resemanticize the silenced "preying" woman, whose image the warriors had reviled, as a "praying" woman. Although Helen is threatened by an event that can be said to symbolize women's historical silencing, at the same time Helen makes visible (albeit inaudible: unheard [of?]) an empowered relationship to language and representation that recalls the ludic potential of both a revised Echo and Irigaray's notion of mimetic repetition. The same words, but in Helen's mouth, suggest that her ability to claim the power to transfigure the demeaning tales lies in the very incapacity to defend herself in any way *but* words: through her repetition of the tales, their inherited meanings can be transformed.

Women who refuse to reflect men back to themselves in language, H.D.'s text makes clear, threaten men, who recognize them no longer as women, but as "witches," "vultures."[38] Equally clear is that such defemininized "texts" aren't altogether reclaimable, giving rise to defensively masterful readings. Women's troubling of androcentric interpretative boxes is articulated through the putting into discourse of their own readings. As a striking example, consider how H.D.'s epic reformulates Freud's famous equation in "Medusa's Head," "To decapitate = to castrate," by reasserting the link Freud suppressed: to strangle = to rape = to castrate (women).

In that essay, Freud draws an analogy between the sight of Medusa's severed head and the child's traumatic first glimpse of the mother's Medusan genitals: "To decapitate = to castrate. The terror of Medusa is thus a terror of castration that is linked to the sight of . . . the female genitals, . . . and essentially those of his mother."[39] According to Freud, women's "lack" is paradoxically the very source of their power for men. Hertz elaborates: "the strength contained in the woman's weakness is the power to frighten the man by revealing to him the possibility of his castration."[40] But what these readings don't specifically address is whether there is any alternative to this "strength," which is, once again, woman's strength as it seems to *man*: the power to frighten someone with your fate is, as in "tough love," the "power" of the already disempowered.

H.D. observes the slippage in Freud's thinking.[41] Conflating an actual violence toward a feminine figure (Medusa's decapitation) with man's potential emasculation, Freud reverses the direction of the attack: the violent silencing of women signified by beheading in the Medusa myth is always the upwardly displaced sign of woman's castration ("Medusa's head takes the place of a representation of the female genitals"),[42] rather than of the other literal aggression portrayed in the myth, which Freud suppresses and H.D.'s epic restores: rape.[43] In suggesting through the insistent re-presentation of such upward displacement (the return throughout the poem to the strangulation scene) that the "fact" of castration has been projected onto women, H.D.'s critique of Freud resembles Cixous's in the essay from which the passage quoted as epigraph to this section was taken.[44] Seeing woman's difference as both castrated and potentially castrating, the man misreads seeing "nothing" as nothing *to see.*

This notion helps to throw further light on H.D.'s portraits of Helen and Achilles and on what she was up to in herself poetically reinterpreting Freud. That H.D. discussed with Freud his theories about girls' penis envy, women's castration, and feminine sexuality in general has been over the years thoroughly established by Friedman's and DuPlessis's foundational work, especially their article "'Woman is Perfect': H.D.'s Debate with Freud." They document through H.D.'s unpublished letters and the posthumously published poem "The Master" that, as H.D. quipped to Bryher in the letter quoted at the beginning of this chapter, "we argued about it [femininity]."[45] In *Tribute to Freud,* H.D. subtly complicates his representation of femininity as deficient, a version, she implies, trying to impose itself on her as truth. Her self-portrait inscribes a female subject who vexes definitions of castrated and not castrated as they pertain to women.

In the scene from *Tribute to Freud* most often cited as Freud's attempt to demonstrate to her, by analogy, the origins of women's penis envy, for example, H.D. tells how he one day showed her a flawless small bronze statue of Pallas Athena, "venerated as a projection of abstract thought . . . born without human or even without divine mother," a fathered, as H.D. is at pains to point out, but not mothered, being (*TF,* 70).[46] Appropriating Freud's own method of analogy, she counters that like Athena the theory of penis envy is actually "a projection of abstract thought" as and onto woman, and as such is a fathered–but not *mothered*–invention. Freud indicates a loss, but H.D. exposes his apparent statement of fact as interpretation, a fictive account whose version is subject to H.D.'s subtle revision:

> It was a little bronze statue, helmeted, clothed to the foot in carved robe with the upper incised chiton or peplum. One hand was extended as if holding a staff or rod. 'She is perfect,' he said, '*only she has lost her spear.*' I did not say anything. (*TF,* 68–69; H.D.'s emphasis)

Coinciding with Freud's designation of the absence as a missing "spear" is H.D.'s suggestion of "staff or rod," words with quite different connotations. She does not contradict him directly; by (apparently) quoting him, H.D. allows the reader to see that he contradicts himself: "perfection" cannot, by definition, be open to qualification, or it isn't perfect. Nor does the passage determine for the reader, who must decide–or not–for herself, which of the three possibilities offered for what's missing is correct. What, the passage subtly asks, has woman (really) lost?

"She has lost her spear. He might have been talking Greek," H.D. continues in the next section (*TF,* 69). What follows this statement is an extended figural association describing how Freud

> had dipped the grey web of conventionally woven thought and with it, conventionally *spoken* thought, into a vat of his own brewing . . . in order to draw it [language] forth dyed blue or scarlet[.] (*TF,* 69; H.D.'s emphasis)

This fabulously refurbished "scrap of thought" is "a pennant, a standard, a *sign* again, to indicate a direction or, fluttering aloft on a pole, to lead an army" (*TF,* 69; H.D.'s emphasis). Into the conventional metaphor for the male artist's intricate poetics, the fabric of androcentric discourse, erupts a particularly withering feminist critique. Despite their beautiful dye, Freud's words reproduce normative (masculinist) standards; they are seductively flashy, but point in the same direction in which thinking has always led its army of logical conclusions: the subjugation of (feminine) difference.

H.D.'s imagery in this passage draws a connection between language's materiality and materialism. In the following excerpt, she characterizes Freud's materialistic tendencies, and then, transmuting the terms, the standards by which he assesses value, she dematerializes them:

> 'She is perfect,' he said and he meant that the image was of the accepted classic period, Periclean or just pre-Periclean . . . he was speaking of value, the actual intrinsic value of the piece; like a Jew, he was assessing its worth. . . . He knew his material pound, his pound of flesh, if you will, but this pound of flesh was a *pound of spirit* between us, something tangible, to be weighed and measured, to be weighed in the balance and—pray God—not to be found wanting! (*TF,* 70; H.D.'s emphasis)

The "pound of flesh" is a paradoxical figure: both patriarchal and liminal, as an uncharacteristic eruption of anti-Semitic stereotyping of Freud on H.D.'s part indicates; both material, something that can be "weighed and measured," and immaterial, uncannily doubled into its ghostly equivalent, "a *pound of spirit.*" Though inscribed rhetorically as the same, the two "pounds" do not equate but equivocate. H.D. asserts their difference through parallelism, which simultaneously establishes resemblance and opens a breach that holds difference in suspension "between us."

Her allusion to *The Merchant of Venice* implies that Freud's insistence on the materiality of the "pound of flesh" that women lack can be undermined in the same way as Portia frustrated Shylock's insistence, by a woman's dramatic rereading of the letter of Law and exposing the gaps in Freud's reasoning. The "pound of flesh" (penis) can only be established as "a pound of spirit" (phallus) semantically, and women can only be "found wanting" by evaluating them solely in terms of a male-defined dialectical materialism. "Symmetry," as Jane Gallop recounts in her discussion of Irigaray's "The Blind Spot of an Old Dream of Symmetry," stems etymologically from the Greek, *summetros,* for "like measure."[47] As in the obfuscating logic of Aristotle's concept of metaphor (as discussed in chapter 1 above), for symmetry to be achieved, similarity and balance must be imposed. Two things must be equated, judged by the dominant measuring rod: "for example the feminine judged by masculine standards."[48] As in Freud's account of female castration, the missing "spear" isn't visible; lack can only be located by a resort to language. Freud "cites" (as well as sights) what is, in his view, absent. That is, he materializes the "immaterial."

His words, colored as they are, though beautifully, by conventional thinking, refer to an already preexisting drama in the face of which H.D. represents herself as silent or silenced before the "Master" ("I did not say anything"). Her silence might be duplicitous, seeming tacitly to be acquiescence (being silenced by a master discoursing), at the same time as it suggests a deliberate resistance to commitment (choosing to remain silent as an evasion of committing herself one way or the other on the question of sexual difference), but silent she is. His English is "perfect," moreover, "without a perceptible trace of accent, yet he was speaking a foreign language" (*TF*, 69). He is using the same language as she, one in which her command (at least, in poetry) has been said to be "perfect," and which is foreign to him, though he speaks it without accent. But in the paradoxical reversal H.D.'s wordplay effects, she both does and does not have access to this language he speaks. In other words, it is foreign *to her*. Although she echoes his words ("She has lost her spear"), it should not surprise us by now that she repeats them with a difference—with, we might ourselves say, echoing Woolf, a different *accent*.[49] And what her accent falls on is that process of representation to which Freud has had to resort to define woman's "deficiency."

As such ventriloquizing of Freud implies, H.D. equivocally invests in his thinking (just as, through another strategic equivocal moment, the anti-Semitism in the passage above, H.D. ambiguously decentralizes Freud's authoritative position).[50] She recounts that Freud was disturbed by her vision of the "writing on the wall," considering it, in fact, a sign of her mother fixation, and labeling it her only "dangerous symptom" (*TF*, 51). Her account of this "vision or symptom" (she never determines which) is worth looking at more closely for a moment, for it will help us to begin to unravel the connections between female subjectivity, femininity, and the rhetorical strategy of equivocation I have so far only implied is a feature of H.D.'s methodology.

The vision consisted of images and hieroglyphic inscriptions that seemed projected, like moving pictures, across the wall. As H.D. essayed to understand it, as she describes in a passage that recalls "Medusa's Head," she becomes aware of how rigid her face has become with the effort. Such a sensation causes her to associate her vision with seeing Medusa:

> I am perfectly well aware that this concentration is a diffi-cult matter. My facial muscles seem stiff with the effort and I may become frozen like one of those enemies of Athené, the goddess of wisdom, to whom Perseus showed the Gor-gon head. Am I looking at the Gorgon head, a suspect, an enemy to be dealt with? Or am I myself Perseus, the hero who is fighting for Truth and Wisdom? But Perseus could find his way about with winged sandals and the cloak of invisibility. Moreover, he himself could wield the ugly weapon of the Gorgon's severed head, because Athené (or was it Hermes, Mercury?) had told him what to do. He was himself to manipulate his weapon, this ugly severed head of the enemy of Wisdom and Beauty, by looking at it in the polished metal of his shield. Even he, the half-god or hero, would be turned to stone, frozen if he regarded too closely and without the shield to protect him, in its new quality of looking-glass or reflector, the ugly Head or Source of evil. So I, though I did not make this parallel at the time, still wondered. But even as I wondered, I kept the steady con-centrated gaze at the wall before me. (*TF*, 52–53)

At first, H.D. cannot decide which "head," an enemy or defender of "Truth and Wisdom," she might be. But she finally distinguishes herself from Perseus, for "he could find his way about" and "Athené . . . had told him what to do." Perseus stands in a privi-leged relation to "Wisdom and Beauty," to which she does not have access. In his role as hero, he has a set of instructions for what to do, and she doesn't.

Such a distinction, however, does not resolve the problem of her relation to the Gorgon head. She stands in a different position not only to patriarchal instruction but to both the "writing on the wall" and Medusa's head than the heroic male figure. Simultaneously gazing upon and, as her description of her quite literally petrifying face implies, embodying the head, her position corresponds to "the double or split identification," as de Lauretis argues, that cinema "offers the female spectator: identification with the look of the camera, apprehended as temporal, active or in movement, and identification with the image on the screen, perceived as spatially static, fixed, in frame."[51] Double identification is the operation, she elaborates, "by which narrative and cinema . . . seduce women into femininity."[52] In a similar operation, H.D. represents herself as absorbed in reflecting (upon) a cultural version, by implication, of fearsome femininity.

In contrast, manipulating his weapon ("the ugly, severed head"), the male figure is depicted as first bestowing (as author) and then appropriating (as hero) Medusa's power to petrify her enemies. But even by her killer, she can be viewed only indirectly, through the mediation of a reflection from a "protective shield." The removal of that shield would effect a reversal: having turned Medusa's head into stone (figuratively speaking) by decapitating her, Perseus himself would be turned to stone (*petrified*) were he to risk unmediated beholding. As de Lauretis comments, in the legend of Perseus in which Medusa is inscribed, it is clear that the threat "is to man's vision, and [her] power consists in [her] enigma . . . , [her] luring of man's gaze into the 'dark continent,' as Freud puts it [in "Femininity"], the enigma of femininity."[53] Men can also can be seduced "into femininity," it would seem, but the implications for them are more ominous: it is a seduction, of course, into death. Medusa–the feminine sex–can only be viewed as a reflection because without mediation she effects a lethal reversal of reflection: the beholder, lured into a no-man's land of no return, reflects *her.*

But in H.D.'s case, the sight was never mediated. A figurative reflection becomes concretized, implying that the Medusa's head already mirrors the female beholder. In the dominant structure, de Lauretis makes clear, such a specular relation is also deadly. Freud certainly saw H.D.'s vision as symptomatic of the latent desire for union with her mother (*TF*, 44) and the accompanying loss of the capacity to differentiate herself from her mother. Such a loss of boundaries was in Freud's eyes the source of the danger, for it threatens the stability that repression and representation have achieved.

In another sense, however, H.D.'s "reflection" is indeed mediated, not by space but by time ("I did not make this parallel at the time"). Her head grew rigid prior to her association of it with Medusa's. An elapse of time took place between the initial sensations and her interpretation of them. H.D. here dramatizes Freud's notion of *nachtraglichkeit*, or deferred action, the subject's revision of past events at a later date that invests them with significance:[54] for example, the time it takes for the boy to give the first sight of female genitals the traumatic meaning of the "fact" of castration. Through retrospection, the boy's initial irresolution about what he saw (or rather, didn't see) is decided. The meaning he eventually attaches to the sight "arouses a terrible storm of emotion in him,"[55] for he at last perceives the apparent threat of castration to himself.[56] But as Kofman cautions, one finds "a perpetual slippage in Freud's texts from what children 'imagine'—on the basis of their castration anxiety, for example—to the simple fact. . . . Freud passes from these 'theories' forged to protect himself against anxiety to their truth, to the affirmation of the 'reality' of the girl's castration."[57]

In "Medusa's Head," Freud asserts that the male viewer's reaction to the sight, his stiffening with "terror," is simultaneously reassuring, for "becoming stiff means an erection," which offers to the male spectator the consolation that "he is still in possession of a penis."[58] Like the boy's, the viewer's initial indecision about what the sight means—oscillating between terror and reassurance, horror and consolation—is restabilized by both retrospective interpretation and representation: *something* is substituted for *nothing* ("Medusa's head takes the place of a representation of the female genitals"). But H.D.'s passage revises Freud's own retrospective interpretation that attaches a meaning that so excludes the possibility that women experience seeing their (mothers') genitals differently. In her version, retrospection allows her to reinterpret the primal scene as evidence not of the mother's lack of a penis, but of her own lack of "lack." Although there's indeterminacy in H.D.'s representation—

she never decides if her vision is "symptom or inspiration" or upon which side of "Truth and Wisdom" her head lands–there's no threat, horror, or reassurance, but "concentration" and "wonder." H.D. sustains the initial undecidability, so disturbing to the male spectator that he must turn his interpretation into fact, as a mode of frustrating the dominant fiction. The moment inscribes another gaze than that of the hegemonic male.

The split in H.D.'s passage between identification with the subject and object of the gaze is ambiguous, or as I have been calling such rhetorical duplicity, equivocal. This ambiguity is specifically productive of sexual difference as well as of female subjectivity. Like the female film spectator, H.D. is both obstructed and enabled by the double identification.[59] Gazing dangerously "straight on" (Freud warns against the dangers of looking closely at female genitals in their "apotropaic act"),[60] she confronts the psychoanalytic specter of what has been said to be woman's already-accomplished castration, a state she seems to contradict: she too has stiffened. Collapsing the distinction between castrated and not castrated, she collapses on the bed, suggestively postcoital, "exhausted" with the effort of reading, her physical strain insistently calling her away from interpretation and back to her body. The scene at once embodies and exceeds the framework of (theoretical) reflection, "the writing on the wall" and the woman "in frame."

The transference this act of reading femininity catalyzes is not onto the figure of Perseus–"trembling," as Cixous puts it in her essay, "The Laugh of the Medusa," "moving backward toward us, clad in apotropes"[61]–but from one woman to another: her lover and patron, Bryher, completes the vision. This eroticized moment the two women share and complete might be regarded as imaging lesbian sexuality, symbolized as a fluid, mutual exchange that blurs the boundaries between self and other that Freud would erect as necessarily (that is, *normatively*) separate and distinct, and that H.D. implies is a privileged site of female specificity. But H.D. does *not* clearly adjudicate between the two "views." Instead, she constitutes herself in the scene in multiple positions: in relation to a woman (Bryher), femininity (Medusa), and in resistance to the theory that would consolidate and contain them. She thereby denaturalizes the androcentric frame in which Freud interprets femininity and

replaces it, like Dickinson and Moore before her, with other epistemological and rhetorical possibilities.

H.D. depicts Helen as experiencing a similarly split identification that operates as both paralyzing and enabling. Helen's strug-
gles as speaking subject and the violent attempts to silence her suggest H.D.'s concern to portray her personal experience of various
sociocultural obstructions to women's expressions of self, desire,
origins–the ones put up by such authority figures in her life as her
father (her biological "papa" Professor), her mentor (Pound), and
her husband (Aldington), as well as Freud. Irigaray describes how
such obstructions have been prohibitive, "the hole, the lack, . . . the
'castration'" greeting the girl "as she enters as a subject into representative systems."[62] At the time when H.D. was writing *Helen in
Egypt*, psychoanalytic theory was quite unable to "see" women; its
"blind spot," as Gallop puts it, was the "female sex organs."[63] As
Helen enters the "system" as subject, she encounters the masculine
desire to stifle the woman who goes behind the looking glass that
supports dominant fictions.

In so doing, however, she poses the possibility of a gaze that
allows the reader not only to "*see, with the eyes of Achilles, Helen*" (*HE*,
49), but to watch, with the eyes of Helen, Achilles:[64]

> As a circlet may break
> in the heat of the smelting-fire,
> or a plate of armour crack
>
> or a buckler snap
> or an axle-tree give way
> or a wheel-rim twist awry,
>
> so it seemed to me
> that I had watched,
> as a careful craftsman,
>
> the pattern shape,
> Achilles' history,
> that I had seen him . . .
> . . . .

baffled and lost,
but I was a phantom Helen
and he was Achilles' ghost.

(*HE*, 262–63)

Helen watches like a "craftsman" for an imperfection to emerge in
the pattern, which may already be present in the structure, as the
"cross-dressing" simile and imperfect rhymes that run through
these tercets imply (break / crack, way / awry, lost / ghost). What
undoes the craft's "perfection" is not simply represented at the figurative level in this passage, the metonymic chain of threats to the
finished "piece." At the aural level as well, the passage recalls
Kristeva's notion of *herethics*: the semiotic that poetic language at
once contains and releases, (de)structuring the symbolic realm and
its totalizing subject. The vowel shifts render the rhymes imperfect
and inconsistent, unsettling the process whereby well-crafted symbolic patterns of identification take (or keep) their "shape."[65] Nor is
Helen, who looks for a figurative crack in Achilles' psychological
armor, gazing in fetishizing ways that would reproduce the gender
asymmetry that the male gaze supports and defines. "*Is the last
enlightenment that of the woman Helen?*" asks the prose passage that
precedes the poetic passage quoted above, referring to her attempts
to understand Achilles. But to assess the difference between the
scopic and subjective positions that the two figures may be said to
represent, we need to consider what happens when Helen returns
Achilles' look.

WHEN THE WOMAN LOOKS

The title of the final part, "Eidolon," indicates that in this section
H.D. examines the dynamics of iconography, but not of woman as
spectacle (however subversive) but of woman as spectator-analyst
of, as well as participant in, the heterosexual construct. Helen's
encounter with Achilles dramatically reveals that his manhood is
on the line of ambiguous sexual difference. As Paris rather crassly
suggests, "the brand he would proffer / is burnt out, extinguished"
(*HE*, 217). The "wavering" for which he was "shot" (*HE*, 60) is a

vacillation not of will but of gender. Helen perceives that his "anger and sudden terror" at the sound of his mother's name, "the one word that would turn and bind / and blind him to any other" (*HE*, 277), is because her invocation of Thetis at the moment of his attack causes him to remember a loss that preceded the loss of his status in the warriors' world.

As Coppélia Kahn has observed, psychoanalysis does not theorize male "identification with the mother," which is the "unknown" to Freud, "not because it is unknowable but because . . . manhood as patriarchal culture creates it depends on denying, in myriad ways, the powerful ambivalence that the mother inspires."[66] The name of his mother is "unspeakable" to Achilles (*HE*, 253) because his identification with Thetis preceded the positing of his gender identity in language. His separation from his mother was accompanied by his being forced verbally into both masculinity and the patriarchal hierarchy:

> and he forgot his mother
> when the heroes mocked
> at the half-god hidden in Scyros.
>
> (*HE*, 292)

Achilles was mocked, as we know from the canonical tale, because Thetis had disguised him in a woman's dress to hide him from the warriors. But he did not attain manhood by proving himself somehow distinctly identifiable as male; rather, mockery caused him to re-dress himself with signs of distinctly dominant masculinity.

His cross-dressing and the crisis of gender catalyzed by his "death" put a different face (the mother's) on the recognition scene between Achilles and Helen. His aggression toward Helen can be construed as an attempt to reestablish his masculinity, on one level played out as an hystericized attempt to reappropriate the body of the lost mother (H.D.'s ironic inversion of her own "dangerous" symptom). But his hostile ambivalence toward the maternal figure who returns as both linguistic trace in Helen's prayer (*Thetis*) and sign of lack of mastery in / over language in Achilles' own curses (the repeated "are you Hecate? are you a witch? / a vulture, a hieroglyph?" [*HE*, 261]) strikingly resembles Lacan's phallocentric notion of symbolic castration. According to Gallop, however, Lacan's ethical purpose as well as therapeutic goal is that

> one must assume one's castration. Women have always been considered [sexually] "castrated" in psychoanalytic thinking. But castration for Lacan is not only sexual; more important, it is also linguistic: we are inevitably bereft of any masterful understanding of language, and can only signify ourselves in a symbolic system that we do not command, that, rather, commands us. . . . Only this realization . . . can release us from "phallocentrism," one of the effects of which is that one must constantly cover one's inevitable inadequacy in order to have the right to speak.[67]

Historically, as Gallop implies, "one" hasn't had to assume one's castration if one has one (although one of course *should*). Historically, H.D. suggests through Helen's analysis of Achilles, one's defense of oneself from that assumption constitutes a mortal combat.

Until he dies out of the Command, Achilles fends off recognition of loss with a series of fetishes that substitute for the mother's genitals (which return in the figure of the monstrous face he cannot countenance seeing). The gap opened up by the head that "takes the place of" the female sex organs, in H.D.'s astute representation of the masculine primal scene, indicates the absence in phallocentric representation itself that Irigaray and Gallop remark as well. As a boy Achilles carved "an idol / / or eidolon, not much more than a doll" (*HE,* 244) that replaced the mother "whole." As a warrior, he also carves his mother's "mermaid body" on the prow of his ship ("his love, his beloved" [*HE,* 248]), but we get only the details of a bust: "her mermaid hair," "her arms, her shoulders," "her eyes," "her high breasts [that] meet the spray" (*HE,* 245, 246). As in the upward displacement in the strangulation scene, Achilles' whole ship becomes the mother's unrepresented "hole": the mother-figure does not exist below the waist, or becomes something else when represented. She is, in a word, a "*figurehead*" (*HE,* 245): something must replace the "nothing" that is (not) there.

The eidolon is thus, "To put it more plainly," a fetish in Freud's sense of the term: "a substitute for the woman's (the mother's) penis that the little boy once believed in and—for reasons familiar to us—does not want to give up."[68] But by its very nature, Kofman points out, the fetish is ambiguous, leaving "room for doubt as to the woman's castration or noncastration, and thus as to the potential castration of the man." The fetishist is split between "denial and affirmation of castration" of the woman and therefore of himself.[69] Feeling that Thetis "cheated" him of the promised immortality (phallus) (*HE,* 253), Achilles has repressed her memory. But in fetishizing and hoarding her image—that is, in maintaining the fiction that she still possesses (and therefore he cannot lose) the "something forgotten or lost" (*HE,* 282)—he has left room for doubt as to the woman's castrated or noncastrated state.

In her unsettling capacity to deflect Achilles, Helen has reminded him not only of his loss of status, but of the moment he first confronted undecidability, before recourse to the interpretation of loss, a patently violent moment that repeats the boy's first "terrible storm of emotion" at the discovery of his mother's "castration."[70] Achilles' confusion of his mother with Helen images the desire to be whole, to master castration anxiety through representation. If language fails him at this crucial moment, it is in the sense that he is no longer able to employ it, as he could in the Command, either to fantasize wholeness through a maternal fetish or to pass off loss (the division instituted in the subject by its constitution in the symbolic order) onto woman in order to be a man's man.

What Helen sees, not when she confronts a male-constructed mirror image of herself, as did the "intellectual" and "transcendental" Helens of the first two sections (*HE,* 258), but when she looks against the (Freudian) theoretical grain, is that "heroic" (*érotic*) man is locked into the (in)determinate fictions of his own making, which his "terror" has constructed. She sees his investment in not seeing her ("the blindness of the seeing eye").[71] Is it "death to stay here?" she asks (*HE,* 301).

SAYING NO TO POWER

The narrative thrust for much of *Helen in Egypt* is, to be sure, to press Helen back into the preferred category of "gender" available to

women in the social as well as Freudian scenario: mother. The
problem of representing otherwise, most specifically explored as
the problem of representing a mother figure who isn't threatening
or threatened, who isn't, that is, subject to the phallic term, is unresolved, albeit explored at length in the poem. Like many readers of
this poem, I find its epistemology mystical and matrifocal as well as
psychoanalytical.[72] But I also find the maternal images in relation
to both Helen and Achilles ambivalent rather than securely affirmative, subject to repeated thematic and technical dislocations and
interrupted resolutions. Helen's own mother, Leda, obliquely
invoked in H.D.'s text, was, after all, raped by Zeus. And Helen's
sister, Clytaemnestra, because she transgressed gender conventions
and "struck with her mind, / with the Will-to-Power" (*HE*, 97), was
murdered by her son. Thetis is fetishized and thus disrupts the fixity
of woman's positioning as castrated. And as nurturingly androgynous as Theseus appears to be, he also smothers Helen, as the following scene suggests:

> Rest here; shall I draw out
> the low couch, nearer the brazier,
> or will you lie there
>
> against the folds of purple
> by the wall? you tremble,
> can you stand? walk then,
>
> O, sleep-walker; is this fleece
> too heavy? here is soft woven wool;
> wrapped in this shawl, my butterfly,
>
> my Psyche, disappear into the web,
> the shell, re-integrate[.]
>
> (*HE*, 170)

Like the mixed metaphors at the end of this passage, this scene and
similar ones depicting Theseus's ministrations convey both nurturing and nuisancing. His possessive endearments of Helen ("my but-

terfly," "my Psyche") double, as we have seen, as linguistic appropriation.

Subjected to and object of his analysis as well as care, Helen resists his interpretive penetration. To his insistence she remember "the child-mother, yourself" (*HE,* 187), she paradoxically replies (since she is, actually, a mother), "I am only a daughter; / no, no, I am not a mother" (*HE,* 191). At another point, she seems at last to accept Theseus's notion that Paris is her symbolic son by Achilles. But her response, "how can I be his mother?" (*HE,* 156), is cast as a rhetorical question, which effectively interrogates Theseus's triangulating schematization (asking not only *how* to mother but asserting the impossibility that she *could* be Paris's mother). She subsequently refuses to rival her mother for her father (*HE,* 195), the feminine version of the Oedipus complex, as well as the masculine version, Paris's desire to "re-live an old story" (*HE,* 223), "with Helen, not Hecuba for mother" (*HE,* 224). According to Freud, as H.D. dramatizes, man's desire is always for the mother. Helen refuses "translation" into this dynamic, not only with Achilles and Paris, but with a paternalizingly presumptuous Theseus ("you must have loved me a little" [*HE,* 148]), which would consolidate her into the image of a limiting and sexually limited mother figure.

But if Helen is not safely reinscribed in the maternal position, the one in which Freud most consistently located feminine sexuality, what position is she in? And if as subject of the gaze, she is identified with the active masculine position, and alone on her "bier" at the poem's closing, she is also in the conventional feminine position, the very image of a passive romantic heroine who is object of the hero's quest, what are we to make of that contradiction? "How can the female spectator be entertained as subject of the very movement that places her as its object, that makes her the figure of its own closure?" asks de Lauretis of precisely such a problematic relation to narrative closure and the paradox of the female subject that cinema poses for women.[73] If the poem is staged, as I asserted in the beginning of this chapter, after The End, have we gotten, like Helen, nowhere?

If views from elsewhere than the masculine gaze seem nowhere to be seen, it is not that women haven't produced them, as a number of feminist theorists have by now observed. It is that we haven't known how to see them, to recall de Lauretis's assertion quoted in chapter 1.[74] From this standpoint, getting "nowhere" implies that we don't recognize, and therefore don't know, where we have gotten to. H.D. depicts Helen's relation, as well as resistance, to the psychic reality of the oedipal construct, for example, whose terms H.D. can and has been regarded as reiterating.[75] She complicates, rather than replaces, the oedipal dynamic by dramatizing Helen's experience as well as perspective. Telling the tale differently entails immersion in phallogocentric discourse, de Lauretis hypothesizes, as well as engagement in the enunciation of "the question of desire as precisely enigma, contradiction, difference not reducible to sameness."[76] Her notion offers a useful approach to H.D.'s narrative strategy of saturating Helen almost inextricably in masterful interpretations. It is such saturation that eventually enables Helen to distinguish herself from *Helena* and to see that the castration anxiety projected onto woman is a misrecognition at the heart of the oedipal construct. Through this immersion of Helen, moreover, H.D. renders visible the sociosymbolic structures by which individual women are subsumed under the rubric of "woman."

Helen raises an analogous epistemological issue in relation to the heterosexual construct when she says of Achilles, "this is Love, this is Death, / this is my last Lover" (*HE*, 268), but asks as well, "was it desire?" (*HE*, 288). She questions not only whether the dream of symmetry can contain (her) desire, since it is not accounted for in that structure. She also asks whether feminine desire exists, whether we can know it precisely as desire, outside that familiar ordering of knowledge. To wit, her attempts to reach her mythic (and mystified) Lover always lead back to the (in)difference of love and death, highlighted by the aural indifference of "*La Mort, L'Amour*" (*HE*, 288) in hegemonic plots. But at the same time, her efforts also lead to the potential, (im)perceptible difference of what Woolf calls at the end of her last novel, *Between the Acts*, "a new plot," and Rich will call, in the decade following H.D.'s completion of *Helen in Egypt*, "a whole new poetry." As Chisholm persuasively argues, such punning homonyms–and, I might add, such translinguistic, cognative puns as "hero" and "éros"–potentially enable the release of vital forces that have been aggressively sublimated into empire building.[77] In Helen's confrontation with Achilles' displaced castration anxiety, H.D. dramatically envisions an imaginative restructuring of heterosexual relations as well as of masculinist theory.

Helen's parenthetical description of the Trojan "maze" she remembers trying to escape as "Theseus' Labyrinth" (*HE,* 232) associates Troy with the Minoan region "almost impossible to revivify," as Freud said of the preoedipal in "Feminine Sexuality."[78] Her physical wanderings and psychic wonderings are nonetheless situated in the symbolic order ("*Theseus'* Labyrinth"), as should by now be clear, which has "possessed" that libidinal geography through its definitions. The plot traces the imaginary space of H.D.'s revisionist debate with Freud over his notions of "how the child with bisexual tendencies *becomes* a woman," to quote Kofman's emphatic reiteration.[79] Helen is "called back to the Walls" that contained her; she must "return and sort over and over, / my bracelets, sandals and scarves" (*HE,* 232), the signifiers of a privileged, epistemologically assured femininity:

> O, I knew my way,
> O, I knew my ways[.]
>
> (*HE,* 265)

To assume those signs knowingly is not simply to accede to woman's place in the frame of gender polarity that structures the dominant order, but to employ consciously the masquerade of femininity. As the punning passage above poetically concretizes, the masquerade is a repetition, but one with a now perceptible *difference.* Such a consciously modulated echo suggests the possibility for the woman so placed of intervening upon the institution of heterosexuality from within, although at the same time it acknowledges the dangers of internalizing dominant beliefs, and thus of co-optation. Helen's position has been precisely equivocal: she has both resisted the maternal fix and acquiesced in creating the feminine mystique.

Although H.D.'s own identification with the "Image" of the Hollywood Star (Garbo and Dietrich especially) was intense, Hirsh tells us,[80] *Helen in Egypt* surprisingly concludes with a cinematic dissolve of the image of Helen as well as of her painstakingly posited voice. Helen is subsumed first into "*One greater than Helen*" and then into its "*Eidolon.*" This problematic image calls attention to its linguistic status as a duplicate. The text, too, foregrounds the coda lexically, by italicizing the whole passage. An eidolon is at once, as Hirsh observes of the irony of the "image" in philosophical as well as Modernist tradition, discursive Idea(l) / icon and mere forgery.[81] The idealization of maternal voice is evident in the penultimate section of *Helen in Egypt*'s third part (the voice is nominally Thetis's), speaking a significance "*we do not wholly understand*":

> so the dart of Love
> is the dart of Death,
> and the secret is no secret;
> . . . .
>
> there is no before and no after,
> there is one finite moment
> that no infinite joy can disperse
>
> or thought of past happiness
> tempt from or dissipate;
> now I know the best and the worst;
>
> the seasons revolve around
> a pause in the infinite rhythm
> of the heart and of heaven.

(HE, 303–4)

This passage, the original closing, is a resounding resolution. Its visionary pronouncements are given aural weight and resonant emphasis through the measured simplicity of its diction, as well as through the schematic balance of grammatic parallels and nuanced alliteration. But the coda, uncertain, even untenable, though its status be, as we have seen, attentuates the statement's semantic assurance. The privileged icon of (white) feminine beauty within a heterosexual construct has been schematically, as well as thematically, dislodged. In her place is a displaced copy, not of Helen but of that which replaced her, which effectively dissolves the image of the final "One."

The sense of woman and / in her place in *Helen in Egypt*'s concluding movement is decentered. The shifts from identification to disidentification (and back and so forth), which suggest a woman's negotiation of masculinist constructs, also enact an unsettling of any poetic identity—male or female—the text would conventionally reassert. H.D. may proffer thematically the resolution of mystical Oneness based on the ideal of heterosexual love modeled by Helen and Achilles, for example, but she unravels the promise of fixity and stasis at the formal level. She resists the narrative desire to close with the satisfying revelation of and resolution to mysteries. Such textual shifts produce the ambivalence of avowal and disavowal of absence associated with (de)fetishized cultural images—the defetishization, in other words, of the masquerade. Like the text's graphic alternation between apparently authoritative prose commentary and multivocal lyric sections that at once repeat and contradict each other as well as the prose passages at times, Helen's performance of femininity renders her relation to it untenable. Through a (capricious) oscillation that never reassuringly settles into mirroring the man, Helen is never one with her femininity. As Mary Russo has suggested, the hopeful power of the masquerade for women resides in the notion that if they can put on femininity, they can also take it off.[82] A woman can, "as a careful craftsman," we might say, have masculinity on.

Helen's and Achilles' relationships to the defining tropes of femininity and masculinity alter in the course of the poem. Crossdressing, as they both do (Helen arrives at Theseus's door in huntsman's gear), represents not only a crisis of gender for Achilles. It also suggests Helen's double-crossing of the signs that organize gender difference hierarchically. Cross-dressing exposes such signs as put-ons, and their hierarchization as an interested construction of the dominant order.[83] Like Moore's equivocal poetic subjectivity, H.D.'s depiction of Helen's transvestism suggests the semiotic introduction of a third position in *Helen in Egypt,* distinct from the hysteric or "criminal" narcissist (the two other positions Freud assigns women).[84] As I have been implying, this position represents another perspective than that of "the masculine point of view" that articulates the masculinist system.[85]

What is at stake for H.D., as for Moore, is her relation to authorial identity and sexual categorization by (entry into) poetic language, an entanglement that she was to tease out with Freud's help (as well as in his terms). In a letter to Bryher, she writes:

> I have gone terribly deep with papa. He says, "You had two things to hide, one that you were a girl, the other that you were a boy." It appears that I am that all but extinct phenomenon, the perfect bi-. Well, this is terribly exciting, but for the moment, PLEASE do not speak of my own MSS. [Bryher was urging H.D. at the time to publish "The Master"], for it seems the conflict consists partly that what I write commits me—to one sex, or the other, I no longer HIDE.

The issues of rhetorical equivocation, gender difference, and H.D.'s ambiguous refusal to enter into a master('s) discourse converge in this passage.[86] Prior to the entry into public discourse, she can be "that all but extinct phenomenon, the perfect bi-," whose very existence contradicts the orthodox theory that the in-between cannot be sustained (femininity, that is, requires the assumption of castration on the woman's part; if she denies castration she is not "bi" but masculine).

Unlike Moore's performative and liberating positionality, however, H.D.'s problem is that language constitutes an act of coming out, requiring precisely that one take one's place on one side or other of the gender divide. She suppressed the poem ("The Master") in which she countered Freud's androcentrism with her own overt gynocentrism. In the text she did publish on Freud, as discussed earlier, she equivocally disturbs his view of women as deficient by repeating the holes in his logic. Such equivocation epitomizes the nuanced methodological as well as thematic concerns of H.D.'s later work. Like her surrogate, Helen, H.D. quietly unsettles the (a)symmetry of Freud's analogy and unmans the Master's discourse. But in her self-portrait, her very equivocation—she leaves unanswered the question of whether her silence ("I did not say anything") is out of resistance or acquiescence—vexes the attempt to characterize her work as unequivocally validating conventionally feminine over masculine values. In her public, as in her private, discourse, it would seem, she managed not to commit "to one sex, or the other."

But as Kofman has thoroughly demonstrated, it is in fact women's indeterminate oscillation between masculinity and femininity, in a word, their *bisexuality,* that comprised the disturbing enigma of women for Freud.[87] We might therefore consider that the third position *Helen in Egypt* introduces is neither a "masculine" nor a "feminine" but a "female" point of view. By this term I mean to locate the specificity of the poem's deconstruction of androcentric theory, not universalize it as representative of all women's oppositional positions (*a,* not *the,* female point of view). I am not suggesting the opposite of "*the* masculine point of view" that Jeffords theorizes, because the former is not a consolidation of differences under one rubric, as is the latter, and cannot be defined by its ideological articulation of the patriarchy's opposite (for example, "the matriarchy"). A female point of view would therefore not constitute a mechanism for dominance that merely reverses the terms. Rather, it indicates a mode not only of resisting dominance, but of divesting oneself of the will to domination, by a rhetorical strategy I have characterized as equivocation. Through its capacity to sustain contradictory views, equivocation can be regarded as a strategy elicited by a female point of view to render visible the ideological biases dominant fictions naturalize, putting into discourse other, opposing, and possible meanings.

To construe the poem primarily as replacing conventionally "masculine" with "feminine" values, as do Friedman and DuPlessis, among others, is to reduce the complexity of the text's disruption of this naturalizing tendency and of the woman validated by and within the patriarchy. The point of view that *Helen in Egypt* articulates and the female gaze Helen mobilizes refuse uncritically to reproduce the conventional plots, metaphoric or otherwise, that support women's subjugation. In the place of the familiar resolution is an unresolved suspension in which the woman sees that the seductions of normative femininity require her acceptance of the *"fact"* of castration and the hero confronts the consequences of his fantasized emasculation.

At the end of the poem, Helen contemplates Achilles' disavowal of castration, countering Theseus's determining logic. Via
the revised figure of the hero as fetishist, the text opens imaginatively to the possibilities for life after The End, which is indeed a
reconnoiter with "castration," H.D. suggests, for male as well as
female subjects. As Gallop's Lacanian insight helps us to conceptualize in this instance, the notion of symbolic castration, though it
does not free us from the phallic term, constitutes an ethical
assumption on the part of the man's man from which women stand
to gain. Silverman describes such ethically motivated, marginal
positions for male subjects as the encounter of "femininity from
within a male body," but not as "disenfranchisement and subordination, but rather as phallic divestiture, as a way of saying 'no' to
power."[88] Such positions, she asserts, provide a potential means of
decentralizing the conventional tropes of masculinity. This encounter of a third kind transfigures the notion of (f)actual castration into
the symbolic order, where the Law of the Father can and must be
transformed.

But just as Silverman's redefinition of masculinity's "femininity," not as the alienating difference within but as a necessary divestment of the phallus, skirts a reinscription of femininity as disempowered, so to imagine a new world free of phallic dominance is as
difficult an undertaking as its contradictory inscription suggests.
H.D. also leaves us in that liminal space in which the schematic
divisions of gender conventions are gone, and it feels dangerous,
because conventions of dominant poetic representation have disappeared as well. Free of the "pitiful" and "monstrous" trappings that
construct worldly status and privilege and hierarchize gender relations in peace as well as war, Helen is haunted by the sense that
nothing is left and it *is* indeed "death to stay here" (*HE*, 301).

But in repeatedly depicting the stranglehold of the fetishized
phallus in its various manifestations (among them war and woman),
H.D. suggests that the danger is not the crisis of gender that the
male subject's destabilization catalyzes. Death (*La Mort*), after all,
can be transmuted into love (*L'Amour*) in the symbolic realm—at
least, in (one) poetic language. The persistence of Achilles' phantas-
matic identification with hegemonic masculinity breaks not only
his own heart but "*the world for a token*" (*HE*, 304) that upholds the

order whose power depends on a fantasized belief in the other's castration. The text leaves the reader, like Achilles, to identify this "token" or sign of superiority as psychic defense: there is no "nothing" that "something" must replace; there is only difference(s). The poem keeps undecidability in play through its thematic and formal equivocations: exceeding the penultimate section's vision of sacred union in the timeless, converting poetic resolution to rhetorical question and riddle. H.D.'s text dramatizes not only a refusal on the woman's part to be seduced (back) into the conventions of femininity. H.D. also replaces the assimilation of the feminine into the mystic (male-defined) One with the possibility posed for a world beyond the heterosexual woman's investment in her privileged status by reason of her relation to a man, and significantly, beyond the man's attachment to power.

5 Living with/in Difference

ADRIENNE RICH'S DOUBLE VISION

Re-vision—the act of looking back, of seeing with fresh eyes, of entering an old text from a new critical direction—is for women . . . an act of survival. Until we can understand the assumptions in which we are drenched we cannot know ourselves. . . . A radical critique of literature, feminist in its impulse, would take the work first of all as a clue to how we live, how we have been living, how we have been led to imagine ourselves, how our language has trapped as well as liberated us, how the very act of naming has been till now a male prerogative, and how we can begin to see and name—and therefore live—afresh. A change in the concept of sexual identity is essential if we are not going to see the old political order reassert itself in every new revolution.

—Adrienne Rich, "When We Dead Awaken"

[I]t is in the aspiration towards artistic and, in particular, literary creation that woman's desire for affirmation now manifests itself. Why literature?

Is it because, faced with social norms, literature reveals a certain knowledge and sometimes the truth itself about an otherwise repressed, nocturnal, secret and unconscious universe? Because it thus redoubles the social contract by exposing the unsaid, the uncanny? . . . This identification with the potency of the imaginary . . . bears witness to women's desire to lift the weight of what is sacrificial in the social contract from their shoulders, to nourish our societies with a more flexible and free discourse, one able to name what has thus far never been an object of circulation in the community: the enigmas of the body, the dreams, secret joys, shames, hatreds of the second sex.

—Julia Kristeva, "Women's Time"

⇛

*T*o begin this last chapter with a re-vision, I have juxtaposed Adrienne Rich's now-classic definition (1972) with a passage from Kristeva's equally classic "Women's Time" (1979) quoted in chapter 1. These excerpts echo, as well as complement, each other. Rich's pertains to the revolutionary act on women's part of reading with "fresh eyes" in order to "break" tradition (*LSS*, 35); Kristeva's analyzes those feminists who, identifying with the "myth of the archaic mother," wish to restore her power through their art.[1] Rich is such a feminist; perhaps Kristeva, albeit steadily demurring, is as well. In any event, both are ambivalent not about the maternal body but about the paternal word.

Both passages describe not only women's desire, like Dickinson's, to change the way they are identified in the dominant system, but the wish, like Moore's, to change the system itself. And like H.D., both Rich and Kristeva believed in the 1970s that poetry could transform society. Rich believed it could do this by changing the concept of sexual identity, Kristeva by "pulverizing" the subject's relation to totalizing constructions of identity and attachment to power. For Rich, the reader sees herself and, through a critical reorientation to the literary text, constructs her identity anew. For Kristeva, a revolutionary textual dynamic that enacts identity as mobile and unstable is transferred via readerly identification to the reader. She in turn modifies her relation to word and world, which are then modified by her. Rich's concept of naming, which theoretically enables readers to see with new eyes,[2] constitutes a feminist poetic practice that, at once conservative and radical, resembles the poetic projects of the earlier American women poets we have discussed.

But with a difference: thematically the most radical (she effects the imaginative break with masculine authority, for example, that the other poets do not), Rich has seemed the least innovative technically. Traditional formal elements in her poetry have in fact drawn criticism. Her poetic subject claims to be a postmodern in search of "new forms," as Rich states in "Paula Becker to Clara Westhoff," but attempts again and again to unify the mind/body split in old ways. Neglecting the lessons of the revisionary modernism of Moore and H.D. (among others),[3] Rich seeks an originary truth about women, "the thing itself and not the myth" (*DW*, 22), arguably following her modernist fathers, for whom there were "no ideas but in things" (or so they pronounced). Although, like Dickinson, Moore, and H.D., Rich also intervenes in the dynamics of specularization that structure the lyric, she seems at times rather to endorse in her poetry what she rejects in her politics. She engages in a sustained critical reconstruction of the maternal figure, yet her work persistently associates woman with qualities traditionally coded as feminine, as Margaret Homans contends.[4] Thus, some critics have found her feminism essentialist, arguing that it reduces her poetry.[5]

In an important article devoted to a reconsideration of the issue of essentialism, however, de Lauretis deconstructs the very charge itself. Through an elaboration of the philosophical definition of "essence," she suggests another approach to what cultural feminists like Rich (and H.D., I might add), charged with reifying woman, might be up to.[6] Consulting the *Oxford English Dictionary*, de Lauretis draws on Locke's distinction between "nominal essence" (the totality of an entity's properties) and "real essence" (an entity's intrinsic nature, the thing-in-itself). She asserts that since most feminists of whatever ilk agree that gender is a "sociocultural construction" rather than "an innate feature," the "essence of woman" described by "so-called essentialists is not the *real essence*, in Locke's terms, but more likely a *nominal* one."[7] She argues that the feminist project of these "so-called essentialists" indicates their appropriation of the means to define the attributes of "woman," historically defined by men and in relation to the male term. Like Rich's act of "naming," de Lauretis's use of *nominal* suggests not only that representation is the arena in which the struggle is taking place: who controls (or has the semblance of controlling) the discourse, who occupies the position from which the power to *name* and determine meaning hails?[8] Her argument also implies that Rich's "essentialism" might be discursive performance, a politically as well as poetically strategic stance. "This is the war of the images," Rich belligerently declares in "The Images" (*WP,* 5).

To be sure, the strategies of subversive performance that characterize the other poets' self-representations—Dickinson's poetics of withholding presence (Emily in white), Moore's revolutionary masquerade (Marianne in her founding father's tricorne), and H.D. the "perfect" bi- (Hilda as poetic Blue Angel)—are more than outmoded for Rich. Adrienne is out to dismantle the "mode" altogether, to be at last outside the representational framework of heterosexual constructs, out of the closet, imaginatively outside male-dominated thinking, law, and language. Refusing the male gaze the other poets subverted, she unequivocally calls such performance lying. Women "have been expected to lie with our bodies," she remarks of makeup, fashion, and orgasm in "Women and Honor: Some Notes on Lying" (*LSS,* 189). Telling the truth to as well as about women, in one's poetry as in one's life, entails the honorable occupation, it would seem, of one stance, one truth.

But Rich's "truth," it turns out, is mutable as well as multiple, a truth which is not one. And like Woolf, whose acute consciousness of "masculine presences" caused her to stifle her anger when she addressed her female audience in *A Room of One's Own,* as Rich argues (*LSS,* 37), Adrienne's rejection of posing is also a pose.[9] Though addressing other women, Adrienne knows and does not know (to paraphrase "Paula Becker to Clara Westhoff") that men will see, not least because of her will to change *them.* "I wanted to choose words that even you [a male addressee] / would have to be changed by," the speaker of "Implosions" asserts (*FD,* 95). Rich is at least of two minds about that desire.

In a critical reassessment of Rich, Elizabeth Meese asserts that we have failed to understand the lessons of Rich's poetic development.[10] Meese demonstrates that Rich's poetry evidences an expanding complexity, rather than the reduction (often attributed to her radical lesbian feminism) which some critics have found.[11] She enacts contra/dictions, as Meese lexically indicates Rich's poetic methodology. In a statement that endorses not only maternal essence but unalienated selfhood, Rich claims in *Of Woman Born,* for example, her brilliant study of "motherhood as experience and institution," that gynocentric images give a woman back "aspects of herself" (*OWB,* 81). But a nonfiction work of such scope cannot, of course, be reduced to one statement and gestures toward the sense of poetic complexity Meese restores. As a relatively conventional fifties wife and mother, Rich, unlike Dickinson, Moore, or even H.D. (whose poetic surrogate, Helen, protests she is "only a daughter"), was identified by her maternal and heterosexual roles. But out of that very different personal experience, she came to a corresponding recognition of the necessity for women to disentangle their identity from oppressive conventions, in particular those of femininity and motherhood as masochistic. As she puts it, "The identification of womanhood with suffering—by women as well as men—has been tied to the concept of woman-as-mother" (*OWB,* 163). Like Dickinson's, Moore's, and H.D.'s poetry, Rich's work is characterized by the dual attempt to identify women with new images and disidentify them from old ones.

Rich terms an analogous dual consciousness "double vision," which she specifically defines as women's ability to understand analytically their mothers' oppression at the same time as women acknowledge the unfulfilled need for strong mothering (*OWB,* 225). As its title declares, this chapter will critically and poetically take up Rich's notion of "double vision" to indicate moments of dual consciousness. Such a capacity to engage, rather than abject, division and contradiction is what I have termed "equivocation" for the purposes of this study. (It is, for example, worth noting that Rich invokes a term for feminist vision that conveys the sense not only of dual consciousness but of blurred sight.) The chapter is structured around analyses of three feminine "double visions": mother and daughter, lesbian and mother, and white woman and black. Rich exemplifies, I shall argue, the subject's divestment of heterosexual, white privilege.

A WOMAN IN THE SHAPE OF A MONSTER, A MONSTER IN THE SHAPE OF A WOMAN

The title of this section is taken from the opening lines of "Planetarium," a poem that Rich wrote with the astronomer Caroline Herschel in mind (*FD,* 114). The lines are unattributed to any speaker, and without the attribution of source that might allow us to locate the perspective they express, they are rendered in the context of the poem literally universal: "the skies are full of them [women and/as monsters]" (*FD,* 114). No accident, perhaps, since astronomers—etymologically, "star-namers"—have been men (Caroline became an astronomer incidentally, the notes in the Norton edition tell us, as she helped her brother, William [*ARP,* 45]). The seeing "eye" of the poem, "virile, precise and absolutely certain"(*FD,* 115), is also unattributed. Although the notes suggest these words are "applicable" to Caroline, they are actually a quotation from sixteenth-century Danish astronomer, Tycho Brahe, describing his own "observations" (*ARP,* 45 n.2). Claiming astronomy, a new science at the time, as a masculine ("virile") pursuit, Brahe stands in the text as syndecdoche for the male gaze as well as empirical science:

> What we see, we see
> and seeing is changing[.]
>
> (*FD,* 115)

Seeing a constellation in the shape of a woman, men see a monster (or vice versa), and it becomes the truth. The problematic issue Rich's poem poses is how women, demonized or idealized in the name of knowledge, might begin to imag(in)e themselves into the historical field of their symbolic erasure.[12]

Much in the transitional poem "Snapshots of a Daughter-in-Law" (1958–60) indicates that Rich was cognizant, early on, that there was "little in the past to support" a feminist poetics concerned to "find language and images" for "a whole new psychic geography," as she would later write in "When We Dead Awaken" (*LSS,* 35). The project of mapping this geography will come to characterize her poetic career at the level of figuration (a recent collection, for example, is entitled *An Atlas of the Difficult World* [1991]). As Deborah Kelly Kloepfer remarks in her Kristevan analysis of H.D.'s hieroglyphic "visible language," "Rich's sense of mapping ["a topography of language"] is perhaps a useful analogy to writing that might be an alternative to representation premised on loss."[13] Mapping also suggests the act of rendering the unknown known, indicating the epistemological nature of Rich's project. The (re)visionary resolution of "Snapshots" anticipates Rich's attempts to find images that would accurately depict women as well as liberate them from the dominant ideology of heterosexuality that interpellates them.[14] As such, it gestures toward the "lesbian continuum" of woman-identified experience, as she will eventually term it in her essay entitled "Compulsory Heterosexuality."[15] Like Dickinson, Kristeva, and H.D., Rich puts into symbolic play the imaginary of redemptive maternal plenitude in the poem's closing, although that image's answer to symbolic loss is perhaps "no answer" ("Contradictions: Tracking Poems").[16]

Whether it is or not is the instructive question "Snapshots" compels us to ask. Although Rich will eventually reject this poem's own blind spot, its universalizing white, heterosexual feminism, and thus the vision of woman with which it closes, the poem is exemplary of Rich's figurative project, the "war of images" she fights politically as well as aesthetically. It is representative as well of the formal complexity of her best poetry.[17] The poem's title calls our attention immediately to the figure of woman as spectacle, as well as doubles it, for the daughter is ambiguously the genetive subject and object both of the pictures and of the gaze. Except for a passage that construes her as the mother's sister (*"ma semblable, ma soeur!"*), a reformulation of Baudelaire (literally and figuratively a foreign language), the text insistently supplements the mother-daughter relationship by reminding us that it is established through a man. The ur-feminist speaker rejects the mother-in-law who complies, as well as inherited images of woman, only to discover that she cannot see her difference from them, gesturing toward the difficulty of actualizing the performative claim Rich makes elsewhere (in "Transcendental Etude") to writing "a whole new poetry."

The poem invokes a poetic language whose figurations would not reproduce the same old tale in which, when the woman "sings / neither words nor music are her own" (*ARP*, 14). Influenced by Simone de Beauvoir's *The Second Sex*, Rich critically depicts how this stereotype is constituted, in the *mise en abîme* of lyric "Corinnas," as a specular image "adjusted in reflections of an eye." As "part legend, part convention," part reflection, this image has no actual relation to the women it purports to represent, as the poem makes clear. A construction like Moore's unicorn and H.D.'s Helen, "Corinna" has no existence outside representation, and can be similarly dislodged from the prohibitive distinctions of "true" and "false" that historically have excluded women from the scene of representation. Like Moore and H.D., Rich quotes, mimes, paraphrases, and rewrites a variety of male-authored and feminist passages, creating a Bakhtinian text of multiple discourses and competing ideologies that fractures woman schematically even as it arguably reinscribes her thematically in the poem's closing, apocalyptic burst.

In the words of Mary Wollstonecraft, whom Rich quotes, "To have in this uncertain world some stay" (*ARP*, 14) to support this discursive project is, in terms of the text's own desire for an assured alternative image to the ones it jettisons, a tenuous undertaking. The portrait of maternal complicity in women's devaluation by the male-dominated system, women's own acceptance of compromise, concludes in no uncertain terms that "Our blight has been our sinecure."[18] In *Of Woman Born*, Rich discusses poet Lynn Sukenick's term for the rejection of one's mother, *matrophobia*, which is "the fear not of one's mother or of motherhood but of *becoming one's mother*" (*OWB*, 237; Rich's emphasis). Due in large part to the dissemination of Freud's theories of normative sexual identity, matrophobia is, according to Rich, a twentieth-century phenomenon. The pervasive labeling of women's friendships as lesbian and therefore, in Freud's terms, perverse or immature, for example, gained currency after the women in Rich's mother's generation acquired the vote. Such labeling effectively divided women, controlling any threatening solidarity among them, as Rich recounts.[19]

Matrophobia is a hatred of women that is different in kind from misogyny, in the same way that women's relationship to power, language, and meaning differs from men's. Misogyny, as Rich defines it, following Karen Horney's revision of Freud, is "the resentment and anxiety harbored by all men toward women" because the mother's original power over her son is transferred to all women as threat to male supremacy (*OWB*, 99). (We might recall Moore's depiction in "Marriage" of Adam's resentment for being "unfathered by a woman.") Rich observes that the mother, posing no threat to her daughter's access to power (since the mother has none), is herself oppressed. But it is easier for the daughter "to hate and reject a mother outright than to see beyond her to the forces acting upon her" (*OWB*, 237). Refusing to see that mothers cannot transmit knowledge that they do not have, women resent their mothers for teaching them the survival skills that reproduce the conditions of oppression. Mothers have compromised, and enjoined their daughters to compromise, rather than helping them to become the "Amazons" who could significantly change the system (*OWB*, 225). Whatever their "rational forgiveness," women grow up in a male-dominated world feeling "wildly unmothered." The mother-daughter relationship–"the great unwritten story," as Rich calls it (*OWB*, 226)–has crucial political as well as personal implications for Rich. She locates the source of dissension among women in feminist movements, for example, in the failure to resolve the mother-daughter conflict: "When we can confront and unravel this paradox, this contradiction [of having mothers but feeling unmothered], . . . we can begin to transmute it, and the blind anger and bitterness that have repetitiously erupted among women trying to build a movement together can be alchemized" (*OWB*, 226).

This statement throws light on the unresolved generational tension "Snapshots" portrays. The speaker's mother-in-law, a metapoetic figure for the conventional lyric the text resists,[20] still fashions herself like the "belle in Shreveport" she once was, "still hav[ing] your dresses copied from that time" (*ARP*, 12). But her mind,

> heavy with useless experience, rich
> with suspicion, rumor, fantasy,
>
> (*ARP*, 12)

molders "like wedding-cake." In the prime of her life, the mother is able to reproduce through artifice a simulacrum of seamless youthful beauty. But from her daughter's perspective, she embodies the aging, increasingly indisposed Southern belle, personified as "Nature":

> that sprung-lidded, still commodious
> steamer-trunk of *tempora* and *mores*
> gets stuffed with it all: the mildewed orange-flowers,
> the female pills, the terrible breasts
> of Boadicea beneath flat foxes' heads and orchids.
>
> (*ARP*, 12–13)

Crumbling "to pieces under the knife-edge / of mere fact" (*ARP*, 12), the mother is not beautified by her continuing attempts to keep up appearances. Rather, as the passage above suggests, she is increasingly uncannily put together.

Observing the mother's mistakes, the daughter tries to grow "another way." "Nervy" as opposed to nervous, "glowering" as opposed to hysterical, she refuses to reproduce the signs of femininity (or lyric tradition, except piecemeal) by fashioning herself in the conventional mold. Her "angels" are twentieth-century, feminist ones, chiding her to "*Have no patience*" and "*Be insatiable*" (*ARP*, 12). She observes the connections among hysteria, chronic invalidism, and men's invalidation of women:

> Bemused by gallantry, we hear
> our mediocrities over-praised,
> indolence read as abnegation,
> slattern thought styled intuition,
> every lapse forgiven[.]
>
> (*ARP*, 15)

But the alternative posed by "thinking" women who "cast too bold a shadow / or smash the mold straight off" is, to say the least, a vexed one:

> For that, solitary confinement,
> tear gas, attrition shelling.
> Few applicants for that honor.
>
> (*ARP*, 15)

As such passages indicate, it is risky for a woman to define herself not only in relation to, but in rejection of, how the female body is coded and displayed in male-dominated culture—in effect, in relation to the masquerade of femininity, in Lacan's sense of the term. This dynamic is depicted in the poem as destructive of the complicitous mother and the rebellious thinking woman alike.

In contrast, the speaker chooses the only alternative she sees at this stage, being dissociated from her body. The text, however, does not portray this choice as any more viable than the others. Representing herself grammatically as a shifting and insecure other—at times objectifying herself in the third person, at other times indicating her presence solely through the angels that address her—the daughter oscillates between rhetorical positions, none of which frees her. She accedes only precariously and temporarily to a first-person subjectivity based on bodily senses ("I hear," "I drive," "I see") she paradoxically can't feel ("since nothing hurts her anymore"):

> Sometimes she's let the tapstream scald her arm,
> a match burn to her thumbnail,
>
> or held her hand above the kettle's snout
> right in the woolly steam.
>
> *(ARP,* 12)

As the speaker discovers, growing another way is not accompanied by linguistic coordinates to help her find the road out of women's traditional lot. Rather, she encounters the paucity of representations. Her attempts to render the "whole psychic geography" by filling in the holes are frustrated by an ineluctable return to the Same, as described in Irigaray's poetic summary of the dilemma women confront:

> So any move toward the other means turning back to the attraction of one's own mirage. A (scarcely) living mirror, she/it is frozen, mute. More lifelike. The ebb and flow of our lives spent in the exhausting labor of copying, miming. Dedicated to re-producing–the sameness in which we have remained for centuries, as the other.[21]

Trying to reflect something other than "the other," women are inexorably returned to the alterity that is the "feminine" in dominant constructions, in spite of themselves.

Rich observes that women's hatred of their mothers screens a threatening absence of difference that psychoanalysis finds dangerous as well (though not for the same reasons):

> where a mother is hated to the point of matrophobia there may also be . . . a dread that if one relaxes one's guard one will identify with her completely. (*OWB,* 237)

Identifying with the mother "completely," the daughter cannot become anything else. "I struggle to describe what it felt like to be

her daughter," Rich writes, "but I find myself divided, slipping
under her skin; a part of me identifies too much with her" (*OWB,*
224).

"Snapshots" engages this problem early on. Although the
speaker has seemed to distinguish herself from the mother, she is,
in fact, her mother's mirror image. The text indicates schematically
and grammatically that she reflects the older woman, as the following passage illustrates:

> Two handsome women, gripped in argument,
> each proud, acute, subtle, I hear scream
> across the cut glass and majolica
> like Furies cornered from their prey:
> The argument *ad feminam,* all the old knives
> that have rusted in my back, I drive in yours,
> *ma semblable, ma soeur!*
>
> (*ARP,* 13)

This scene depicts the imaginary reciprocity of mother-daughter
relations as mutually destructive. The women portrayed in the passage do not speak themselves, but are contained by a self-reflexive
system that iterates them, as the passage's chiastic structure suggests. Chiasmus, to recall the discussion in chapter 1, configures
"the structure of phallogocentrism itself."[22] The replacement in the
passage above of masculine words with their feminine grammatical
counterparts maintains, rather than subverts, the structure. A mere
reversal of terms does nothing to change the normative order of
things. Inhabiting the same space, obviating even generational difference, the women occupy the same symbolic position. Only the
lexical shift to other languages indicates a difference (although the
semantics of the language of *différance* ironically repeat the women's
indifferentiation). Attempting to constitute herself in daughterly
separation, the speaker encounters her inseparability from the
mother.

Disturbing as well is Rich's implication that all too often women
of the class that produces southern (and northern) "belles" and their
daughters are not only indifferent from and to each other. They are
also indistinguishable from the hegemonic system of "a world mas-

culinity made," as Rich puts it in a distinction reminiscent of H.D., "unfit for men and women" (*DW*, 35).[23] The thinking woman who sleeps with the "monsters" of repressed desires becomes the phallic "beak that grips her": she both assumes as her own and embodies the very portrait of herself as "harpy, shrew and whore" that male-dominated culture has presented of her (*ARP*, 12). And, like the mother, the speaker herself is situated in the paradoxes of her own symbolic relationship to a man. As a married woman, she is defined literally in-(the)-Law (the absent husband, who is present solely in the dash's lexical trace, is thus symbolically replaced by the patri-archal system). But the competing discursive registers in the poem render her a subject-in-contradiction. She represents the vexed desire to break the Law that has stifled and defeated age after age of young women, as the following passage implies:

> Deliciously, all that we might have been,
> all that we were—fire, tears,
> wit, taste, martyred ambition—
> stirs like the memory of refused adultery
> the drained and flagging bosom of our middle years.
>
> (*ARP*, 14–15)

The issue Rich poses in this poem is whether it is possible to inscribe a poetic subjectivity that is not ineluctably returned to the male term, how a woman might represent, see, read in / differently.

Summarizing the problem of "feminine identity and the mas-querade in the male system of the woman," Heath observes that the ways out female artists and theorists have come up with raise two questions: What are alternative images, alternatives to the image? ("a question of representation"), and What are the inconsistencies, the disruptions in the system? ("a question in representation"): "The former is the utopian actuality of a new spectatorship, the latter the current disturbance of the old positions."[24] Rich's text begins in the disruption of images saturated in misogyny and closes with the attempt to inscribe a feminine, or "womanly," gaze (as she calls it in "North American Time"). The poem's conclusion epitomizes the feminist dilemma toward which Heath summarily gestures. There is, on the one hand, the desire to participate in the project of *mater-*

ializing "new" or "true" images of women, and, on the other hand,
the tendency to (re)mystify woman, which an Irigarayan deconstruction of inconsistencies in the system risks. Here's Rich's closing passage:

> Well,
> she's long about her coming, who must be
> more merciless to herself than history.
> Her mind full to the wind, I see her plunge
> breasted and glancing through the currents,
> taking the light upon her
> at least as beautiful as any boy
> or helicopter,
>
> poised, still coming,
> her fine blades making the air wince
> but her cargo
> no promise then:
> delivered
> palpable
> ours.
>
> (*ARP*, 15–16)

The urgency of the tone and the elevated, visionary quality of the
central image in this passage suggest that the resolution tries to
deliver into representation the promise of that new psychic geography of alternative images that Rich will continue to envision. The
passage's epiphany insists on its resolution of the formal problem of
women's conflation with woman, but its gestural flourish paradoxically reifies the woman for our readerly pleasure and consumption.

The difficulty in representing both difference and differently
has, in fact, been concretized earlier as a trope of vision. Eyes "inac-
curately dream / behind closed windows blankening with steam"
(*ARP*, 14) that rises from the countless irons, sinks, and washtubs
that have obscured the view from those very kitchen windows
through which women have historically seen the world. The formal
conventions of rhymed pentameter to which section 8 of "Snapshots" returns us are paradigmatic of the persistent textual recon-
tainment of the new subject straining to be released here, the reso-

nant "dream" rhymed with the banal "steam" subtly emptying out ("blankening") women's escapist fantasies of significance. Defined in the *OED* as "minute particles produced by attrition or disintegration," the "grit" that blows each morning in the speaker's eyes, the only thing that "hurts her anymore," concretizes the "attrition shelling" and "solitary confinement" that is the fate of those women who "cast too bold a shadow"–who see, in other words, and are seen, altogether too clearly.

When the speaker suddenly and inexplicably accedes to unobstructed sight in the text's closing ("I see her"), her capacity to see clearly is punningly doubled and, since double vision is unclear, thereby doubly suspicious: the woman in the vision, too, is "glancing," at once seeing and reflecting something. Rich's pun complicates the effect of the utopian resolution because the wordplay is so visually oriented that it reproduces a specularization of woman the rest of the poem calls to account. Trying to see its way to a female subject, the text seems blind to its own fetishizing moves and comes titillatingly close to subjecting this newly imaged woman to the old moves. Ostensibly formulating a new subject, the speaker reconfigures the aging and menopausal (castrated) mother into the mother who has still got the goods, a phallicized as well as revalorized maternal figure. Producing this "new" image, "Snapshots" trots out one with which we are familiar: woman idealized for her reproductive powers. Rich's attempts to inscribe woman/women another way operate at cross purposes, working both to detach women from, and to restore them to, their association with the maternal. Like the woman "coming" in its visionary resolution, the text both plays off and is captivated by woman, both recognizes and is blinded by the same old fix. Oscillating between the desire for "stays" and for deliverance from them, however, "Snapshots" suggests the ways a female-authored text might specify difference by negotiating a distance with in/difference–for example, the figure of woman constructed in the paradoxes of its own undecidable status in relation to the male term.

Doane argues that the "effectivity of masquerade lies precisely in its potential to manufacture a distance from the image, to generate a problematic within which the image is manipulable, producible, and readable" by a female spectator.[25] In its undecidable complexity, the conclusion to Rich's poem produces such a problematic, "readable" within the framework of the poem by the female speaker-as-spectator and thereby potentially "manipulable," as I have been implying, by a female reader outside the text. The final passage can certainly be read with the "old" eyes of the fetishizing gaze, revealing how Rich gets captivated by the seductions of the very spectacle of femininity she wishes to see changed. Following Doane's hypothesis, however, we can also approach the conclusion with "new" feminist eyes, in which case the poem helps us to consider a "womanly" gaze as productive of an altogether more complicated (in)sight than the one the helicopter-woman at first glance seems to be. The climactic impulse of the final two stanzas is a utopian vision/version that is figuratively complete, for example, but literally incomplete (or anticlimactic). The patterns of theme and imagery and the rhythmic, evocative language refuse at the last moment to identify (with) the all-important "palpable" and "delivered" cargo that is already "ours." The text suspends and resists its own stereotypical conclusion.

Its complexity exposes what we might call its "female complexes," to play on another stereotype. As the etymology of *complex* suggests, that is, the text embraces the plurality of discourses noted earlier, fixing on none of them, enacting a linguistic braiding that models the most radical aspects of Rich's poetic methodology. To return for a moment to the Woolf passage that opened this study, we might reconsider how "Snapshots" structures and destructures that "very queer, composite being," woman:

> Imaginatively, she is of the highest importance; practically,
> she is completely insignificant. She pervades poetry from
> cover to cover; she is all but absent from history.[26]

Both there and not there, romantically present and historically absent, Woolf's "she" differs from herself: "she" is the same grammatically, but not rhetorically. Figuratively and linguistically, "she" is a shifter. "She" is not exposed but "composed," made up of several coexisting "poses" that are not self-consistent, shifting among different lexical voices, no one fully privileged.

Rich similarly posits a female subject *between* two familiar extremes, hysterical and idealized mothers, schematized in the poem by the grammatic shifts and the rhetorical oscillation between the two. This subject has discovered that her eyes were closed, but when she opens them, she realizes that her sight is still obscured. Deposing woman, she finds she can hardly see anything else. Obscurely then, she composes–and decomposes–her text, mobilizing the tension as well as the promise of "double vision" that Rich figures. Analogous to Doane's feminist reconsideration of the masquerade, the poetic subject is the daughterly double of contrasting "mothers." She produces a distance from her identification with the one, generating a trace of what will eventually "out" as her desire for the other. (To wit, Rich's revision of de Beauvoir's passage, "she is a helicopter and she is a bird; . . . and words issue from her breasts," sexualizes de Beauvoir's textualization of the goddess's breasts.)

The interaction of formal and thematic elements in the closing of "Snapshots," reminiscent of the structuring and destructuring dynamic of semiotic and symbolic registers, establishes what Kristeva calls the "split unity" of the revolutionary poetic text. In a 1978 interview with Wendy Martin, Rich describes her notion that form should emerge from the interactive dynamic between the unconscious and language:

> A poem can't exist without form, but it should be the result
> of a dynamic or dialogue between what is coming out of the
> unconscious and what is coming out of language, and
> everything that means–rhythm and sound and tone and
> repetition and the way words can ring off each other and
> clash against each other.[27]

Although Rich's general sense is modernist in its orientation (that form should emerge from content), she depicts language in this passage as signifying in excess–and separate from the control–of conscious intentionality. In addition, poetic form is not the mimetic record, but the product, of the "dialogue" (to recall Kristeva, the "discharge") between signifying (symbolic) and nonsignifying (semiotic) meaning-effects of language. The resolution of "Snapshots" releases an explosive nonsignifying, but meaningful, aural energy ("copter," "blades," "coming," "cargo," "delivered," "palpable"). This dynamic shatters the ecstatic symbolic "content" that provides the poem its climax (which I'm tempted to translate as meaning that the "not yet" of female subjectivity is really an "already," but I won't), which the poem's form nevertheless keeps comprehensible (or it would be nonsense). The individuated words—or pulverized utterances—are separated graphically by lines, and meaningfully related by logical association, but detached from syntactic relation. At the formal level, the metonymic structure helps the poem grammatically to vex the rhetorical reassimilation of content and image back in service to the symbolic structure of metaphor. At the thematic level, the woman comes into her own self-sufficient, fecund space, which is neither a place nor a "maternal" language, but, like the *semiotic chora*, a maternally connoted register of discourse constitutive, but also straining the limits, of the poetic form itself. The semiotic energy that the resolution expends, the reactivation of the repressed maternal element it signifies, disrupts the symbolic closure that would restore the woman fully to herself or to us as readers (she is, though morphologically reconstituted, still, as it were, spoken for). The mutual structuring and destructuring action of the unconscious and language, or the semiotic and symbolic elements, works to prevent the reader's identification with the woman posited in the text's closing from being reified.

Chapter 1's feminist rereading of Kristeva postulated that, for women, the way in which a text might "revolutionize" the symbolic order is not through an excavation of some archaic feminine power that could give a female reader back "herself." There is no *there* there, as Gertrude Stein might say and Rich intimates. Rather, a revolutionary feminist poetics that puts the maternal imaginary into circulation frees it from its singular symbolic status as empty—the uncanny, repressed, or absent in Western culture, as we have seen that Moore's and H.D.'s work exposed.

Naming the "enigmas . . . of the second sex," as Rich discovers, is easier said (so to speak) than done. But through an engagement of the psychic processes that constitute meaning, sense, and identity, the processes that symbolic discourse tries to gloss over in the name of coherence, a woman's poetic language potentially re-forms women's identification with the equation that associates all women with the oppressive conventions of maternal function, and by extension of those powers, as fantasized by the adult male, with the monstrous (women = mothers = monsters *encore*).

By way of an illustrative transition, I would like to take a brief detour into another genre concerned with male fantasies and female images, that of the Hollywood classic film, in which the issues of female subjectivity in the symbolic realm that Rich engages in "Snapshots" summarily coalesce. Examining Alfred Hitchcock's *Rebecca* (1940), Tania Modleski remarks that the film and psychoanalysis treat the second Mrs. de Winter's narcissistic identification with the first Mrs. de Winter as a problem. The heroine has a disturbing mother fixation. The solution the film proposes is broadly Freudian in its outlines.[28] The daughter replaces the mother, as the repetition of the name indicates, by marrying the father. She pleases him precisely because she is no match for him. At once daughter, other woman, and "vacuous self" in comparison to the mother, Modleski observes,[29] the girl will become a woman who can *really* mind her manners, looks, and words, unlike Rebecca, who only pretended to and was therefore at last exposed as a monster masquerading as a woman (like Helen or the thinking woman in "Snapshots," inappropriate mirrors of man). When the heroine learns of the mother's true nature from the father, the girl is his for life.

But there is a residue of "indigestible" femininity, Modleski asserts, from Daphne du Maurier's Gothic feminine novel that Hitchcock found impossible to purge.[30] In learning so well how to put herself together, the heroine has had to give up, it turns out, "that funny, young, lost look" her husband loved; he laments that she has "grown so much older." Much as the film tries to cover it up, she arguably has not assumed a more appropriate look at the end for Maxim. He never wanted that look, in both senses of the word, because it might be Rebecca's "look," which threatened the smooth flow of the master's life by being a desiring subject and by returning his gaze not as mirror but as carnival: as Mrs. Danvers tells the male characters, Rebecca "used to sit on her bed and rock with laughter at the lot of you."[31] Maxim may well be mourning the loss of the "look" on the heroine's part that is solely for him, that does not return his gaze with the knowledge and power to see for herself, and will not laugh at him. He has said, after all, that he does not want a *femme de trente(-six) ans.* There's "something potentially more subversive" to this film, Modleski observes, than its representation of "a woman's problems of 'overidentification' with another woman": namely, "the desire of women for other women."[32]

As Rich's analysis of matrophobia discussed earlier reveals, she also treats an overidentification with the mother as a problem. And it is interesting that the solution she eventually poses is precisely the subversively "indigestible" desire the film, *Rebecca,* cannot completely repress: "to recognize and act upon the breadth and depth of [women's] feelings for women" (*OWB,* 234). The conversion of the imaginary "lesbian continuum" of woman-identified experience into an actualized "lesbian existence" de-fuses the *either/or* construct that frames the woman's identity in the institution of heterosexuality (as in *Rebecca,* to accede to normative heterosexuality, according to Freud, the girl must make the transfer from mother to father as erotic object choice). In contrast to this "contradiction between lesbian and mother," as poet Sue Silvermarie, whom Rich quotes, asserts, there is for lesbians "an overlapping" of identities between mother, lover, and self (*OWB,* 234).

With "Snapshots of a Daughter-in-Law," Rich intimates that matrophobia can be resolved not by suppressing overidentification or abjecting the mother, but by pluralizing the desire to materialize a unified, stable subject. The famous line from the later "Diving into the Wreck," often understood as figuring "the primal wholeness that predates the dualities," as Martin asserts[33]–"I am she: I am he" (*DW,* 24)–does not simply fuse the line into an image of androgynous identity. It con/fuses and doubles identity. The two gender indicators are graphically separated as well as associated by the colon between them. The line renders the very notion of stable gender identity problematic. And the line closest to such fusion, "the one who find our way," is literally a grammatical sex which is not one.

It is the engagement with, not the denial of, a divided subjectivity that provides Rich, as it did Dickinson, Moore, and H.D., with the poetic resources she needs to revise the feminine version of the maternal and heterosexual fixes. The woman in "Transcendental Etude," for example, exceeds at the structural level of figure (in this instance, metonymic displacement) the stereotypical maternal imagery (metaphoric replacement) with which Rich depicts her. The "image of mother as nature," to which Homans claims the poem reduces her,[34] is mutable, as suggested by the assertion that the woman "finds herself" in what is in effect a series of multiple tropes for the self:

> becoming now the sherd of broken glass
> slicing light in a corner, dangerous
> to flesh, now the plentiful, soft leaf
> that wrapped round the throbbing finger, soothes the wound;
> and now the stone foundation, rockshelf further
> forming underneath everything that grows.
>
> (*FD,* 269)

The woman is not simply "passive and stereotypically lacking in an identity of her own,"[35] as her association with the traditionally feminine images of "yarn, calico, and velvet" into which she disappears suggests. In Rich's revision of poetic tradition's Laura-in-pieces, the woman's "experienced fingers" are also pushing

> dark against bright, silk against roughness,
> pulling the tenets of a life together[.]
>
> (*FD,* 269)

She is, as the passages above suggest, re-presented as creatively active. The metonymic chain of figures that she becomes at the end, although "poetically terminal," as Homans remarks,[36] construes a notion of identity that is not illusorily stabilized: "the many-lived, unending / forms in which she finds herself" (*FD,* 269). "Finds" is, in this context, an ambiguous verb, connoting both the woman's passive (as a reflexive) and active (as a transitive) engagement with the materials that make up her work, her life, and by analogy, the poem itself.

The speaker gestures rhetorically toward the utopian "cure" to self-division that a revised reflexivity of lesbian relation beyond or beside the male term might offer. Unlike the mother-daughter in "Snapshots," the two women in "Transcendental Etude" nourishingly mirror each other: "eye to eye / measuring each other's spirit, each other's / limitless desire" (*FD*, 268). They are specifically subject to maternal ("mus[e]ing"), not paternal ("argument and jargon"), law. The text portrays how two women can find in each other the (m)other. At once the same and different, however, the (m)other figure is more analogous structurally to the Kristevan mother as symbolic of divided subjectivity than to the imaginary maternal plenitude of mutual reflection, which the text posits thematically. The claim to a singular identity—the speaker both

> *the lover and the loved,*
> *home and wanderer, she who splits*
> *firewood and she who knocks, a stranger*
>
> (*FD*, 268; emphasis in original)

—is a performative one, as the crucial line break on "splits" implies. Although rhetorically unified, the speaker is grammatically divided into parts, representing an internal difference that is reconfigured externally with the (m)other woman (and vice versa), indicative of the psychic processes of identification and separation the word *and* marks. The remarkable percussive and sibilant sounds the final section orchestrates ("dark," "petal," "domestic," "silver," "soft," "soothes," to name but a few) compose an aural collage that displays a semiotic element. The closing thereby transgresses the ideological underpinnings of the text's own conventional symbolism ("the musing of a mind / one with her body" [*FD*, 268–69]), moving text and reader alike away from as well as toward a Romantic resolution.

Like Kristeva's contemplation of nationalism,[37] Rich's project entails a detachment from identificatory cultural as well as gender blinders. Rich takes up this point in an exemplary earlier poem in *The Dream of a Common Language*, "Hunger," dedicated to Audre Lorde, in which we recognize the structure and the problematic of the Dickinsonian sublime. Dickinson's nineteenth-century refusal to abject the maternal in order to consolidate the self has in this poem become Rich's twentieth-century grounding of an irresolvable "end-of-the-line" moment of self-loss in "the sociohistorical realities of injustice, brutality, and terror," as Diehl remarks in another context.[38] Viewing a Chinese ink drawing (and thus poised

to revise the "hysterical women" with which Yeats's "Lapis Lazuli"
opens), the speaker is disoriented by the "scene of desolation" that
the drawing portrays, in which two tiny "human figures [are] reck-
lessly exposed" in the foreground. She suddenly identifies herself
and her lover with the two figures "leaning together," their intima-
cies "rigged with terror" (*FD*, 230, 231). At the same time, the "film
of domesticity" that enculturates as well as protects her from the
knowledge of the fragility of such sheltering constructions recedes.
A literally split subject, she loses the sense of cultural identity that
positions her as "Western":

> I know I'm partly somewhere else—
> huts strung across a drought-stretched land
> not mine, dried breasts, mine and not mine, a mother
> watching my children shrink with hunger.
> I live in my Western skin,
> my Western vision, torn
> and flung to what I can't control or even fathom.
>
> (*FD*, 230)

The other is not, as it were, *othered* in this passage; rather, the
speaker is herself inscribed by and in / difference. Extending Dickinson's sense of the "stranger" within, this moment of global identification with a material elsewhere that is lethal to women and children dislocates the speaker from her sense of place in the world.
This dislocation tears off the blinders that her privileged position
has afforded her.

The simultaneity of perceptions in this divided state enables the
speaker to see with the other's—specifically, with another mother's—
eyes. She thereby has imaginative access to the other's experience
of the effects of power and oppression, to borrow DuPlessis's apt
observation of Moore's animal poems. She receives "in imagination the pressure of dumbness, the accumulation of unrecorded
life," as Woolf, whom DuPlessis quotes, puts it.[39] "As with a number
of women writers influenced by feminism or working out of an
implicit feminist critique," DuPlessis remarks, "the invention of stories, images and voices for the semi-silenced or silent, the unheard
and formerly invisible creates major revisionary statements."[40] In

lieu of the protection the speaker's tangible domesticity afforded her, for example, she is located solely by intangibles (her dreams, her fears, her beliefs):

> I stand convicted by all my convictions—
> you, too. We shrink from touching
> our power, we shrink away, we starve ourselves
> and each other, we're scared shitless
> of what it could be to take and use our love,
> hose it on a city, on a world,
> to wield and guide its spray, destroying
> poisons, parasites, rats, viruses—
> like the terrible mothers we long and dread to be.
>
> (*FD,* 231)

With their experience, both fantasized and real, in symbolic circulation, women simply will not stand for lack. The speaker in this passage stands for, as well as stands (convicted) by, her beliefs.

Because of the ambiguity of the first line in the passage above, however, it is impossible to say which conviction we are "supposed" to understand as "the one." The speaker might well be "convicted" because she is detached from (though not, symbolically speaking, outside of) the hegemony of imperialism and heterosexuality. The dual grammatical function of *touching* as both transitive participle and gerund, rendered by its lexical placement, certainly implies as much. But she might also be "convicted" because the Western "skin" that, she acknowledges, she must inhabit in order to live obstructs her ability to "change reality" for her children, her lover, in the world ("We shrink from touching / our *power.*"). Rather than settle on either reading, however, I think it more useful to consider that the vision in the passage above is associated not only with the lesbian continuum of a woman-identified epistemology, but with the ontology of a lesbian existence.

Lesbian desire as well as subjectivity are often associated in Rich's work with the maternal, as I observed earlier without comment, in discussing *Of Woman Born.* But it should be noted that such fantasized, affirmative fusion of lesbian and maternal love poses a problematic alternative to heterosexuality for many of Rich's readers, since such a conflation seems once again to enmesh women in the maternal fix. Rich's attempts to represent "the truth" of lesbian desire as maternally connoted are more reminiscent of Kristeva's notion of the "homosexual-maternal facet,"[41] for example, than of de Lauretis's more recent theorization of desire between women. De Lauretis cautions that the inscription of lesbian sexuality as maternal indicates the persistent confusion of desire with identification, which is culturally coded as narcissistic and therefore immature. Rich also complicates the issue of women's identification with the mother, as we have seen, and posits women's desire for each other as an alternative, but one that seems always to be reclaimed for the maternal in her work. De Lauretis argues that such a confusion of lesbian and maternal keeps the representation of "homosexual-lesbian desire," as distinct from lesbian desire conceived within the framework and institution of heterosexuality, invisible and/or unrecognizable.[42] According to de Lauretis, Kristeva contributes, of course, to maintaining lesbian invisibility by reproducing the prevailing cultural coding of women's desire for each other as a mother-daughter structure. And certainly Kristeva's characterization of male-authored poetic language as "the *equivalent of incest*" should be applied to female-authored poetry, if at all, with caution.[43]

But Kristeva's theory, including that of poetic language, has significantly contributed to the visibility of the *mother* outside the mother-daughter relation. In hypothesizing the altruism of the mother's desire beyond figural and discursive conventions of maternal masochism, Kristeva suggests a paradigm shift that could potentially transform the symbolic order. The distinction she makes between maternal and filial desire provides an approach, I suggest, to the specificity of the lesbian subject that Rich (albeit not de Lauretis) represents. The desire of the speaker in "Hunger," for example, is not posited in *daughterly* identification *with* a mother figure; rather, her identification *as* a *mother* inscribes her desire. As both lesbian and mother, she evinces a desire that is not as a mother for a child, or the reverse, but rather for another woman who happens also to be a mother.

In addition, Rich poses a figural alternative in the passage quoted earlier that (literally) explodes the canonical mystification of the mother as either comforting or devouring. Performing a hyperbolized reversal of woman as contamination, the speaker imagines the two women's love as a purgative wash that would decontaminate the world the "male State" has made. The text comprises a far more complex association of maternal and lesbian desire than orthodox psychoanalytic theory has been able to imagine. These Amazons join in a furious desire to destroy the destructive. Her use of the overdetermined word *terrible* at once turns man's fantasized fear of the mother into the two women's experience of fear, both personal and global, as both mothers and lesbians in the world; revises the gynophobic (monstrous), and homophobic, undertones of the (uncanny) word; and bears a trace of the awesome power the word denotes etymologically and the poem as a whole connotes.

There is an altruistic, ethical imperative in this revisionary aesthetic, which the next section will specifically take up, as the speaker's realization of her protected status (and the guilt that accompanies it) indicates:

> I'm alive to want more than life,
> want it for others starving and unborn,
> to name the deprivations boring
> into my will, my affections, into the brains
> of daughters, sisters, lovers caught in the crossfire
> of terrorists of the mind.
>
> (*FD*, 231)

The language of this passage flattens out, "boring" in its (failed) attempts "to name the deprivations." But the question Rich raises is the one that obtains implicitly throughout the poem: How does one meet the poetic challenge of finding a language that will render another's suffering so present that a reader might feel impelled to action?[44] If we do not "find each other," "Hunger" concludes, "we are alone" (*FD*, 232). In loving another woman and projecting that love as both lesbian and matriarchal "antidote" to patriarchal poisons, to recall both Dickinson and H.D., the speaker is not, however transferentially, committing an incest the social contract prohibits (as, perhaps, are the male poets about whom Kristeva theorizes). That economy does not pertain when lesbians accede openly to subjective agency. Rather, she inscribes the perspectival shifts, the overlapping of lesbian and maternal identities, her "double vision" enacts. Without the enactment of shifting identificatory positions that deprivilege the attachment to the very notion of fixed identity itself, the text suggests, we cannot "change reality," a crucial concern in Rich's work to which we now turn.

CHANGING THE SUBJECT

> *Some women wait for something*
> *to change   and nothing*
> *does change*
> *so they change*
> *themselves.*
>
> —Audre Lorde, "Stations"

➳

Rich has claimed that no inherited ethical ideal has deserved women's unconditional respect because all ethics gloss over crimes against women (*OWB*, 276). Her aesthetic is, like Moore's and H.D.'s, nevertheless highly ethical, as the project to participate in changing (our) minds in order to revolutionize internalized masculinist thinking and the reproduction of patriarchal social systems that characterizes Rich's career might suggest. But that project also generates contradictions. Words do not translate unproblematically into material change. Rich longs spiritually for "the pure annunciations to the eye / / the *visio beatifica*" (*FD*, 236). To counter the negative representations that dismember women "on the cinema screens, the white expensive walls / of collectors, the newsrags blowing the streets," as she writes in "The Images," she infuses her poetry with positive, sometimes mesmerizing, idealizations of woman:

> When I saw hér face, she of the several faces
>   staring   indrawn   in judgment   laughing for joy
>   her serpents twisting   her arms raised
>   her breasts gazing
>   when I looked into hér world

I wished to cry loose my soul
    into her, to become
        free of speech   at last.

(WP, 5)

Such representations of woman are not so much instances of unconscious essentialization on Rich's part, but rather, like Moore's revisionary discursive masquerade, a strategic figural performance of women's reclamation of the means (language) to name feminine "properties" (nominal essence) for themselves. The passage above additionally suggests Rich's desire to saturate a symbolic contract premised on feminine sacrifice with more-nourishing images of women, to invoke the excerpt from Kristeva's "Women's Time" that opened this chapter.

The stanza's formal symmetry, reasserted by the desire to fix meaning (albeit differently) and aligned with the figural mystification of the feminine, must be read against the grain of the grammatical and syntactic laws this passage breaks. The image's effect, moreover, is temporary. Far from projecting us permanently into another world "free of speech" (a maternal haven/heaven), we are soon returned to the one in which we are never free of the belief systems language expresses. "And so I came home," the speaker continues. Although the paradox of the egotistical sublime, that we have only speech to gesture toward the unspeakable, seems to motivate this text, it is well to recall that Rich is writing about not the unspeakable, but the unspoken, not the unnameable but, in the crucial distinction de Lauretis and Kristeva make as well, the unnamed. She does not have unconscious repression but conscious suppression in mind, as the following passage from "Women and Honor: Some Notes on Lying" exemplifies:

Patriarchal lying has manipulated women both through falsehood and through silence. Facts we needed have been withheld from us. False witness has been borne against us. *(LSS,* 189)

We (women) need the very language whose symbolic structures translate "violence into patterns so powerful and pure / we continually fail to ask are they true for us" (*WP*, 4). As Rich asserts in "The Burning of Paper instead of Children," "this is the oppressor's language // yet I need it to talk to you" (*FD*, 117). Diehl contends that the issue for Rich is "how to control distrust of the very language the woman poet must invoke."[45] I would add, however, that she is arguably more aware of the possibility that the infusion of the same structures with new images might not change the structural patterns of violence than Diehl gives her credit for. Language is not a static entity for Rich,[46] who constantly renegotiates her sense of it, as well as her relation to it: "Only where there is language is there world," she writes in "The Demon Lover" (*FD*, 84); in "Cartographies" she states, "Language cannot do everything" (*FD*, 235).

Language is nevertheless a vexed point in Rich's work, in part because distinctions between oppressor and oppressed, or male and female authored representations of woman, blur. Women are spoken by, as well as speak, "the oppressor's language." They have been socialized to lie as well as been lied to:

> It has been difficult . . . to know the lies of our complicity from the lies we believed. The lie of the "happy marriage," of domesticity—we have been complicit, have acted out the fiction of a well-lived life, until the day we testify in court of rapes, beatings, psychic cruelties, public and private humiliations. (*LSS*, 189)

Although the passage elides the class and racial differences among women that inflect subjectivity, which Rich eventually acknowledges, it aptly characterizes the kind of position I have called "equivocal"–the one(s) occupied by women who are not simply oppressed by gender discrimination, but well placed by class and race. Women who not only lie to men "for survival," but who are complicit in the male-dominated system. Women who also lie to each other, a learned response they must "unlearn" (*LSS*, 189).

The linguistic structures of violence that these women have internalized and themselves reproduce must be changed. Because "*the master's tools will never dismantle the master's house,*" as Lorde has famously put it,[47] the "mistresses" of the house must stop conforming to their real position: the semblance of privilege, to recall Hurtado's point. To do so, these women must reorient their sense of honor, traditionally a moot point for them as long as they demonstrated "chastity" or "fidelity to a husband" (*LSS*, 186), and redefine it in relation to other women, not as a feminine version of the masculine code.

Rich's ideas seem to presuppose a univocal truth: "The unconscious wants truth, as does the body" (*LSS*, 188). There are many lies, but only one truth. But here Rich herself equivocates:

> "Women have always lied to each other."
> "Women have always whispered the truth to each other."
> Both of these axioms are true. (*LSS*, 189)

For any of these axioms to be true, and Rich does not adjudicate, truth must shift diachronically. Each line's truth cancels out, or supplements, the previous line's truth. In deciphering the unity within contradiction in a text, Kristeva writes, we find that unity is constituted by "*moments* in the subject's experience-in-practice."[48] For Rich, truth is similarly a moment of unity, like the tenuous linguistic "stays" that support and produce the changes in consciousness to which she has devoted herself. As the etymology of the word suggests, "stays" are contingent, temporary stops in the generation of significance, resembling Kristeva's notion of provisional identity and de Lauretis's Peircean *interpretant.* "Stays" are pauses as well as stands, like Rich's sense of identity itself.

Kristeva's definition of the "herethical" function of art offers an approach to understanding the way the notion of truth might operate as an ethical component in Rich's texts:

> a practice is ethical when it dissolves those narcissistic fixations (ones that are narrowly confined to the subject) to which the signifying process succumbs in its socio-symbolic realization. Practice . . . positing and dissolving meaning and the unity of the subject, therefore encompasses the ethical.[49]

Rich's work enacts how any truth a text reveals is a temporary "stand" in the larger poetic process, how the sense of unified identity, or identification with an "essentializing" image, is a momentary "stay" within the constitutive dynamic of a subject-in-practice. Experiencing a division of perception that is at once an outward expansion of and an internal reorientation to alterity, a revision of perspective that I have called, following Rich herself, "double vision," the speaking subject of "Hunger," for example, dissolves the culturally specific indicators that at the same time posit her as "Western." She is still positioned by that identity, but she is also, through a renegotiation of her relation to it, and to the location from which she speaks, beside herself (as it were). Rich's poetic practice has political implications analogous to those of Kristeva's antitotalitarian redefinition of the symbolic order. Rich observes in "Women and Honor" that much of what has been "narrowly termed 'politics' seems to rest on a longing for certainty even at the cost of honesty, for an analysis which, once given, need not be reexamined" (*LSS*, 193). Honesty requires critical reexamination, a disengagement from the attachment to "certainty."

As noted earlier, Meese terms the oppositions Rich puts into play and undoes "contra/dictions." For Rich, Meese suggests and "Hunger" illustrates, "the separation from the other is a separation within the self, requiring us to undertake multiple, unending negotiations with the logic of identity."[50] Once Rich conceives of identity as a field of shifting locations, Meese contends, the positioning of "the other" as the point against which to fix one's own identity can be exposed. Rich's exposure of this identificatory strategy amplifies Dickinson's inscription of the stranger within to include a tolerance of and for external differences from oneself, dehierarchizing them. In attending to that which locates her, Rich continually reveals her "truth" as contingent, her position(s) as performative pauses in the process of her own consciousness-raising. As she comments in a later essay, "Blood, Bread, and Poetry: The Location of the Poet (1984)," "I am telling you this from a backward perspective, from where I stand *now*" (*BBP*, 177–78; emphasis added).

De Lauretis, on the other hand, terms the subject of multiple dislocations of the hegemonic center that Rich enacts "eccentric" (or ex-centric). Building on Rich's own theoretical thinking, de Lauretis addresses the problem of heterosexual, middle-class hegemony within feminism, asserting that the position of white feminism is "much less pure" than the earlier notion of woman as absolute other (to which Rich once subscribed). It is "ideologically complicit with 'the oppressor,'" she elaborates, echoing Rich, "whose position it may occupy in certain sociosexual relations (if not others)."[51] Observing that "the view of a single, totalizing, 'Western' feminism" is "oppressive or at best irrelevant to women of color in the world," de Lauretis advocates a revised white feminism that would be "self-critical" as well as critical, have "agency (rather than 'choice')," and bear "social accountability."[52]

To be sure, as de Lauretis notes, gender is a significant determining factor shared by women in relation to power. To take a famous example, the conservative, devout Anita Hill was made over into a vengeful, spurned woman, and this, in spite (or perhaps because) of her consistently dignified deportment, in order to confirm Clarence Thomas's nomination to the U.S. Supreme Court.[53] When push came to shove, in the form of Thomas's representation of himself as the victim of a Congressional "high-tech lynching," the men consolidated not only political differences but class and racial differences as well. They demonstrated, in short, a collective blindness to the gendered issue of sexual harassment Hill raised, remarkable only in being unusually public. But gender is not the only factor that impacts subjectivity, as white, middle-class feminists have been challenged to confront in the past decade.

Rich's very public account of her own constantly revising, insistently self-criticizing process constitutes a conscientious white feminist's response to the challenge posed by women of color. Her work has increasingly addressed the need for "enlarging the range of accountability" as well as recognizing agency on the part of women most closely associated with—and in positions to benefit most from their proximity to—hegemonic masculinity. She has, in both her poetry and essays, asserted the ethical necessity for more and more examination, as opposed to naturalization, of the truth of personal and political stands.

This aspect of her project to "change reality" is a difficult as well as self-critical undertaking, which Rich herself admits in her essay, "Split at the Root: An Essay on Jewish Identity (1982)," because "There is no purity." Her Jewish father's insistence on assimilation into the dominant Gentile culture "has affected *my* perceptions," she confesses (*BBP*, 123; Rich's emphasis). The essay tracks her development from a belief in (some) unified, if as yet unattained, identity to an awareness that the positions one occupies in the world are multiple, specific, and shifting. At first she rejected the "split" between "Gentile" and "Jew," in her case, as "trying to have it both ways" (*BBP*, 101). She then began to realize how she had been "controlled" as the "favored" daughter, "rewarded" as the "special" woman (*BBP*, 116). In a position historically to influence as well as be influenced by second-wave and poststructuralist feminisms, Rich has addressed not simply the disadvantage of her place as a woman in a male-dominated society. She has also confronted the status that she has been granted because of her class, the seductions of rewards for compliance from which she has had to extricate her thinking. In so doing, she has consciously tried to detach herself from the security attached to any one fixed position. The essay concludes with the assertion that the paradoxes of her identity—"white, Jewish, anti-Semite, racist, anti-racist, once-married, lesbian, middle-class, feminist, exmatriate southerner, *split at the root*" (*BBP*, 122; Rich's emphasis)—"will have to be engaged" in the necessary, ongoing process of one woman's trying "to clean up her act" (*BBP*, 123). To be conscious of the specificity of one's position at any given time and place is, for a woman in Rich's position, to refuse to ignore the reality that she is not absolutely victimized, any more than she is absolutely favored. Her status, that is, is equivocal: contradictory as well as eccentric.

Both Meese and de Lauretis are thus useful in approaching this self-critical aspect of Rich's project. By foregrounding her physical as well as psychic location, she confronts the implications of her placement. Like "Hunger," the later poem "Frame" (1980) evinces Rich's ethical aesthetic, treating the problematic position of being a politically committed white woman who attempts to represent the victimization of a silenced woman of color without speaking for her. "Frame" focuses on the internal cultural politics of the United States—the "stranger," as it were, within white hegemony. The speaker is a white woman who is "*not supposed to be / there*" (*FD*, 304; Rich's italics). She watches a white campus security guard and a white policeman harass and brutally arrest a black female student who had found shelter from the winter wind by standing inside an empty campus building while she waited for the bus. The speaker is *"just outside the frame / of this action,"* which she can't hear, but which she witnesses (*FD,* 304; Rich's italics). Rich's feminist poetics have evolved far beyond the early speaker of "Snapshots," for in witnessing the action, the speaker of "Frame" accedes not only to unobstructed vision, but to the knowledge of localized oppression she can no longer abstract simply as a blanket sexism.

The speaker's knowledge in "Frame" derives very specifically from her location: all she knows *"is what / I can see from this position,"* which is as *"a white woman who they will say / was never there"* (*FD,* 305; Rich's italics). She is not "there" because, *as* a white woman, she is not supposed to see the racist sadism in a white supremacist society. But the speaker insists *"I am there,"* as much to admit accountability for being (able to be) outside the frame of this event as to claim a position as witness. Race, not gender, constitutes both her difference from the other woman and her relation to the men, a crucial as well as unsettling realization for the white female witness.

Rich has said elsewhere that the only grounding she can now find is in "the history of the dispossessed" (*BBP,* 176). "Frame" epitomizes the possibilities for and the constraints upon enacting that sensibility. The speaker narrates what happens to the disenfranchised woman whose fate she observes. She neither appropriates the woman's voice nor shares the woman's experience except vicariously. The history of the silenced has itself been silenced, as the speaker makes eloquently clear in her insistent litany of the victimization that takes place "in silence":

> *I can see from this position there is no soundtrack*
> *to go with this and I understand at once*
> *it is meant to be in silence that this happens*
> in silence that he pushes her into the car
> banging her head in silence that she cries out
> · · · · · · · · · · · · · · · ·   ·   · · ·
> in silence that he twists the flesh of her thigh
> with his nails in silence that her tears begin to flow
> that she pleads with the other policeman as if
> he could be trusted to see her at all
> in silence that in the precinct she refuses to give her name

in silence that they throw her into the cell
in silence that she stares him
straight in the face in silence that he sprays her
in her eyes with Mace in silence that she sinks her teeth
into his hand in silence that she is charged
with trespass assault and battery[.]

(*FD*, 304–5; Rich's italics)

In this passage, the men are in effect blind and the speaker occupies
a foregrounded position of "double vision": the speaker both sees
the woman the police do not (except as the unruly colored body they
torture in order to control) and "sees" the future (what happens after
the police have hauled the black student away). The repeated "in
silence" rhetorically and rhythmically, as well as thematically, inten-
sifies the emphasis on the necessity for white women to expose the
men who see without seeing–to see, that is, with a politicized gaze.

In her record of this event, the speaker invokes synecdochically
the sexualization of white male violence against black women historically: the hand that pushes and the nails that twist the student's
flesh. In another furious revision of Laura-in-pieces, the text depicts
the black woman's body fragmenting into parts (head, flesh, thigh,
teeth, eyes) as she is physically, not erotically, violated. The credibility of the speaker's words is undermined (" *What I am telling you /
is told by a white woman who they will say / was never there*" [*FD*, 305;
italics in original]), but not, like the speaker of Dickinson's "I think
I was enchanted," by the speaker herself. Rather, her words are inval-
idated by the system the law-enforcement officers represent. Thus,
when the speaker proclaims herself a presence ("*I say I am there*"),
she performatively claims herself *present*. At once inside the event,
because of her gender identification, and outside it, because of her
racial difference from the student, she provides a perspectival frame
that throws the action into stark relief.[54] The fact that she has broken
the white (female) silence that has always protected the white (male)
perpetrators of racial violence is a "stand" for women in *her* position
to continue to take. The text resists the urge to perform a universal-
ization of woman's voice from a white feminist standpoint, to speak
for others, as Meese comments in another context.[55] To insist on
acknowledging the conditions under which certain statements are

true is to work toward a specificity attentive to differences, as well as commonality, among women. We must commend Rich for the ethical urgency and the conscientious anger she epitomizes.

But the scene also demonstrates the problems with her methodology. It is important to remember, for instance, that it is another story for the black woman. At the end of the poem, she is, as the title implies, still framed by white hegemony as concretely as by the bars of her jail cell. And to represent her without a "soundtrack" may seem literally honest (that is, antiperformative and thereby "real") in the particulars of the white woman's experience (because she couldn't hear anything), but it is constrained by its adherence to literality. Rehearsing the black student's silencing, Rich reproduces it, and in the name of truth the text reduces the student's violation to the status of spectacle that a concerned but paralyzed white feminist spectator watches, as if viewing actors in a silent flick. In lingering over the bodily violation because that is "all" the speaker "knows," Rich poses as truthful while in fact performing a lie. The speaker of "Frame" not only represents the black woman's experience as silenced, that is, but misrepresents it as *silent* (which it surely was not). The text claims to document only what the white woman could see, presenting itself not as an interested representation, however well-meaning in this case, but as reality.

In reality, of course, the text brackets the black woman's perspective while centralizing highly selective details of her ordeal. Since the speaker cannot in all honesty identify with the black woman's victimization, cannot represent anything but what it *looks like* to her, Rich's depiction of the women's in/difference all but succumbs to hegemonic indifference. Framed by the particulars of the white woman's perspective, the student is rendered completely—and within the context of the poem, permanently—without agency, caught in, as well as by, a moment of victimization (like a Moorish fly in amber), voiceless. In relegating the black woman so fully to the status of victim, the text arguably does not see beyond its liberal white feminist impulses. Rich's sympathetic "double vision" has, in this instance, blurred her sight. As such, "Frame" dramatizes the need for some imaginative passage between the absolutes of "truly" particularized and "falsely" universalized subjects that Rich's conscientious positioning of the speaker does not here resolve.

The extreme adoption of such a localized position is a strategic pose masquerading as the renunciation of posing, an (anti-)performance of limited vision that equivocally (de)fetishizes the black woman as spectacle. Although she is not presented for *erotic* readerly consumption, as was the (white) woman in the resolution of "Snapshots," she is nonetheless *food* for white feminist thought (obviously, mine included). Rich has destroyed any possible *pleasure* readers might take in the narrative, which Mulvey asserts is a "radical weapon" for undoing the workings of dominant ideology.[56] White and black female readers of the poem, however, experience the violence it describes very differently, as Sonia Saldívar-Hull's critique of recent white feminist critical celebrations of Gertrude Stein's "Melanctha" might suggest.[57] Rich deuniversalizes knowledge, rendering it the basis for a transformation of "objective" poetry based on observable reality into a politicized and honorable white feminist poetics attentive to context. But she has not enacted the metamorphosis itself.

I suggest that what she does achieve in playing it both ways, truth telling and lying, however, is the anatomization of the specularizing mechanization's sadism without assuming the power of its gaze. "Sadism demands a story," Mulvey observes and Rich's text illustrates.[58] But as her poem suggests, recalling Barrett Browning's version of Syrinx's tale, that story needn't reproduce *the* story. "Frame" attributes the sexist operation of sadism, for example, not to an interaction with its feminine counterpart, masochism, which renders the woman complicitous, but to its rightful place in a white supremacist system that uses sadistic brutality to regulate and control differences, which the poem specifically exposes as racialized.

In a statement reminiscent of a stunned Helen in mortal danger early on in H.D.'s epic, the speaker in the title series of *An Atlas of the Difficult World* states, when she hears of the murders of a lesbian on a camping trip with her lover and of a battered wife, that she doesn't "want to know / wreckage, dreck and waste" (*ADW,* 4). But, the speaker admits, such knowledge is the stuff of (feminist) poetry: "these [facts] are the materials" (*ADW,* 14). Political action generated by epistemological specificity "leads to poetry, the deed to word," Rich observes in "Toward a More Feminist Criticism," "when the poet identifies with others like and unlike herself who are trying to transform an oppressive order" (*BBP,* 90). The problem is not *that* the poet imaginatively identifies with others unlike as well as like herself (in/difference); rather, when her imagination is so rigidly constrained by adherence to literal circumstance, the text falls problematically short of its project, and the interpretive projection that identification entails (as in the phrase *I am there* in "Frame") is *covered up* or gets the last word (indifference). Such are the risks of Rich's methodology.

The very irresolvability of the issues about the positioning of poetic subjectivity, representational control, and epistemological integrity that Rich raises and with which she wrestles is paradigmatic of how difficult the terrain she has chosen to traverse continues to be. It is precisely such utopian *will* to change the oppressive order that associates her most with the other poets in this study. "If the 'women's tradition' means anything," writes Loeffelholz, "it means a common set of problems—of definitions and ambivalence. It is a relational, not an absolute, identity."[59] I have identified these poets as related through the strategies they share that undo positions of poetic privilege and dissociate women from woman, productive of other subjects and poetic language that neither uncritically reproduce dominant structures nor replace them with "feminine" equivalents. Their projects—Dickinson's divided Romantic subject and (de)valorized poetic source, Moore's dialogizing of poetic language, and H.D.'s decentering of hegemonic femininity and masculinity—coalesce and extend in Rich, whose poetic and autobiographical subject continues to seek ways honestly (that is, not illusorily) of divesting herself of white privilege and the specificity of power accorded its perspective. She writes of the lesbian and activist pacifist, Barbara Deming, in a statement that could characterize the complex aspects of Rich's own activist poetics: "An activist's faith can never be unquestioning, can never stop responding to 'new passions and new forces,' can never oversimplify."[60]

AFTER WORDS

By way of closing, I would like to return for a moment to the poem that opened this chapter, "Planetarium," and consider the obvious grammatical ambiguity of the line, "seeing is changing," which I previously neglected in order to read it as representative of the male gaze. Through the lens of the discussion above, we might now observe that the change in seeing, or the seeing of / that is changing, mobilizes a shift of the all-seeing "eye" into a localized "I" who intercedes at the end. The speaker tells us,

> I have been standing all my life in the
> direct path of a battery of signals[.]
>
> (*FD*, 116)

Unlike the speakers of "Snapshots," "Hunger," or "Frame," this speaker is not in the position of a feminine, or even a revised white feminist, gaze. Rather, a figure for the female poet herself, the speaker is a translating medium (for example, of the lines, "A woman in the shape of a monster / a monster in the shape of a woman," with which the poem opens):

> I am an instrument in the shape
> of a woman trying to translate pulsations
> into images   for the relief of the body
> and the reconstruction of the mind.
>
> (*FD*, 116)

Bombarded by such signs as *women are monsters are women* from the symbolic cosmos, in Rich's reorientation of the Emersonian eye / I, this poetic subject-in-process is in a position to transform the seeing of others, in all senses of the phrase.

Rich's changed (and changing) subject translates, I suggest, into a reader whose mind has been changed. It is to her the "double visions" of, or equivocations among, (dis)identification with maternal / feminine dominant conventions, epistemological and ontological (re)construction, and (de)structuring of privilege that Rich's texts enact transfer. "I do believe that words *can* help us move," she punningly continues in "Feminist Criticism" (*BBP*, 90; emphasis in original)–that is, to activism. But what "*is political activism, anyway?*" she emphatically states that she has been asking herself. The answer she poses not only evinces hope, or faith, as she revises herself,[61] but equivocates: "It's something both prepared for and spontaneous–like making poetry."[62] The analogy, pivoting on the crucial "like," establishes similarity but also sustains the difference between the two activities. Rich stakes her performative claim to poetry's activism on its capacity to *move* readers: not only preparing them for, but catalyzing them to, change both an inequitable social order and themselves in relation to it, as the lines from Lorde's poem, "Stations," that opened the previous section convey.[63] Just as, through the poet's identification with "others like and unlike herself," act leads to word, so, for the exchange between text and reader to be not only mutual but productive of realizable impact, word must inspire deed. After words, that is, action.

The speaker of the Whitmanian address to the reader that concludes the title series of *An Atlas of the Difficult World* apostrophizes, among other things, that

> you are reading this poem listening for something, torn
> between bitterness and hope
> turning back once again to the task you cannot refuse.
>
> (*ADW*, 26)

Such an imaginary interaction between reader and poetic text generates a potential for "revolutionary" action, or magical transformation, as Rich implies in "Women and Honor": "The possibilities that exist between two people, or among a group of people, are a kind of alchemy" (*LSS,* 193). Alchemy, as we know, changes a baser metal into a valuable one.[64] According to Rich, this metaphorical (ex)change is creative: "Truthfulness, honor, is not something which springs ablaze of itself; it has to be created between people" (*LSS,* 193). The alchemy between Rich's reader and text creates what was not there before: the "gold" of feminist honor, women's truths.

Although Rich's "double vision" continues to move me personally, I sometimes think (as another white feminist activist-poet as well as academic) that it is too late in the century, in the progress of capitalism, for revolutions of consciousness or dominant systems. As Rich comments:

> When we do and think and feel certain things privately and in secret, even when thousands of people are doing, thinking, whispering these things privately and in secret, there is still no general, collective understanding from which to move.[65]

What can poetry do anyway? I've been asking myself throughout the writing of this book. Like most American poets writing today, Rich writes fully aware of poetry's status as specialized speech to many audiences—at best, exotic; at worst, incomprehensible. Yet her individual career attests to poetry's odd and enduring power to create something out of nothing—mere words, sparingly used, that move us. Rich suggests that the igniting efficacy of "so-called political poems" comes from the powerful, alchemical connections they build out of a "listen[ing] back and forth" between text and world. She poetically continues:

> But these thoughts and feelings, suppressed and stored up and whispered, have an incendiary component. You cannot tell where or how they will connect, spreading underground from rootlet to rootlet till every grassblade is afire from every other. This is that "spontaneity" which party "leaders," secret governments, and closed systems dread. Poetry, in its own way, is a carrier of the sparks, because it too comes out of silence, seeking connections with unseen others.[66]

An ethical, feminist poetic practice seeks to establish "connections with unseen others" so that eventually the unseen will be seen. To render the invisible visible in turn opens readers' eyes, especially, in Rich's case, the eyes of white, middle-class, heterosexuals/feminists, to the enculturated blind spots of privilege. Rich's additions to the visible world have surely caused much shuffling around of feet still in step with dominant conventions, poetic and otherwise.

But on a humbler note, Rich casts her "lot" with those who would "reconstitute the world" (*FD,* 264). Among them are the "scheming women" of this study. Others are the fellow Amazons Rich honors in "The Hermit's Scream": Barbara Deming, Alva Myrdal, the Swedish pacifist, and the late Lorde (1934–92). The example of connections that Rich and Lorde sought as poets and radical visionaries to build between them of powerful public and personal opening and dialogue provides a paradigm for the reformulation of relations between races, sexes, classes, identities. One is neither benefited nor empowered by the other's disenfranchisement. Empowerment evolves through exchange based on listening to, not talking at—a disengagement from the structures of dominance. Listening is not passive but actively builds bridges between subjects positioned by, as well as shifting between, internal and external differences (whether we define them as natural or contructed, whether established through processes of inclusion/exclusion or identification/abjection). In respect to and of each other, these poets inscribe visions that amplify, extend, double each other in a practice of revolutionary poetic and political commitment to changing the system. In Lorde's harrowing and exhilarating words:

> Once you live any piece of your vision it opens you to a constant onslaught. Of necessities, of horrors, but of wonders too. . . . Of wonders, absolute wonders, possibilities, like meteor showers all the time, bombardment, constant connections.[67]

Notes

PREFACE

1. In conceptualizing, writing, and completing this study, I have benefited from a number of foundational feminist critics and more recent theorists of women's poetry, whose work has variously influenced and inspired me. Among them are Joanne Feit Diehl, *Women Poets and the American Sublime;* Rachel Blau DuPlessis, *The Pink Guitar;* Sandra Gilbert and Susan Gubar, *The Madwoman in the Attic;* Gilbert and Gubar, eds., *Shakespeare's Sisters;* Margaret Homans, *Women Writers and Poetic Identity;* Suzanne Juhasz, *Naked and Fiery Forms;* Jan Montefiore, *Feminism and Poetry;* Alicia Ostriker, *Stealing the Language.*

2. For a compelling argument that the male modernists confused subjectivity with subjectivism, see Andrew Ross, *The Failure of Modernism,* 209–20.

3. For a feminist discussion of modern and postmodern poetic subjectivity, see Joan Retallack, "Post-Scriptum-High-Modern."

4. For an argument that Dickinson, for example, was a "willful" woman poet of her class, see Martha Nell Smith's superb *Rowing in Eden,* 13. The point here is that although these poets all experienced gender bias, they have in common a poetic and intellectual confidence stemming in part from the class-specific advantages to which they had access.

5. Jonathan Culler, *The Pursuit of Signs,* 143.

6. For historically nuanced work on American women's poetic tradition, see especially Betsy Erkkila's excellent study, *The Wicked Sisters,*

Cheryl Walker, *The Nightingale's Burden*, and Emily Stipes Watts, *The Poetry of American Women*.

7. On the paradox of women = woman = mother, see Teresa de Lauretis, *Technologies of Gender*, 20; and Mary Jacobus, *Reading Woman*, 138.

8. Darlene Clark Hines, "Rape and the Inner Lives of Black Women in the Middle West"; Gloria Anzaldúa, *Borderlands: La Frontera*. For a cogent contribution to theorizing the destructuring of white privilege, see Marilyn Frye, "White Woman Feminist."

9. Aída Hurtado, "Relating to Privilege." The limitation of this excellent theoretical article is that it is inattentive to class differences among women of color as well as among white women.

10. For an account of how Rich's early poetry won high praise from male critics for its modesty as well as craft, see Wendy Martin, *An American Triptych*, 173–75.

CHAPTER 1. CONCEIVING A GIRL
INTRODUCTION TO A FEMALE POETIC SUBJECTIVITY

1. On the child's primordial demand for a presence that turns the absent mother into a signifying form, see Lacan, *Écrits*, 286. On the analogous linguistic effect in poetry, see Barbara Johnson, *A World of Difference*, 199.

2. This intolerance is also the problem with Lacan's point about femininity defined solely in relation to the male term, that is, the masquerade of femininity. He asserts in "The Meaning of the Phallus" (*Feminine Sexuality*, 84) that "it is in order to be the phallus, . . . the signifier of the desire of the Other, that the woman will reject an essential part of her femininity, notably all its attributes through masquerade. It is for what she is not that she expects to be desired as well as loved." But as Stephen Heath points out, Lacan and the theorist he follows, Joan Riviere, mistake sexual politics for a psychology of gender, an error that becomes the foundation for Lacan's influential misreading of gender. See Joan Riviere, "Womanliness As a Masquerade"; and Heath, "Joan Riviere and the Masquerade."

3. Irigaray, *Speculum of the Other Woman*, 165.

4. On H.D.'s refusal to represent the familiar trajectory of violence in her figuration of Leda, an image that functioned in her work, in contrast to its function as symbol of inspiration for the male modernists, as "anti-inspiration," see Helen Sword, "Leda and the Modernists." For critiques of masculinist criticism for reproducing the slippage from sexual domina-

tion to the production of poetry, see Nancy K. Miller, "Arachnologies"; and Patricia Klindienst Joplin, "Epilogue."

5. See Johnson, *A World of Difference*, 184; de Lauretis, *Technologies of Gender*, 31–50; and Helena Michie, *The Flesh Made Word*, 88, 159 n. 13. I treat this point at more length in chapter 4.

6. Vickers, "Diana Described," 95–96, 98–99.

7. For an analysis of Ovid's tale of Philomela as one of gender violence that catalyzes a feminist poetics, see Joplin, "The Voice of the Shuttle Is Ours."

8. Ovid, *The Metamorphoses*, p. 51.

9. Ibid.

10. Lacan "God and the Jouissance of the Woman," in *Feminine Sexuality*, 141.

11. Vickers, "Diana Described," 102, 105–6.

12. Homans, *Women Writers and Poetic Identity*, 12. For a discussion of Romantic poetic subjectivity as an intertextual construction that subverts unifying gestures, see Tilottama Rajan, "Romanticism and the Death of Lyric Consciousness." For a study of emerging gay subjectivity in Victorian poetry, see Richard Dellamora, *Masculine Desire*.

13. Diehl, *Women Poets and the American Sublime*, 5.

14. Nyquist is writing about Wallace Stevens and the tradition of poetic muse he inherits. See her insightful discussion, "Musing on Susanna's Music"; see also Patricia Parker's introduction to *Lyric Poetry*, 26.

15. Fineman, "Shakespeare's Sonnets' Perjured Eye," 126.

16. See Lévi-Strauss, *Structural Anthropology*, 61; Lévi-Strauss, *The Elementary Structures of Kinship*, 495–97. For other feminist critiques of Lévi-Strauss, see especially Gayle Rubin, "The Traffic in Women"; and de Lauretis, *Technologies of Gender*, 44–47. For an important theorization of differing relations to power and discourse among men, which builds on Rubin's work, see Eve Kosofsky Sedgwick, *Between Men*.

17. De Lauretis, *Alice Doesn't*, 160–61.

18. Irigaray, *This Sex Which Is Not One*, 31–32.

19. David Perkins, ed., *English Romantic Writers*, 1037.

20. Culler, *The Pursuit of Signs*, 143.

21. For an analysis of Whitman's employment of the feminine figure to reaffirm his own poetic priority, one that also makes the link in this poem between sexuality and textuality, see Diehl, *Women Poets and the American Sublime*, 1–25.

22. Alexander W. Allison et al., *The Norton Anthology of Poetry*, 770–74.

23. On the constative and performative aspects of language, see J.

L. Austin, *How to Do Things with Words,* 1–66; on those aspects specifically examined in terms of lyric poetry, see especially J. Hillis Miller, *The Linguistic Moment;* and Paul de Man, "Anthropomorphism and Trope in the Lyric." On the alternating expansive and anxious performative claims to full and timeless poetic presence of an embodied voice in Whitman, see Tenney Nathanson's *Whitman's Presence,* 85–161.

24. On the generic process of substitution whereby the more durable poem comes to replace the mortal beloved, see Sharon Cameron, *Lyric Time.*

25. Jardine, *Gynesis,* 25, 161, 102.

26. Rukeyser, *Breaking Open,* 20.

27. Owens, "The Discourse of Others: Feminists and Postmodernism," 71; Owens's emphasis.

28. Yeats, *Collected Poems,* 89.

29. Friedman, *Psyche Reborn,* 233–35.

30. De Lauretis, "Eccentric Subjects," 119, 128. De Lauretis is influenced by MacKinnon's "Feminism, Marxism, Method, and the State," 26 n. 59; MacKinnon herself builds on John Berger's *Ways of Seeing,* and Berger on Simone de Beauvoir's *The Second Sex.* Beauvoir notes critically (*pace* Freud) that a woman becomes a woman by turning herself into an erotic object for men (301).

31. De Lauretis, "Eccentric Subjects," 115.

32. De Lauretis, *Alice Doesn't,* 186.

33. De Lauretis, *Technologies of Gender,* 25.

34. For a redefinition of the Western concept of mimesis, whereby through "playful repetition" a woman both makes visible "the place of her exploitation" in dominant representation and exceeds that framework, which might aptly characterize Barrett Browning's technique in this poem, see Irigaray, *This Sex,* 76.

35. Allison et al., *Norton Anthology of Poetry,* 675–76.

36. For a compelling Lacanian analysis that also reads this poem as reworking primal castration fantasies as they pertain to the construction of gender identity, see John Fletcher, "Poetry, Gender and Primal Fantasy," 126–33.

37. For a discussion of the Victorian poetic ideals on which was based the belief that women are more "naturally" adapted to being poets than men are, see Joyce Zonana, "The Embodied Muse." For the Victorians, Zonana recounts, "It is not so much 'unfeminine' to be a poet as 'unmasculine'" (249).

38. Barrett Browning's depiction of the reed pipe startlingly illustrates Irigaray's notion of woman's uncanniness for the male subject: a

woman's "entry into a dominant scopic economy signifies, again, her consignment to passivity: she is to be the beautiful object of contemplation [the implicit aggression of the gaze that the mutilation in Barrett Browning's poem literalizes]. While her body finds itself thus eroticized, and called to a double movement of exhibition and of chaste retreat . . . , her sexual organ represents *the horror of nothing to see*" (*This Sex*, 26; Irigaray's emphasis).

39. On women's bisexual mobility as an uncomfortable defining feature for Freud, see Sarah Kofman, *The Enigma of Woman*, 223. I explore the implications of this notion more fully in chapter 4; here I wish to demonstrate how Barrett Browning problematizes the "universal voice."

40. Fletcher, "Poetry, Gender and Primal Fantasy," 133.

41. Browning, *Letters*, 1:231–32; I quote the passage as it appears in Helen Cooper, "Working into Light," 65; Cooper's ellipses. On Barrett Browning's feminist revisions of canonical conventions, see Cooper, *Elizabeth Barrett Browning*; Sandra M. Gilbert, "From *Patria* to *Matria*." On her influence on Dickinson, see Mary Loeffelholz, *Dickinson and the Boundaries of Feminist Theory*, 67–76.

42. De Man, "Semiology and Rhetoric," 129–30.

43. Ibid., 140.

44. Johnson, *A World of Difference*, 40.

45. Jacobus, *Reading Woman*, 247.

46. For a discussion of Kristeva as "a paradox, an anomaly, or a 'man,'" see Kelly Oliver, *Reading Kristeva*, 107. For the final stages of this section and the next, I have benefited from Oliver's lucid and comprehensive study, whose understanding of Kristeva, close in spirit to my own, helped me to advance my argument (see especially pp. 163–81 of Oliver's book).

47. The question is Irigaray's, posed with reference to what she claims is the scientific definition of the female sex as determined by chromosomal anomaly (see Irigaray, *Speculum of the Other Woman*, 167). While her claim is scientifically erroneous (the male Y, not the female X, chromosome is anomalous), it is culturally accurate.

48. Kristeva, *Revolution in Poetic Language*, 143.

49. On the dynamic "transposition" of influence from the revolutionary text to the social and material context in Kristeva's version of reader-response theory, see Rajan, "Intertextuality," 66. See also Oliver, who explains that, for Kristeva, the textual subject-in-process with which the reader identifies puts the reader herself "in process": Kristeva's hope was that "this revolutionary subject could subvert capitalism" (Oliver, *Reading Kristeva*, 100).

50. Kristeva, *Revolution in Poetic Language*, 235 n. 8.

51. Ibid., 46–47.

52. On Kristeva's retheorization of the maternal and paternal functions, see Oliver, *Reading Kristeva*, 18–90. The evolution of Kristeva's thought tells the story of her challenge not only to the political ideology of the Left but to traditional psychoanalytic theory (both male-dominated). Her location of the subject's division earlier than the mirror stage, in a material negativity (drive rejection) regulated by the mother that prefigures rejection in the symbolic order, is an attempt, as Oliver elaborates, to expose the traditional emphasis on the paternal function as masculinist fantasy, and to theorize what the Law of the Father represses–both the maternal and its function.

53. Kristeva, *Revolution in Poetic Language*, 48–49.

54. Ibid., 48.

55. Oliver, *Reading Kristeva*, 149.

56. Rose, *Sexuality in the Field of Vision*, 146.

57. Kristeva, "Women's Time," 198.

58. Kristeva, *Revolution in Poetic Language*, 26, 27.

59. Ibid., 41.

60. Ibid., 147.

61. Ibid., 17; Kristeva's emphasis.

62. Ibid., 164.

63. Oliver, *Reading Kristeva*, 182.

64. Kristeva, *Revolution in Poetic Language*, 185.

65. Kristeva, "Women's Time," 210.

66. Rose, *Sexuality in the Field of Vision*, 146; Rose's emphasis. For a heated debate about Kristeva's usefulness to the study of poetry, see Toril Moi's indignant exchange with Calvin Bedient: Moi, "Reading Kristeva"; and Bedient, "How I Slugged It Out."

67. Kristeva, *Revolution in Poetic Language*, 79–80.

68. Ibid., 145–46.

69. Ibid., 187.

70. De Lauretis, "Feminism, Lesbianism." See also de Lauretis, "The Female Body."

71. On Kristeva's argument that the crisis in religious representations of the maternal leads to a misplaced "denigration of women" and antifeminism, see Oliver, *Reading Kristeva*, 161.

72. Kristeva, "Women's Time," 207.

73. Kristeva, "From One Identity to an Other," 146.

74. Kristeva, "Women's Time," 196; Kristeva's emphasis.

75. Ibid., 193; Kristeva's emphasis.

76. Kristeva, *Revolution in Poetic Language,* 233.
77. Ibid., 205.
78. Ibid., 195–96.
79. Oliver, *Reading Kristeva,* 101.
80. De Lauretis, *Alice Doesn't,* 165–67.
81. Ibid., 172. For this quotation and the discussion in this section, I am, of course, indebted to de Lauretis, and direct the reader to her chapter (ibid., 158–86). My purpose is not to replace her discussion, but to analyze how she makes use of Peirce's thinking. See also Peirce, *Collected Papers.*
82. De Lauretis, *Alice Doesn't,* 173–74.
83. Ibid., 178.
84. Ibid., 178–79; de Lauretis's emphasis.
85. Ibid., 159; de Lauretis's emphasis.
86. See de Lauretis, *Technologies of Gender,* 110–24.
87. Meese, *(Ex)tensions,* 171.
88. On women novelists (not poets) as being by definition hysterics because they at once accept the woman's world (by writing about it) and refuse it (by being novelists), see Lynda Zwinger, *Daughters, Fathers, and the Novel;* Juliet Mitchell, *Women: The Longest Revolution;* and Jacobus, *Reading Woman,* 197–274. Cf. Kofman, who observes the disturbing way Freud's female "criminals" are made over into "hysterics" (*Enigma of Woman,* 66–67), a makeover this project resists.
89. In "Linguistics and the Feminist Challenge," Sally McConnell-Ginet asserts that (white, middle-class) women have influenced "linguistic development through their ... preference for refined and (in certain spheres) veiled and indirect expression" (14).

CHAPTER 2. "I DID'NT BE—MYSELF"
EMILY DICKINSON'S SEMIOTICS OF PRESENCE

1. On Dickinson's language as peculiar but not "unique either in most of its particulars or in its designs," see Cristanne Miller, *Emily Dickinson,* 160.
2. Stonum, *The Dickinson Sublime,* 99–100.
3. Among the earlier feminist studies on Dickinson from which I have benefited over the years are Diehl, *Dickinson and the Romantic Imagination;* Jane Donahue Eberwein, *Dickinson's Strategies of Limitation;* Homans, "'Oh, Vision of Language!'"; Juhasz, *The Undiscovered Continent;* Juhasz, introduction to *Feminist Critics Read Emily Dickinson;* Vivian Pollak,

Dickinson. Among more-recent studies important to my work are Paula Bennett, *Emily Dickinson*; Margaret Dickie, *Lyric Contingencies;* and Joanna Dobson, *Dickinson and the Strategies of Reticence.*

4. Cristanne Miller, *Emily Dickinson,* 185.

5. Diehl, *Women Poets and the American Sublime,* 26.

6. Diehl, "In the Twilight of the Gods," 173–75.

7. Loeffelholz, *Dickinson,* 10; see also Erkkila's excellent "Emily Dickinson and Class."

8. Smith-Rosenberg, *Disorderly Conduct,* 42.

9. Ibid., 144–45. Smith-Rosenberg contends that upper- and middle-class Victorian girls were socialized into being timid, dependent, anxious, and sensitive to rejection (214).

10. See Dobson, *Strategies of Reticence,* 56.

11. Loeffelholz, 10.

12. Diehl, *Dickinson and the Romantic Imagination,* 183.

13. I build on, and depart from, both Diehl's and Stonum's important studies. Both scholars locate Dickinson within a poetics of difference/ deference and resistance: the countersublime. Following Harold Bloom's, *The Anxiety of Influence,* 99–112, Stonum cautions that *all* American poetry exemplifies the countersublime: repression of derivativeness is necessary to produce resolution in the sublime moment. See Stonum, *The Dickinson Sublime,* 110–87. Revising Bloom, Diehl defines a feminist countersublime that Dickinson, and eventually her "literary daughters," elaborated as challenging the masculinist American Sublime. See Diehl, *Women Poets and the American Sublime,* 1–43. See also Thomas Weiskel's pioneering *The Romantic Sublime;* and Neil Hertz's extension of Weiskel's work, *The End of the Line.*

14. On this point, see Cameron, *Lyric Time,* 190.

15. Scholars generally, though cautiously, agree that Dickinson's dictionary was the 1844 issue of the 1841 edition of Noah Webster's *An American Dictionary of the English Language,* published by J. S. Adams and C. Adams in Amherst, which this study uses. On Dickinson's creative use of etymological nuances in her poems, see Richard Benvenuto, "Words within Words." On the notion of *caprice,* cf. Susan Hardy Aiken, *Isak Dinesen,* 23–25.

16. Dobson, *Strategies of Reticence,* 56–57.

17. See Bennett, who argues convincingly that, because nineteenth-century women poets' cliterocentric flower imagery is incomprehensible to men, its implications have been ignored (Bennett, *Emily Dickinson,* 1–23, 150–80); and Smith, who makes a fascinating case based on the Dickinson manuscripts that she was angered by the conventionalizing of her printed

poems' punctuation and grammar, and therefore "published" herself alternatively, in letters (Smith, *Rowing in Eden,* 11–50).

18. Smith, ibid., 125. See also Gilbert and Gubar, *Madwoman in the Attic;* Homans, *Women Writers and Poetic Identity,* 166–73; and Ostriker, *Stealing the Language,* 38–43.

19. Kofman, *The Enigma of Woman,* 145–46.

20. For a different employment of the Freudian paradigm to read Dickinson, see Loeffelholz, *Dickinson,* 24. For a study that takes issue with both object-relations psychoanalytic and Anglo-American feminist theoretical approaches to Dickinson's poetic "I," see Dickie, *Lyric Contingencies,* 16–17.

21. Dickinson's behavior, as Dobson observes in *Strategies of Reticence,* "appears . . . strongly acquiescent to cultural demands"; her poetry, on the other hand, does not (46–47). For additional work on Dickinson's poetic subjectivity as particularized and contingent, see Dickie, "Reperiodization"; on her poetic and epistolary "I" as literary and "carefully constructed," see Smith, *Rowing in Eden,* 112, 124.

22. La Place, "Producing and Consuming Woman's Film," 152.

23. On nineteenth-century women's fiction that evinces a pragmatic feminism valorizing a bourgeois image of the self-made *woman* instead of man, see Nina Baym, *Woman's Fiction,* 3. For studies that situate Dickinson in relation to the literary conventions and the cultural context in which she worked, see Barton Levi St. Armand, *Emily Dickinson;* and Dickinson's most recent biographer, Cynthia Griffin Wolff, *Emily Dickinson.*

24. For the argument that "seeing" was a form of power for Dickinson, see Wolff, *Emily Dickinson,* 53–57, 226–27. I think that the link between seeing and power is more complicated than Wolff acknowledges, but her insightful biography was helpful in formulating my ideas. See also Dobson, who remarks that the sensational press of Dickinson's day, which she did not read but would have known about in general, routinely published works that objectified women, and that these lurid images were clearly male fantasies *about* women (Dobson, *Strategies of Reticence,* 61, 144–45 n. 1).

25. Mulvey, "Visual Pleasure and Narrative Cinema," 19. On the "gaze" as constitutive of castration, see Jacques Lacan, *Four Fundamental Concepts of Psycho-analysis,* 103; on woman's castration, see Irigaray, *Speculum of the Other Woman,* 47–48. My point in this section is that Dickinson's and Higginson's epistolary exchanges, as well as the poetry that I shall presently discuss, unsettle the dynamics of the patriarchal (castrating) gaze. On the relevance of feminist film criticism to a reading of Dickinson's culture, see Loeffelholz, *Dickinson,* 50.

26. On the "Master" figure in Dickinson's poems and letters as largely symbolic—"insubstantial," Smith notes—see Smith, *Rowing in Eden,* 17–18. For a Hegelian discussion of mastery in Dickinson's work, see Stonum, *The Dickinson Sublime,* 149–87.

27. For a different reading of how Dickinson represents herself as both powerful and powerless in her letters, see S. Jaret McKinstry, "'How Lovely Are the Wiles of Words!'"

28. Hertz, *The End of the Line,* 40–41. See also Weiskel, *The Romantic Sublime,* 28–29.

29. Hertz, *The End of the Line,* 60, 214.

30. Larsen, "Text and Matrix," 253.

31. See Wolff, *Emily Dickinson,* 141–43, who suggests that Dickinson was alluding to Emerson's famous assertion that "The poet is representative" in his essay "The Poet." Cf. Loeffelholz, who contends that Dickinson calls into question Emerson's figuration of the American primal scene (*Dickinson,* 7–39); and Dickie, who argues that lyric identity in Dickinson's work asserts a "powerful indictment of [Emerson's] confidence in the discrete subject of the *Cogito*" (*Lyric Contingencies,* 16–18).

32. For an extensive technical discussion of this method in Dickinson's work, see Miller, *Emily Dickinson,* 30–37.

33. On Dickinson's preference for metonymy and indirection over metaphor, see Roland Hagenbüchle, "Precision and Indeterminacy"; taking issue with Hagenbüchle, Dickie views "Dickinson's use of metonymy as an effort to retain a hold on this world" (*Lyric Contingencies,* 180 n. 7); on metonymy as a dominant trope in women's poetry as well as in Dickinson's specifically, see Cristanne Miller, *Emily Dickinson,* 111.

34. Miller observes that this "hole of meaning which, filled, would explain the relation of one event or proposition to the next" is typically left unfilled in Dickinson's work (Cristanne Miller, *Emily Dickinson,* 32). On Dickinson's development of this strategy, arguably in reaction to the expressive restrictions on women writers in her day, see Dobson, *Strategies of Reticence,* 123.

35. For an analysis of Dickinson's use of etymological connotations in this poem, see Benvenuto, "Words within Words," 52–53. This section owes much to his excellent article.

36. Barbara Antonina Clarke Mossberg, *Emily Dickinson,* 12. See also Erkkila, *The Wicked Sisters,* 45.

37. Miller, *Emily Dickinson,* 166, 167.

38. On Edward Dickinson's at-times contradictory attitude toward his children's reading, see Jack L. Capps, *Emily Dickinson's Reading,* 11–16; and Dickie, *Lyric Contingencies,* 60, 181 n. 10.

39. On the quest for the identity of Dickinson's lover, see Smith, *Rowing in Eden,* who reviews, not without irony, the preoccupation in Dickinson scholarship with the three "Master" letters and the scarce attention given to "thirty years worth of prose, poems, and poems woven into prose" sent to "the housewife next door," Dickinson's sister-in-law, Sue (99). See also Susan Howe's astute discussion of the "Master" as an intertextual construction, in *My Emily Dickinson,* 24–27. Cf. William H. Shurr, *The Marriage of Emily Dickinson.* My reading focuses on the (trope of) heterosexual structure of these letters, as representative of larger cultural forces to which Dickinson's work variously responds, rather than on the Master's identity. My examination of this dominant structure that bears on all subjects thus does not preclude the possibility of Dickinson's lesbianism. See Rebecca Patterson's *The Riddle of Emily Dickinson;* Lillian Faderman's "Emily Dickinson's Homoerotic Poetry"; and Smith, *Rowing in Eden,* 97–154.

40. Since the pattern the Master letters seem to follow resembles Irigaray's characterization of the girl's denarcissization in the feminine version of oedipal transition, a characterization that has generated the implications on which I build my reading, it might be useful to review her point briefly. Observing that the Oedipus complex functions for the boy as "narcissistic protection," Irigaray asserts that, for the girl, the castration complex is not protection but subjection to "the harsh reality of a sexual 'mutilation,'" a wound to her narcissism that leaves the woman with a "scar" (*Speculum of the Other Woman,* 87). Cf. Freud, "Some Psychical Consequences," 253.

41. For very different readings of the Daisy figure as a subversive, and thereby empowered, position, see Homans, "'Syllables of Velvet'"; and McKinstry, "'How Lovely Are the Wiles of Words!'", 203–5.

42. Kristeva, *Powers of Horror,* 11, 12.

43. Hertz, *The End of the Line,* 223, 53. Because I am concerned with the gender dynamics that Hertz has uncovered, and because the enormous amount of work on the sublime in the last decade precludes thorough citation, I sketch the sublime scenario only briefly here. Weiskel delineates three phases that structure the literature of the sublime: (1) the normative phase, before alterity has been perceived; (2) the traumatic phase, when the object of perception is apprehended as other; and (3) the reactive phase, when sublimation takes place, and the subject experiences empowerment and release. See also Mary Arensberg's introduction to *The American Sublime,* especially pp. 2–3; and Longinus, *Longinus on the Sublime.*

44. Hertz, *The End of the Line,* 222–23. Hertz has borrowed the notion of end-of-the-line textual moments, or "nonreflective opacity,"

from Kenneth Burke's "On Methodology." On autobiographical moments of such "unreadable" opacity, see de Man (who also influenced Hertz), "Autobiography As De-facement." Hertz is fascinated not only by "the specularity of reading" that absorbed de Man's attention, but by the violence that accompanies the operation.

45. Weiskel, *The Romantic Sublime*, 105.

46. Ibid., 105.

47. Hertz, *The End of the Line*, 230.

48. Kristeva, *Powers of Horror*, 13, 15; Kristeva's emphasis.

49. Kristeva, "L'Abjet d'amour," *Tel Quel* 91 (1982): 20; quoted in Hertz, *The End of the Line*, 231–32.

50. Hertz, *The End of the Line*, 233, 214.

51. If we take Freud at his word, Irigaray points out, the girl will "have very little narcissistic ego for sublimation." See *Speculum of the Other Woman*, 87.

52. Hertz, *The End of the Line*, 233.

53. Doane, *The Desire to Desire*, 19.

54. Kahane, "The Gothic Mirror," 347.

55. Gallop, *The Daughter's Seduction*, 27. As Gallop recounts, the nauseating immediacy of femininity, which the "odor di femina" epitomizes, puts at risk the achievements of repression and sublimation, threatening to return the subject to the powerlessness of its primal connection to the mother's body. While I think the smelly dynamics in Poem 675 are analogous, the elevation in Dickinson's poem from odor to sublime perfume renders the notion of women's anxiety at the very least complex.

56. For important interpretations of this poem as metapoetic, see Charles R. Anderson, *Emily Dickinson's Poetry*, 64; Cameron, *Lyric Time*, 195; and Miller, *Emily Dickinson*, 2–5, 27–28.

57. Cristanne Miller, *Emily Dickinson*, 4, 189 n. 3.

58. Both Madonna and Magdalene, Mary "operates as a subversive image of discontinuity and covert female power," as Aiken observes in "Dinesen's 'Sorrow-Acre,'" 182. For a discussion of Mary's subversion of the patriarchal Judeo-Christian tradition, see Marina Warner, *Alone of All Her Sex*. For an analysis of Dickinson's inscription of herself as a subversive Eve figure, see Homans, *Women Writers and Poetic Identity*, 166–74. My point is that, like the figures to which her name alludes, Dickinson's "Rose-Mary" subverts at all levels the attempts to put her safely away in poem or pall, to sanitize or to suppress her.

59. Kristeva, "Motherhood According to Giovanni Bellini," 238–40.

60. Stonum, *The Dickinson Sublime*, 185.

61. Cristanne Miller, *Emily Dickinson*, 44.

62. On Dickinson's use of economic metaphors to put into discourse a desiring female subject that protests restrictions on women's sexuality, see Joan Burbick, "Economics of Desire."

63. On Dickinson's notion of renunciation, see Mossberg, who contends that "according to Dickinson's aesthetics, she must retain her virginity and obscurity or she will lose her 'gifts,'" (Mossberg, *Emily Dickinson*, 182); and Juhasz, who argues that in response to the constrictions of her life, Dickinson's "successful version" of the virtue of renunciation became a form of "'slant' revolution" (Juhasz, *The Undiscovered Continent*, 174–75).

64. On the affinity of Dickinson's sense of words with Shelley's notion of poems as "seeds," see Dickinson's earlier biographer, Richard Sewall, *The Life of Emily Dickinson*, 676. For a discussion that proposes a dialogical, reader-response model, specifically for feminist readings of women's writing, see Patrocinio P. Schweickart, "Reading Ourselves."

65. Although I here locate Dickinson's ethical discursivity in her own work, anticipatory of Kristevan herethics, also worth noting are influential studies of "feminine" ethics: Carol Gilligan, *In a Different Voice*; and Nancy Chodorow, *The Reproduction of Mothering*.

66. I take the notion of "dowering"–giving without conditions (following Cixous, the gift that gives, not takes)–from Dickinson herself, whose use of the word and variations on it (*munificence, endowment*) figures conceptually in this last section. In a letter to longtime family friend, Mrs. Holland, for example, Dickinson writes, "To live is Endowment" (*L* 399). In one of the definitions offered by her dictionary, *endowment* means "gift of nature," and as Dickinson would have known, its Latin root, like that of *munificence*, means "gift."

67. Gilbert and Gubar use this poem as one of the epigraphs for chapter 2 of *Madwoman in the Attic*. Although my reading of the anxiety evident in the poem differs from their approach, their discussion of the "socially conditioned epidemic of female illness" in the nineteenth century is of interest (45–92). On Dickinson's reader-oriented poetics, see Dickie, who analyzes Poem 1261 as a "powerful indictment of the organic theory of art that informed the work of the male Transcendentalists" ("Reperiodization," 405–6).

68. Dickie, "Reperiodization," 405.

69. Wolff, *Emily Dickinson*, 46.

70. Hertz, *The End of the Line*, 47.

71. Although I take some poetic license with the notion of witchcraft in the pages that follow, most Dickinson scholars give scant consideration to it because there are scant references to witchcraft in Dickinson's oeuvre.

Dickie glosses Poem 593's use of the term as a metaphor for books and the potentially subversive activity, for a woman, of reading itself (*Lyric Contingencies*, 60). Even Erkkila's *The Wicked Sisters*, which plays on the common etymology of *witch* and *wicked*, pays more attention to the sororal than to the wiccan figure as trope for women's poetic tradition (see pp. 4–5, 17–54). Cf. Gilbert's introduction to Cixous and Clément's *The Newly Born Woman* for a discussion of the figure of witch in Dickinson as an exemplary trope for "the woman artist" (xii). But Gilbert slips from *witchcraft*, which does figure in Dickinson's canon, to *witch*, which does not. See Poems 1583 and 1708, and my discussion below, for occurrences of this very overdetermined term. For an analysis of the witch (and the hysteric) as a *conservative* as well as antiestablishment feminine role, see Cixous and Clément, *The Newly Born Woman*, 3–39.

72. Diehl argues of this poem that in "the redemptive possibilities of a woman-to-woman encounter, we discover the seeds of . . . an alternative poetic tradition" (*Women Poets and the American Sublime*, 28–29). For another approach to this poem, Barrett Browning's influence on Dickinson, and women's poetic "witchcraft," see Erkkila, *The Wicked Sisters*, 68–79.

73. Although it is beyond the theoretical scope of this chapter, a fruitful direction to pursue along these lines is provided by Jessica Benjamin, "A Desire of One's Own." Reworking object-relations psychoanalytic theory, Benjamin asserts that female desire can be understood through the notion of an "intersubjective reality, where subject meets subject," each able to be both with and distinct from the other (98). See also her chapter on women's desire in her *The Bonds of Love*, 85–132.

CHAPTER 3. LESS IS MOORE
MARIANNE MOORE'S POETIC SUBJECT

1. As Smith-Rosenberg tells us, a commitment to social service characterizes the first generation of New Women (*Disorderly Conduct*, 176–77). But in addition, Mary Warner Moore, daughter of a Presbyterian minister, also impressed on her children the importance of a Christian life of service. Erkkila argues that, influenced by her pious mother and minister brother, Moore sought to transform the dominant values of the American marketplace with a combination of traditionally feminine and Christian virtues (*The Wicked Sisters*, 102–4).

2. Included among the Moore scholars who have begun to consider gender in the past decade are Charles Altieri ("The Powers of Genuine Place"), who argues that Moore's poems resist gender identification and

self-reflexivity, a traditional masculine construct; Marilyn L. Brownstein ("The Archaic Mother"), who contrasts Moore's "poetics of *jouissance*" with Williams's poetry of oedipal resolution; Bonnie Costello, who has done pioneering work ("The 'Feminine' Language of Marianne Moore") on the language of values and qualities in Moore's work traditionally coded as "feminine"; Carolyn Durham ("Linguistic and Sexual Engendering"); and Leigh Gilmore ("The Gaze of the Other Woman"). See also essays collected in the Moore centennial anthology, Patricia C. Willis, ed., *Marianne Moore.*

3. DuPlessis, "No Moore of the Same," 7–8.

4. For an analysis of the poetic subject in Mina Loy, Moore, and Laura Riding as a shifting discursive position representative of the complex ethics and aesthetics of female modernism, see Carolyn Burke, "Getting Spliced."

5. On Moore's early concern with originality and poetry as a form of self-definition autonomous from the influence of other writers, see John M. Slatin, *The Savage's Romance,* 59–98. As illuminating as Stonum on Dickinson, Slatin falls similarly short in his failure to consider how gender inflects her poetics. For a compelling essay on influence and intertextuality that takes up where Slatin left off, see Lynn Keller, "'For inferior who is free?'"

6. Costello, *Marianne Moore,* 185. See also Slatin, who speculates that Moore's move to free verse during the *Dial* years in the 1920s was an attempt at more-direct treatment (*The Savage's Romance,* 7–8); and the excellent first full-length consideration of gender in Moore's poetry, *Omissions Are Not Accidents,* by Jeanne Heuving, who asserts that Moore's "position in the culture as a woman leads her to write an indirect, complex poetry" (87). The move to free verse interestingly coincides with a period in which Moore most directly treated gender issues.

7. Moore's biographer, Charles Molesworth, *Marianne Moore,* recounts—but does not take into account—Moore's youthful activities as a suffragette and her admiration for the feminist president of Bryn Mawr, M. Carey Thomas, during Moore's college years. Moore's mother left her untenable marriage and raised her children alone, providing a model for her children of maternal strength and female independence. Like her mother, Moore was a suffragette and, as Laurence Stapleton puts it in his *Marianne Moore,* a "confirmed feminist" (38, 4). In addition to Heuving, scholarship that takes Moore's feminism into its account of her poetics includes DuPlessis, "No Moore of the Same," especially 29 n. 28; Erkkila, *The Wicked Sisters,* 99–151; Keller, "'For inferior who is free?'" ; and Sabine Sielke, "Snapshots of Marriage."

8. Moore's unpublished prose and reading notebooks indicate her awareness of what this figure represented in popular culture. A fragment entitled "Girl of Today," written around 1920, for example, strategically negotiates a response to men's dismay with "the independent woman" (*RML*, 2:02:19); about that time Moore also records a passage from a Mary Austin book review, in which Austin protested that the author under review had "not a single example of a modern woman in any" of his books (*RML*, 7:01:04).

9. As Costello puts it, "Moore typically stands on both sides" (Costello, *Marianne Moore*, 44).

10. Burke, "Supposed Persons," 132; "Getting Spliced," 100.

11. DuPlessis, "No Moore of the Same," 6.

12. Ibid.

13. Costello, *Marianne Moore*, 246. Molesworth (*Marianne Moore*, 310) tells us that in the early 1940s Warner had written his sister that George Washington epitomized for him the sense of civic responsibility, which Molesworth suggests Moore transposed to her vocation as a writer. He does not speculate about the connection between this exchange and the final form of Moore's costume, or the (perhaps inexplicable) fact that it followed so soon after her mother's death. (Since her undergraduate days, Moore had worn a black broadcloth cape, to which she later added the broad-brimmed black straw hat that preceded the tricorne, as her niece, Marianne Craig Moore, reminds me in a note dated 17 July 1994.)

14. Photograph by Esther Bubley, reproduced in *Marianne Moore Newsletter* 3 (Fall 1979): 20.

15. Slatin, *The Savage's Romance*, 16.

16. Ibid., 17. For a summary of the critical debate about when Moore did her best work, see Slatin, ibid., 260 n. 28. For the argument that Moore's constant revision makes it impossible to chart the development of her style or keep its periods quite discrete, see Taffy Martin, *Marianne Moore, Subversive Modernist*, xii. I follow Martin in discussing early poetry (but final versions) in light of later comments and moving back and forth through Moore's career, acknowledging that Moore's revision process was indeed complex, ongoing, and *controversial.* It is not unpolemical of me to use the versions revised for the last time by this "kindly old lady."

17. Molesworth, *Marianne Moore*, 436.

18. Frank Parsons, *The Psychology of Dress*, xxii. Moore took copious notes on this book (*RML*, 7:01:03).

19. Parsons, *The Psychology of Dress*, 349.

20. Evelyn Feldman, research associate at the Rosenbach Museum and Library, commented in conversation with me on 20 May 1993 that

Moore was always interested in fashion and enjoyed the dressing up and posing her increasingly public persona entailed. The figure she struck, that is, was calculated; nor was she above an ironic, *conscious* self-parody.

21. Nancy K. Miller, "Changing the Subject," 116.

22. Gilbert, "Marianne Moore As Female Female Impersonator," 31.

23. Ibid., 42.

24. DuPlessis, "No Moore of the Same," 16.

25. Hugh Kenner observes, in *A Homemade World,* that Moore "democratizes 'tradition'" (11) in her poetry of found objects and words: "we are not *meant* to look up the sources" (102; emphasis added). But I concur with Keller ("'For inferior who is free?'"), who argues not only that the sources provide valuable information that allows the reader "to perceive a social context to which the poet is reacting" (229), but that, in response to Eliot's "Tradition and the Individual Talent," Moore "uses quotations and allusions to demonstrate her right [as a woman poet] to a place within the established [male] tradition" (225).

26. Keller, "'For inferior who is free?',"233.

27. Tracing the source of Moore's famous phrase in "An Octopus," *neatness of finish,* to a line ("Neatness and finish"), from William Carlos Williams's *Kora in Hell,* which Moore had reviewed for *Contact* in 1921, Stapleton remarks that it is characteristic of Moore to change quotations. See the "Replies" section of *The Marianne Moore Newsletter* 1, no. 2 (Fall 1977). As Slatin observes, *whenever* the issue of her methodology of quoting came up, Moore "became thoroughly evasive" (Slatin, *The Savage's Romance,* 2).

28. In "No Moore of the Same," DuPlessis describes Moore's textual strategies as "non-masculinist in being anti-authoritarian, and nonfeminine, in calling fixed surfaces of beauty into question" (11), postulating that Moore is "a self-declared 'foreigner' to codes of gender as she assumes a 'foreign' stance to codes of English prosody" (23). "Isn't this androgyny?" DuPlessis asks (11).

29. Costello, *Marianne Moore,* 181.

30. Slatin, *The Savage's Romance,* 89.

31. Ibid., 87; Slatin's emphasis.

32. Although Costello (*Marianne Moore,* 118–20) suggests that the poem alters conventional images of the maternal, she reads the mother figure as unproblematically analogous with poetry; Durham, too, reads the maternal figure as a trope for the female poet as "daring, clever, and mischievous" ("Linguistic and Sexual Engendering," 226); Ostriker notes that "the roles of creation and procreation are for [the mother figure] one" ("What Do Women [Poets] Want?" 5). For work that is more attentive to

the poem's tensions, see Sielke's Irigarayan reading of the remetaphorization of maternity in order to signify "an 'other' economy of desire, discourse, and voice" (Sielke, "Snapshots of Marriage," 93); Diehl's argument that this poem portrays the potentially adversarial relationship between mother and daughter (Diehl, *Women Poets and the American Sublime*, 87–88); and Ostriker's compelling defense of Moore's maternal hero from her critics, "The Maternal Hero."

33. The poem was written in the years just prior to the United States' entrance into World War II, but reflects, as Costello points out, Moore's support of international peace efforts through the adoption of the "feminine ideal" of compassion rather than force, about which she had written in a *Dial* "Comment" ten years earlier. See Costello, *Marianne Moore*, 119, 262 nn. 3,15.

34. See, of course, Adrienne Rich, "When We Dead Awaken," in *On Lies, Secrets, and Silence*, 33–50; Shoshona Felman, "Rereading Femininity"; and Jacobus, *Reading Woman.*

35. On the four types of female figures in Moore's poetry—the ornamental, the maternal, the tempermental, and the artistic—see Margaret Holley, "Portraits of Ladies."

36. Cristanne Miller, "Marianne Moore's Black Maternal Hero." Discussing Moore's poem "The Hero," Miller makes a compelling case for Moore's strategic use of (re)categorization to deconstruct stereotypes of "African Americans, of the maternal, and of emotionality (liking and love)" through redefining the hero (791).

37. Gilbert contends that Moore's unprecedented use of syllabics allowed her "to call attention to the arbitrariness of female poetic identity, as well as to the artifice of 'poetry' itself" (Gilbert, "Female Female Impersonator," 42).

38. For a feminist theorization of female characters and Bakhtinian dialogism in American novels, see Dale Bauer, "Gender in Bakhtin's Carnival."

39. Moore excluded this poem from the *Complete Poems.* All quotations are from the text printed in *Observations.* It is Slatin who suggests that the poem overturns the convention of courtly love that it invokes (*The Savage's Romance*, 61).

40. Taffy Martin, *Marianne Moore, Subversive Modernist,* 100.

41. Heuving, *Omissions Are Not Accidents,* 27; see also her fine discussion of Moore's validation of roses for their "'co-ordination'—their beauty *and* thorniness" (79; Heuving's emphasis).

42. Ibid., 80.

43. DuPlessis, "No Moore of the Same," 22.

44. The analogy might have personal implications as well for Moore, who identified herself as Irish. In response to a letter from Pound, who upon reading the early poem "Black Earth" curiously asked if she were "ethiopian," Moore described herself as "Irish by descent, possibly Schotch [*sic*] also, but purely Celtic" (9 January 1919, *RML*, 5:50:06); see also Cristanne Miller, "Marianne Moore's Black Maternal Hero," 811–12 n. 20.

45. As Taffy Martin (Marianne Moore, *Subversive Modernist*, 123) demonstrates, water is associated with the feminine in Moore's work. For a discussion that specifically images the construction of femininity as fluid, see Irigaray, *Speculum of the Other Woman*, 106–18; for a critique of Irigaray's stereotyping of femininity, see Doane, *The Desire to Desire*, 104.

46. On the rhetorical phenomenon of philosophers like Nietzsche and Derrida speaking from the position of woman (because it "cannot be claimed by women"), see de Lauretis, *Technologies of Gender*, 32.

47. For an alternative approach to Moore's use of repetition, as desire for the mother, cf. Brownstein, "The Archaic Mother," 27–28.

48. Diehl, *Women Poets and the American Sublime*, 47.

49. While I approach the issue of imitation from a very different orientation, I have benefited in the writing of this section from Slatin's thorough discussion of the Romantic influence on "Virginia Britannia" in *The Savage's Romance*, 205–52. See also Cristanne Miller, who confirms, in "Marianne Moore's Black Maternal Hero," 786, that Moore rejects racism in this poem. Miller uses the version in *Complete Poems*, observing that earlier versions limit the condemnation of appropriative economy to a few individuals: "Unlike Slatin, I find Moore's later version of this poem to be . . . a more politically astute . . . document. One must also remember that Moore writes this poem at the end of an age of appalling United States expansionism" (813 n. 29). For a discussion of this poem in the context of hegemonic American literary history, see Slatin, "Advancing Backward in a Circle."

50. J. Hillis Miller, *The Linguistic Moment*, xvi.

51. Rich defines the term as specific to the mother-daughter dynamic, which I address at more length in chapter 5 below; here I borrow the term to refer to a general cultural (male) fear of the maternal. Cf. Sielke, "Snapshots of Marriage," 91.

52. *RML*, 7:04:04. See Patricia Willis, "The Road to Paradise"; and Diehl, *Women Poets and the American Sublime*, 71–72, 177–78 n. 1.

53. See Diehl, who notes that in subsequent drafts of these poems Moore suppressed "the earlier individualized voice in favor of a universalizing 'one'" (*Women Poets and the American Sublime*, 60).

54. I take the notion of dissociation from Moore herself. The notes to "Marriage" and "An Octopus" contemplate the necessity of a dissociating/reassociating activity in order to reconceptualize marriage, the relations between the sexes, and women's equivocal relationship to that "archaic" institution:

> Never despair—too archaic for words
> There is this to be said about it
> the parts must be resolved and dissassociated
> Love, greed, pride, ferocity; sagacity, ~~lust~~, haste,
> cowardice and power
> and be reassorted The mind of man—
> is a problem
> the predatory imagination of these rustics
> this eagle with tigers in its eyes and feet
> these self intensifying pairs **A & Eve**
> must be disformed and reassociated
> pride greed doggedness—ferocity brute force
> skindeep humility gainful love—the getting power lavishness
> the mind of man—is a problem
>
>   (*RML*, 7:04:04)

55. For the argument that Moore's treatment of gender oppositions in the poem is a balanced and equitable one, see Costello, *Marianne Moore*, 176; and Taffy Martin, *Marianne Moore, Subversive Modernist*, 21. On the poem's structure of argumentation, see Lynn Keller and Cristanne Miller, "'The Tooth of Disputation.'" On its feminism, see David Bergman, "The Problem of 'Marriage'"; Keller, "'For inferior who is free?'," 219–39; and Heuving, *Omissions Are Not Accidents*, 123–33.

56. Diehl, *Women Poets and the American Sublime*, 67.

57. Keller and Miller, "'Tooth of Disputation,'" 114.

58. Burke, "Getting Spliced," 114–15. Burke's point is that Moore abjures "amalgamations and prizes the separate integrities" of component elements; on Moore's "chiasmic strategies," her "'genius for disunion' like that of Irish grandmothers in 'Spenser's [and her own] Ireland,'" see Costello, *Marianne Moore*, 160–66; on Webster's words as specious, see Pamela White Hadas, *Marianne Moore*, 175.

59. Sielke, "Snapshots of Marriage," 86.

60. The figure of Eve in this poem is literally transsexual. The lines, "I have seen her / when she was so handsome . . . ," read in the notebook, "I have seen him . . . " : Moore changed the sex of the observed person (*RML*, 7:04:04).

61. "Marriage" is an early example of something that becomes typical of Moore's work after 1930, as Holley recounts: that direct first-person pronouns are almost never used. Moore thereby represents "subjective self-expression as . . . an occurrence in the public world." See Holley, *The Poetry of Marianne Moore*, 81; and Miller, "Marianne Moore's Black Maternal Hero," 809 n. 5.

62. Interestingly, the initial speaker's self-inscription also corresponds to one alternative to hysteria in women posed in Freud's work—the female criminal, or narcissist—as discussed in Elizabeth Berg's Kofmanesque "The Third Woman." Sielke ("Snapshots of Marriage," 86) also notes the speaker's shifts, suggesting that Moore, anticipating Irigaray, playfully repeats and exposes "the conventional structures of poetic authority and voice as well as of marriage."

63. Keller and Miller ponder a repetition in Moore's poetry notebook that I also found curious: "on what appear to be the first twenty-nine pages of her working on this poem—pages which contain relatively few repeated long lines—Moore repeats eight times that 'men have power and sometimes one is made to feel it'" ("'Tooth of Disputation,'" 109; *RML*, 7:04:04). They suggest that the gendered knowledge of male violence against women is an erased subtext of the poem, of which the nightingale (Philomela), Hercules "in the garden of the Hesperides" (doing penance for having killed his wife and children), and Ahasueris (invoking Vashti as well as Esther) stand as synecdoches. On "Marriage" as a strategic debate with and alternative to Eliot's misogyny, see Keller, "'For inferior who is free?'," 236–39.

64. Although H.D. wrote Moore informatively about her sessions during the 1920s and early 1930s with Havelock Ellis and Freud, and Moore's comments on Freud and Jung in her working notes for "Idiosyncrasy and Technique" confirm that she had read into the field of psychology (*RML*, 2:03:05), she was always suspicious of it. See Erkkila, *The Wicked Sisters*, 146–51. The correspondence between this passage's ventriloquizing of Pound's misogyny ("A wife is a coffin" are his words, Moore's notes tell us) and Freud's "The Uncanny" is thus itself rather uncanny:

> Dismembered limbs, a severed head, a hand cut off at the wrist, . . . feet which dance by themselves, . . . all these have something peculiarly uncanny about them, especially when, as in the last instance, they prove capable of independent activity in addition. As we already know, this kind of uncanniness springs from its proximity to the castration complex. To some people the idea of being buried alive by mistake is the most uncanny thing of all. And yet psycho-analysis has taught us that this terrifying phantasy is only a transformation of another phantasy which had

originally nothing terrifying about it at all, but was qualified by a certain
lasciviousness—the phantasy, I mean, of intra-uterine existence. (Freud,
"The Uncanny," 244)

"Marriage" calls attention to the fact that the imaginary fear as well as pleasure are components of male fantasy.

65. On this point see Jacobus, *Reading Woman,* 39.

66. See Diehl, who suggests that this poem be read as a conversation
(*Women Poets and the American Sublime,* 49). Another correlation with Parsons's *The Psychology of Dress* is Moore's development in the 1920s of a
"conversational" poetic structure (she kept conversation, as well as reading, notebooks all her life). Parsons recounts that, like the salons of France
in the eighteenth century, the *conversazione* of Italy, beginning after the
balls and going on all night, were "woman's kingdom" (234): "The philosophy of Voltaire and Rousseau, the theories of paganism in regard to the
marriage contract, individual rights of man and the meaning of nature"
were disseminated through these *conversazione.* Society imbibed the ideas
that would "revolutionize thought and then life" (234–35). If Moore surmised that ritualized and female-dominated conversations were as crucial
to revolutionizing thinking as Enlightenment philosophy itself was, she
may have used a dialogical model to advance her "objectionable" (revolutionary) "hybrid method of composition." Another intellectual antecedent
closer to home is, of course, Margaret Fuller's Conversations for Women,
which Fuller's biographer Charles Capper, in *Margaret Fuller,* characterizes as subversive.

67. Moore is circumspect about her admiration for James and identifies her own tendencies toward accumulation of details with his narrative
methodology, not altogether (un)flatteringly: "one must admit that it is not
in the accepted sense that Henry James was 'big' and did things in a big
way. But he possessed the instinct to amass and reiterate" (*CP,* 316).

68. According to Stapleton, the source of this phrase was Williams's
aestheticizing trope for housework in *Kora in Hell* (see chap. 3, n. 27,
above): "Neatness and finish, the dust out of every corner! You swish from
room to room and find all perfect. The house may now be carefully
wrapped in brown paper and sent to a publisher. It is a work of art" (*Kora
in Hell,* Section 21, part 2). The phrase might have been doubly resonant
in its metapoetic implications for Moore, who also, as we shall see, has a
meditation on the relationship between housework and writing.

69. On the analogy between Milton's *Paradise Lost* and the New
Eden of America, which reinforces the fallen position of the beholder and
criticizes the commodification of the wilderness, see Costello, "Marianne

Moore and the Sublime"; Willis, "The Road to Paradise"; and Slatin, who reads the poem as an ironic revision of *Paradise Lost*, as well as of the Emersonian tradition of the American Adamic sublime (*The Savage's Romance*, 156–72). Heuving discusses the mountain as a figurative "haven for feminine presences" (*Omissions Are Not Accidents*, 133–36).

70. On Moore's ambivalence about conquest, as suggested by a style that "presents a superficial appearance of flux and free association and disguises an elaborate thematic and formal structure," see Costello, *Marianne Moore*, 131.

71. It reflects, Slatin observes, "what you do not recognize as an image of yourself." While my reading has a very different orientation, this section has benefited from Slatin's discussion of the scene of reflection and the linguistic fluidity of the poem more generally. See *The Savage's Romance*, especially 164–68.

72. On this point see de Lauretis, *Alice Doesn't*, 101.

73. Diehl argues that this scene is genealogical–"the primal scene of female poetic origins" (*Women Poets and the American Sublime*, 61), a point that I think misses how Moore typically problematizes representation and the sense of origins and originality, as I have tried to demonstrate.

74. Ibid., 78.

75. Costello, "Marianne Moore and the Sublime," 9. Costello takes persuasive issue with Diehl's assertion that Moore "covertly reinscribes the male imagination's conceptualization of the feminine" (see Diehl, *Women Poets and the Sublime*, 47). While in essence I agree with Costello's critique of Diehl on this point, I would qualify it: as I've argued, Moore does in fact reinscribe hegemonic (or male-defined) femininity (Diehl has a point). But Moore does so critically (rather than uncritically, as Diehl seems to suggest), in order to expose those images as representations having no basis in women's real historical experience.

76. Moore's connection of femininity and the "octopus," and the connotations to which it gives rise, come out in a passage in which she protested the mystifying symbolization of woman in Pound's *Cantos*: "apropos of 'feminolatry,' is not the view of woman expressed by the Cantos older-fashioned than that of Siam and Abyssinia? knowledge of the femaleness of *chaos*, of the *octopus*, of *Our mulberry leaf, woman*, appertaining more to Turkey than to a Roger Ascham?" (*CP*, 272; emphasis in the original). Roger Ascham, a tutor to Elizabeth I, as DuPlessis notes, "presumably believed in female education," and thus as a figure indicates that Moore finds Pound's views toward women "antiquated" (DuPlessis, "No Moore of the Same," 29 n. 30). For the corresponding associations among femininity, maternity, and spider motifs, see Kofman, *The Enigma of Woman*. Kofman recounts that

for Freud the motif of terror provoked by Medusa's head is related to that of the spider, symbol of the phallic mother (83 n. 63).

77. DuPlessis, "No Moore of the Same," 11.

78. Diehl, *Women Poets and the American Sublime*, 78.

79. Freud, "The Uncanny," 245.

80. Felman, "Rereading Femininity," 40; Felman's emphasis.

81. De Lauretis, *Alice Doesn't*, 101.

82. Carolyn Burke, "Getting Spliced," 115.

83. Marianne Moore, "M. Carey Thomas Award Acceptance Speech," transcript in the Marianne Moore Collection, Bryn Mawr College Archive; quoted in Holley, *The Poetry of Marianne Moore*, 3; my ellipses.

84. Kenner, *A Homemade World*, 112.

85. Holley, *The Poetry of Marianne Moore*, 38.

86. On this point, see also DuPlessis, "No Moore of the Same," 19.

87. Holley, *The Poetry of Marianne Moore*, 58.

88. Johnson, *The Critical Difference*, 38.

89. I have embroidered on a line from a lecture delivered by Barbara Babcock entitled "Mud Women and White Men," for the *Arizona Quarterly* Symposium, University of Arizona, Tucson, 2 March 1989. Babcock was referring to Pueblo women potters, the satirism of whose clay figures of Anglos went unnoticed by collectors, who wrote off the figurines as "slight" and "cartoonish." Her original comment was: "These women were manipulating considerably more than clay!"

90. As such, Moore anticipates more-recent feminist projects. Making a distinction between femaleness (biological sex), femininity (narrative trope), and feminism (a critical reading of culture), de Lauretis observes that feminism rewrites our culture's "master narratives" (*Technologies of Gender*, 113); Jacobus states that what "is at stake for both women writing and writing about women is the rewriting of [the inherited] fictions" about woman (*Reading Woman*, 40).

CHAPTER 4. EQUI/VOCATIONS
H.D.'S DEMASCULINIZATION OF THE SUBJECT IN
HELEN IN EGYPT

1. I am playing with this "part," but I am also in part serious because the conception of the androgynous "One that transcends all the dualities of life" has been central to an understanding of H.D.'s poetics since Friedman argued that H.D.'s extensive study of mystical texts offered a model

to resolve successfully all the dialectical conflicts permeating *Helen in Egypt* (Friedman, *Psyche Reborn,* 294). In "H.D.'s Scene of Writing," Joseph Riddel, restoring the textual complexity that Friedman glossed over, contends that the poem anticipates poststructuralism in its concerns: "Helen . . . '*is the writing*' in the sense that she . . . not only represents but disseminates" (51). In phallicizing the figure of Helen, however, he represses the feminism that Friedman uncovered along with H.D.'s mysticism. He makes a *part* over into *the* part, as it were. In *H.D. and Freud,* Claire Buck restores H.D.'s feminist poetics as well as considers the textual complexity of her work. Quoting H.D. herself, who once wrote that "There is a feeling that it is only a *part* of myself there [in her poetry]" (*TF,* 149), Buck speculates that the "part" left out is gender (see especially pp. 13–37).

2. Buck, *H.D. and Freud,* 99. See also Friedman, "Against Discipleship"; and DuPlessis, *H.D.,* 74–77, 81–85.

3. On these lines from "The Master" and H.D. and Freud's theories, see Buck, *H.D. and Freud,* 77–130.

4. Friedman first made this case. See her *Psyche Reborn,* chaps. 1–5; see also her more recent work on H.D.'s prose, *Penelope's Web,* in which she advances her argument that by employing Freud's techniques of transference and working through, H.D. repeats the Father's text (Freud's *Interpretation of Dreams*), "replacing his authority with her own" (312). Among the feminist scholarship on H.D. in the last decade that I have found helpful, in addition to those works cited above, are Diane Chisholm, "H.D.'s Auto*hetero*graphy"; Deborah Kelly Kloepfer, *The Unspeakable Mother;* and many of the essays collected in *Signets: Reading H.D.,* edited by Friedman and DuPlessis.

5. Kofman, *The Enigma of Woman,* 171. Cf. Freud, "On Femininity." On H.D.'s debate with Freud over his definition of femininity, see Friedman and DuPlessis, "'Woman is Perfect.'" For a critique of their article as essentializing, see Buck, "Freud and H.D."

6. Buck, *H.D. and Freud,* 147.

7. On these points see DuPlessis, *H.D.,* 111. "Herself defined" is an allusion to Barbara Guest's excellent biography of H.D., *Herself Defined.*

8. I do not mean to suggest, however, that because the poem analyzes the role of the phallus, the text is phallogocentric. It is my contention that H.D. urges us to understand the dynamic by which women *qua* woman come to stand in for loss in patriarchal culture. Although Riddel tries hard to avoid the sexism of his earlier article, "H.D. and the Poetics of 'Spiritual Realism',", one couldn't find a more apt illustration of a Jardinian instance of *gynesis* at work in postmodernist criticism than Riddel's second article on H.D. For a cogent critique, see Elizabeth Hirsh, "Imaginary Eyes."

9. Although Moore and H.D. were born within a year of each other, Moore's combination of feminism and Christianity characterizes first-generation New Women, while H.D.'s early bohemian feminism characterizes the second generation of New Women. For a discussion of the second generation as emphasizing self-fulfillment, not social service, and presenting itself as cosmopolitan, often lesbian or bisexual, see Smith-Rosenberg, *Disorderly Conduct,* 176–77. The later H.D., although not given to social service, is altruistically visionary in her unique fusion of feminism, mysticism, psychoanalysis, and poetry forged in the face of war. Anticipating the necessity of this work by the early 1930s, H.D. claims to have returned to Freud as his self-declared "student": "to fortify and equip myself to face war when it came, and to help in some subsidiary way . . . with war-shocked and war-shattered people" (*TF,* 93).

10. On H.D.'s connection of fascism and war with the psychodynamics of heterosexuality and the patriarchal family, see Friedman, *Penelope's Web,* 339–40.

11. Chisholm, *H.D.'s Freudian Poetics,* 180. By the time she was writing *Helen in Egypt,* H.D. conceived of herself as poet-analyst, and poetic language, as Chisholm elaborates, as "healing anodyne" (179) and therapeutic "antidote to patriarchy" (177). See her superb discussion of H.D.'s recovery of the antithetical semiotic reserve of the unconscious via poetic language, pp. 161–80.

12. Italics in quotations from *Helen in Egypt* indicate the prose commentary as it appears in the text, not emphasis added.

13. For a discussion of *Helen in Egypt* as an antiwar text that examines the roots of violence in repression of love of the mother, see DuPlessis, *H.D.,* 113–14. DuPlessis's point is persuasive, although I also find H.D.'s dramatic poem more complicated. As H.D. commented in a letter to Bryher written during H.D.'s second set of sessions with Freud, suggesting that the male unconscious was far from clear to her, "as you say, these males and the state of their uc-n. Cess-pits, my dear" (5 November 1934, *YCAL/* Beinecke).

14. For the comparison of H.D.'s "neo-epic" to the those of the male modernists, see Lucy Friebert, "From Semblance to Selfhood." On Achilles and the proto-fascist hierarchy represented in *Helen in Egypt,* see Friedman, *Psyche Reborn,* 256–67; DuPlessis, *H.D.,* 113; and Ostriker, *Stealing the Language,* 224.

15. Friedman interprets the enigma for the child in H.D.'s memoir, *The Gift,* to be violence and death. See *Penelope's Web,* 333.

16. For a discussion of H.D.'s representation of time, see Walker, "Women and Time: H.D. and the Greek Persona," in her *Masks Outrageous*

and Austere, 105–34. Walker analyzes H.D.'s debt to the nineteenth-century sentimental feminine poetic tradition that Walker mapped out in her earlier study, which extends well into the twentieth century, as she convincingly demonstrates.

17. Undated manuscript (*YCAL*/Beinecke). For another approach to the indeterminacies of the closing lines of *Helen in Egypt,* cf. Robert O'Brien Hokanson, "Is It All Story?," 342–44.

18. For the inspiration for this notion, I am indebted to Richard Dellamora, who discussed the question of postapocalyptic gay identity with me during a telephone conversation, 26 March 1992. See his *Apocalyptic Overtures,* which was published after the completion of this text.

19. And, one might add, subjects of fantasy. Although H.D. addresses "the opposition reality-illusion (imaginary)," as Jean Laplanche and Jean-Bertrand Pontalis describe one Freudian dialectic, the poem as a whole functions as fantasy—that is, it has "psychical reality," the structure, according to Freud, that fantasy gives to desire. See LaPlanche and Pontalis, "Fantasy and the Origins of Sexuality," 26–27. Summarizing their point, Kaja Silverman states that the "typical fantasy" works to produce "a conventional subject," who internalizes a pregiven structure from outside, beginning with parental fantasy but derived from "that wealth of representational and signifying practices which make up the dominant fiction" (*Male Subjectivity at the Margins,* 28–29).

20. Following Louis Althusser, Silverman uses the term to signify ideology and the way it functions to create "belief" (Silverman, *Male Subjectivity at the Margins,* 15–51).

21. For a deconstruction of the notion of a prelinguistic origin, see de Man, "The Rhetoric of Blindness"; and Jacques Derrida, *Of Grammatology,* 3–26. For a discussion that connects gender blindness and rhetoric, see Irigaray, *Speculum of the Other Woman,* 111–12; Felman, "Rereading Femininity," 27.

22. Hirsh, "Imaginary Eyes," 441; Hirsh's emphasis.

23. On this point see Hogue, "(Re)Placing Woman."

24. On the lyric characteristic of creating in the space of the poem a timeless world that will preserve the speaker in an eternal present, see Cameron, *Lyric Time,* 201–60.

25. Helen's and Achilles' displacement to Egypt is often understood as a replacement of the paternal with the maternal world, and all that both forces connote culturally. See Friedman, *Psyche Reborn,* 264; DuPlessis, *H.D.,* 113–14; Kloepfer, who builds on Friedman and DuPlessis to argue that H.D. inscribes the story of the daughter's attempt to "speak," as opposed to the son's attempt to "banish," the preoedipal mother (*Unspeak-*

able Mother, 164–71); and Chisholm, who contends that the "displacement of the phallus facilitates Achilles' recovery of oedipal and preoedipal eroticism and his wholehearted conversion to the maternal mysteries, his and civilization's cure" (*H.D.'s Freudian Poetics*, 188). Unlike these discussions, which read the poem as a vision of communion and maternal fusion, my analysis focuses on the unresolved divisions within the poem as well as on the divisiveness between Helen and Achilles that other critics cover over. I agree that the translation of the scene from Troy to Egypt does indeed represent an imaginary displacement, but I locate the imaginary, following Kristeva's rereading of the Lacanian mirror stage discussed in chapter 1, in the symbolic order, and thus in an already divided realm.

26. For an illuminating discussion of H.D.'s use of the various definitions of "projection," see Adelaide Morris, "The Concept of Projection."

27. Irigaray, *Speculum of the Other Woman*, 47; Irigaray's emphasis.

28. See Jeffords, *The Remasculinization of America*, xii, 181–83. At page xii, Jeffords quotes Gerda Lerner, *The Creation of Patriarchy* (239), to define patriarchy as the "institutionalization of male dominance over women in society in general. It implies that men hold power in all the important institutions of society and that women are deprived of access to such power."

29. Homans, "'Syllables of Velvet,'" 573.

30. De Lauretis, *Alice Doesn't*, 155.

31. Buck, *H.D. and Freud*, 147.

32. Hirsh, "Imaginary Eyes," 440.

33. On the "violence of rhetoric," see de Lauretis's chapter of the same title in *Technologies of Gender*, 31–50; Jacobus, *Reading Woman*, 245; and Johnson, *A World of Difference*, 184–99.

34. For a discussion of Marxism and feminism as "theories of power and its distribution . . . [that] argue, respectively, that the relations in which many work and few gain, in which some fuck and others get fucked, are the prime moment of politics," see MacKinnon, "Feminism, Marxism, Method, and the State," 3.

35. Irigaray, *This Sex*, 70.

36. For a cogent discussion that focuses on H.D.'s problematic relation to the Image of Imagism in light of Irigarayan theory, see Hirsh, "Imaginary Eyes," 430–51.

37. On "the pattern of violation [of women]–revenge–violation" in Ovid's *Metamorphoses* and issues of gender violence, like that of woman as battle spoils, that war gives rise to, see Joplin, "The Voice of the Shuttle Is Ours," 45–50. See also Jeffords, who discusses the expendable woman in representations of the Vietnam War, in *The Remasculinization of America*, 133.

38. For an insightful and very different approach to the witch imagery in both *Trilogy* and *Helen in Egypt,* see Chisholm, *H.D.'s Freudian Poetics,* 182–212.

39. Freud, "Medusa's Head," 273.

40. Hertz, *The End of the Line,* 165.

41. For a reading that repeats Freud's slippage, see Norman Holland, "H.D. and the 'Blameless Physician.'"

42. Freud, "Medusa's Head," 274.

43. Joplin restores the original violence, Neptune's rape of the beautiful Medusa, which Freud's account leaves out and H.D., as a student of classical Greek myth, would certainly have known. Joplin speculates that behind the scene of the head that turns men to stone might lie the collective memory trace of both the virgin's sacrifice and the transgressive woman stoned to death by men (Joplin, "The Voice of the Shuttle Is Ours," 49–50 n. 30).

44. Cixous, "Castration or Decapitation?" H.D.'s point of view differs from Lacan's with regard to the notion of a symbolic castration that constitutes subjectivity, although their similarities are instructive, as I shall presently discuss.

45. The unpublished letters to Bryher written during H.D.'s two sets of sessions with Freud relate a fascinating process of initial acceptance of, and excitement about, Freud's theory of penis envy changing to a more equivocal stance. In a letter dated 3 May 1933, after the session in which Freud apparently first talked to her about his theory that penis envy characterized all women, not just homosexual women, H.D. crowed to Bryher that they had influenced his thinking, and thus had been "feeding the light [Freud]" and finding their "niche in the universe." Although Bryher's response is lost, she was apparently not persuaded, because on 12 May, H.D. wrote that Bryher had been "beastly" about "my penis-envy." By 26 May, H.D. had had an important dream about a "band of sisters" watching literary men and "all their little vagaries," and realizing it was only "a performance, something to enjoy really to enjoy, not envy, but to keep out of. Savvy???????" (*YCAL*/Beinecke). For a full discussion of these letters and H.D.'s prose, see Friedman, *Penelope's Web,* 281–354.

46. Critics generally agree that H.D.'s encounter with Freud represented in this scene is about penis envy. See, for example, Holland, "H.D. and the 'Blameless Physician,'" 486; DuPlessis and Friedman, "'Woman is Perfect,'" 417–29; Nora Crowe Jaffe, "'She Herself Is the Writing'"; and Hirsh, "Imaginary Eyes," 435–37. On the centrality of resistance and rebellion for H.D.'s exchange with Freud, as suggested by her unpublished letters to Bryher, see Friedman, "Against Discipleship," 97. For a

critique of DuPlessis's and Friedman's assumption that there is a core feminine identity that H.D.'s text "reveals," see Buck, "Freud and H.D.," 53–66. My concern here is to analyze what has been given little attention to date, H.D.'s subtle equivocation in her representation of the exchange, and to connect her rhetorical ambivalance to sexual difference.

47. See Irigaray, *Speculum of the Other Woman*, 11–132.

48. Gallop, *The Daughter's Seduction*, 57–58.

49. Woolf, *Orlando*, 312.

50. On H.D.'s rejection of Freud's materialist theory of the unconscious, as well as her (contradictory) association of him with the Prophets of Israel as well as with Shakespeare, see Friedman, *Psyche Reborn*, especially 100–120.

51. De Lauretis, *Alice Doesn't*, 123.

52. Ibid., 143.

53. Ibid., 110.

54. See LaPlanche and Pontalis, *The Language of Psycho-analysis*, 111–14. For an analysis of H.D.'s "reconceptualization of the Image in terms of a structure of deferred interpretive action . . . that is very much at odds with the imagism of Pound," see Hirsh, "Imaginary Eyes," 438–49.

55. Freud, "Some Psychical Consequences," 252.

56. For a discussion of Freud's theory of castration, penis envy, and deferred action to which this section of my chapter is indebted, see Jacobus, *Reading Woman*, 112–15.

57. Kofman, *The Enigma of Woman*, 142.

58. Freud, "Medusa's Head," 273.

59. For a consideration of the enabling aspects of such a double identification, see Mulvey, "Afterthoughts."

60. Freud, "Medusa's Head," 274.

61. Cixous, "The Laugh of the Medusa," 255.

62. Irigaray, *Speculum of the Other Woman*, 83.

63. Gallop, *The Daughter's Seduction*, 58.

64. For an excellent analysis of photos in H.D.'s scrapbook posing "a fluid realm of female looking: a mutual beholding which celebrates the object as subject," see Diana Collecott, "Images at the Crossroads."

65. For a Kristevan reading of H.D.'s poetics, see DuPlessis, "Language Acquisition."

66. Kahn, "The Hand That Rocks the Cradle," 88.

67. Gallop, *Reading Lacan*, 20.

68. Freud, "Fetishism," 152–53.

69. Kofman, *The Enigma of Woman*, 86.

70. Freud, "Some Psychical Consequences," 252. For a cogent read-

ing of Achilles as male hysteric (not fetishist) and the flashpoint moment of violence (not lovemaking) to which the poem returns, see Susan Edmunds, "I Read the Writing When He Seized My Throat," 473–80.

71. For a feminist discussion of Freud's analysis of the strange state that afflicted Breuer during his treatment of Anna O, see Jacobus, *Reading Woman*, 225. Anna O's hysteria took the form of a disturbance in and of language, and her treatment produced the historic "talking cure," Jacobus recounts; Breuer's response was, like that of Achilles, finally to be reduced to silence and violence: he broke off the treatment. As Jacobus remarks, Breuer hysterically recoiled from feminine sexuality–in essence, a recoil from the mother (223).

72. On the revelation of the mother/child dyad central to *Helen in Egypt*'s female quest plot, see DuPlessis, *Writing beyond Ending*, 83; and Ostriker, *Stealing the Language*, 225. For insightful discussions of the voice of an "invisible 'm/other text'" in H.D.'s poetics, see Kloepfer, *The Unspeakable Mother*, especially 160–71; and Chisholm, *H.D.'s Freudian Poetics*, 5–6.

73. De Lauretis, *Alice Doesn't*, 141.

74. De Lauretis, *Technologies of Gender*, 25.

75. As Buck observes, building on Riddel, each character is identified with a position within the family romance, "but this [structure] is variable and mobile" (Buck, *H.D. and Freud*, 157).

76. De Lauretis, *Alice Doesn't*, 157.

77. Chisholm, *H.D.'s Freudian Poetics*, 180.

78. Freud, "Feminine Sexuality," 226.

79. Kofman, *The Enigma of Woman*, 122.

80. Hirsh, "Imaginary Eyes," 437.

81. Ibid., 443–48.

82. Russo, "Female Grotesques," 224.

83. On transvestism as a travesty of "an orderly, hierarchical polarity" of gender, see Felman, "Rereading Femininity," 28–29; on the figure of the transvestite (the third position) as that from which binary thinking can be questioned, see Margorie Garber, *Vested Interests*, 1–17.

84. In "The Third Woman," Berg terms this position, following Kofman, "the affirmative woman": "the female equivalent of the fetishist, who treats castration as an undecidable question, concluding that the penis is both there and not there. . . . She is the woman who refuses to be simply castrated" (13).

85. In *The Remasculinization of America*, Jeffords suggests the term, "'the masculine point of view,' which represents the disembodied voice of masculinity, that which no individual man or woman can realize yet which

influences each individually, in order to identify the voice through which dominance is enacted in a narrative representation" (xiii). I will presently suggest the term *a feminine point of view* as functioning similarly, in that no individual character in H.D.'s poem can be said to be synonymous with it. The poem assumes that point of view, I contend, in order to work *against* the reproduction of patriarchy.

86. In this unpublished letter, dated 23 November 1934 (*YCAL/* Beinecke), it is the *public* nature of the commitment to gender fixity with which H.D. is concerned. See, although it is not precisely analogous, Lacan's passage on the laws of public urinary segregation as adducing the linguistic installation of the gendered subject, in *Écrits,* 151. Mitchell and Rose note that although the female subject's entry into language is more problematic than that of the male's, bisexuality in Lacan's rereading of Freud came to stand for "the division and precariousness of human subjectivity." See their Introductions I and II to *Feminine Sexuality,* 12, 29.

87. Kofman, *The Enigma of Woman,* 210–25.

88. Silverman, *Male Subjectivity at the Margins,* 389.

CHAPTER 5. LIVING WITH/IN DIFFERENCE
ADRIENNE RICH'S DOUBLE VISION

1. Kristeva, "Women's Time," 205, 207.

2. I draw a distinction between Rich's readerly and writerly oriented inscriptions of vision. Cf. Albert Gelpi, who elaborates Rich's near-obsession with the idea and the act of "vision," associating seeing with being: "I am eye," as Gelpi puts it in "Adrienne Rich," 134–35.

3. For a discussion of Dickinson's influence on Rich and Rich's changing response to Elizabeth Bishop (if not to Marianne Moore), see Erkkila, *The Wicked Sisters,* 152–84.

4. Homans, *Women Writers and Poetic Identity,* 229.

5. For a critique of Rich as essentializing, see Montefiore, *Feminism and Poetry,* 89–90; for a response to Montefiore's (and Helen Vendler's) criticism of Rich, see Meese, *(Ex)tensions,* 170–73.

6. De Lauretis, "The Essence of the Triangle."

7. Ibid., 5; de Lauretis's emphasis.

8. *Hailing* is the term Althusser specifically uses to describe how we recognize ourselves by the way we are addressed. In "Ideology and Ideological State Apparatuses," Althusser states: "You and I are *always already* subjects, and as such constantly practice the rituals of ideological recognition, which guarantee for us that we are indeed concrete, individual, dis-

tinguishable and (naturally) irreplaceable subjects." Althusser is quoted in Tenney Nathanson, "Collage and Pulverization," 307–8. I take the notion of the importance of women's "naming" themselves from Rich herself, who discusses it in both *Lies, Secrets, and Silence* and *Of Woman Born*. In the latter, she asserts that, despite what men protestingly term their "natural" protective instincts toward women to explain the origins of male dominance, power and force are the real issue (*OWB*, 99–102).

9. See Homans, who observes Rich's analogous rejection of figuration as lying, in *Women Writers and Poetic Identity*, 223. On the performative aspects of gender identity, see Judith Butler, *Gender Trouble*, 128–41.

10. For an analysis of the development of the politics of Rich's aesthetic project, her "negotiating the metalogic" that frames us all, and finally the alternative she poses to dominant white feminism, see Meese, *(Ex)tensions*, 155–79. My own chapter builds on her ground breaking work.

11. See Meese, *(Ex)tensions*, 168. For the argument that Rich's lesbian, separatist poetry is less mature and "empowered" than that postdating her reclamation of her Jewish and heterosexual origins, see Diehl, *Women Poets and the American Sublime*, 159. Although I am also interested in analyzing Rich's fraught relationship to the dominant heterosexual construct, as well as the alternatives to its reproduction she has symbolized, I find Diehl's argument troubling, and these pages take general issue with it.

12. I am paraphrasing Peggy Kamuf's Foucauldian analysis of Woolf's *A Room of One's Own*, which frames the question Woolf poses in that text as the problem of women's subjectivity as fictive invention written into the historical field of its own exclusion. See Kamuf, "Penelope at Work."

13. Kloepfer, *The Unspeakable Mother*, xii.

14. For a related discussion that was helpful in revising this section, see Nathanson, "Collage and Pulverization."

15. Preceding Sedgwick's *Between Men* by some years, Rich makes an analogous distinction between the homosexual ("lesbian existence") and homosocial ("lesbian continuum"), and rejects the term *lesbianism* altogether as having too "clinical and limiting" a ring. Because I have included in this chapter an analysis of the way Rich attempts to inscribe a female subject's resistance to the heterosexual construct, as well as her contradictory relation to other women, I have found Rich's term *lesbian continuum* useful in discussing her poetry. I employ the term as she defines it in "Compulsory Heterosexuality": "a range–through each woman's life and throughout history–of woman-identified experience" (*BBP*, 51).

16. After the speaker, an abused wife, recounts how "Women's Lib"

taught her "the words" with which to defend herself, she adds, bleakly, that "answering back's no answer." See Rich, *Your Native Land, Your Life,* 86.

17. For a critical analysis of Rich's white-centered aesthetic-ethic, see Erkkila, *The Wicked Sisters,* 154.

18. For the argument that Rich "exposes" women's self- indulgence, see DuPlessis, "The Critique of Consciousness," 286. I follow Rich in arguing that historically women compromise rather than indulge themselves, to suggest women's responsibility for their complicity but also the cultural pressure that elicits women's compliance.

19. Rich cites Smith-Rosenberg's "The Female World of Love and Ritual: Relations between Women in Nineteenth-Century America" (1975) to describe how women's friendships were viewed by men, before Freud gave women's relations labels. A later Smith-Rosenberg essay, "The New Woman as Androgyne: Social Disorder and Gender Crisis, 1870–1936" (1985), substantiates Rich's anecdotal evidence. Both essays are collected in *Disorderly Conduct,* 53–76, 245–96.

20. I shall drop the in-law indicator at this point in the discussion for ease of reference, with the caveat that while the text insists the women are related not by blood but via the husband/son, by law, the poetic speaker's mother-in-law resembles Rich's own mother, a Southern "lady," rather than her actual mother-in-law. See "Split at the Root: An Essay on Jewish Identity" (*BBP,* 100–23). In addition, given that Rich's father, Arnold Rich, rigorously instructed her in the tradition of lyric prosody, the figure of the mother that the daughter rejects in "Snapshots" functions as a metapoetic screen-symbol for the daughter's rejection of the father's lessons. The emphasis given Rich's patronym by its placement at the end of the line quoted presently in the text has deliberate metapoetic implications as well.

21. Irigaray, *This Sex,* 207.

22. Jacobus, *Reading Woman,* 247.

23. On Rich's rejection not of men but of the "destructive masculinity" patriarchy has constructed, see Wendy Martin, *An American Tryptich,* 226–31.

24. Heath, "Joan Riviere and the Masquerade," 59.

25. Doane, "Film and the Masquerade," 87.

26. Woolf, *A Room of One's Own,* 45.

27. Wendy Martin, *An American Tryptich,* 169.

28. De Lauretis, for example, argues that the girl symbolically participates in the killing off of the mother, in order to replace her in an unalterable "web of a male Oedipal logic" (*Alice Doesn't,* 152).

29. Modleski, *The Women Who Knew Too Much,* 50.

30. Asserting that the assimilation of femininity into dominant masculine structures can never be complete, Modleski compellingly analyzes the "resistances that disturb the text" of *Rebecca,* and I direct the reader to her chapter (ibid., 43–55).

31. Ibid., 54.

32. Ibid., 44, 51.

33. Wendy Martin, *An American Tryptich,* 190.

34. Although as Homans herself admits, the reduction is not final (*Women Writers and Poetic Identity,* 229).

35. Ibid., 228.

36. Ibid., 229.

37. Kristeva, *Nations without Nationalism.*

38. Diehl, *Women Poets and the American Sublime,* 165.

39. Woolf, *A Room of One's Own,* 93.

40. DuPlessis, "No Moore of the Same," 18.

41. Kristeva, "Motherhood According to Giovanni Bellini," 239.

42. De Lauretis, "Film and the Visible," 252. Although published too recently for this study to take into account, see also de Lauretis's *The Practice of Love.*

43. Kristeva, "From One Identity to Another," 136; emphasis in original. It is important to remember that Kristeva is speaking of the symbolic contract. Alluding to "Transcendental Etude," Kloepfer makes the following analogy: "To rupture the code, linguistic or cultural, by the reinsertion of the mother [name] *is* incest" (*The Unspeakable Mother,* 177). She literalizes Kristeva's point about the symbolic contract, overlooking the fact that Kristeva's subject-in-process is male, and that a female subject's relationship to this "incest" might be differently inflected because females are not under the same pressure of the incest prohibition as male subjects are (which is specifically what Kristeva has in mind). Kloepfer confuses what Kristeva is careful to keep distinct—that poetic language is the linguistic *equivalent* of, not a literal, incest.

44. For a related discussion, see Diehl, *Women Poets and the American Sublime,* 165.

45. Ibid., 150.

46. For a discussion that relates Rich's refusal of abstractions not only to her feminism, but to Dickinson and, through her, the Puritan ideal of "plain speech," see Wendy Martin, *An American Tryptich,* 170–71.

47. Lorde, "The Master's Tools," 99; Lorde's emphasis. For a discussion on Lorde's own revisionary activity, see AnnLouise Keating, "Making 'Our Shattered Faces Whole.'"

48. Kristeva, *Revolution in Poetic Language,* 220; Kristeva's emphasis.
49. Ibid., 232–33.
50. Meese, *(Ex)tensions,* 172, 173.
51. De Lauretis, "Eccentric Subjects," 137.
52. Ibid., 137.
53. For more extensive and varying analyses of the Thomas/Hill hearings than I can address in this chapter, see Toni Morrison, ed., *Race-ing Justice, En-gendering Power.*
54. For this insight I build on Meese's discussion, following Derrida's *The Truth in Painting,* of the frame as at once inside and outside the composition (Meese, *(Ex)tensions,* especially 176).
55. Ibid., 176–77.
56. Mulvey, "Visual Pleasure and Narrative Cinema," 15–16.
57. In "Wrestling Your Ally," Saldívar-Hull argues that white liberal feminism's celebration of "Melanctha" misses—and therefore reproduces—the racism in "Melanctha." Here, I am not suggesting that Rich's text is racist, but rather that it raises (and attempts to resolve via a localized positioning of the speaker) difficult issues about the politics of representational and interpretive control in feminist aesthetic and critical works.
58. Mulvey, "Visual Pleasure and Narrative Cinema," 22.
59. Loeffelholz, *Dickinson,* 110.
60. Rich, "The Hermit's Scream," 1159.
61. Of Deming's activism Rich writes that the "hope was that action informed by the love of justice . . . could teach by example." She then amends: "I wrote 'hope' but I should say more accurately 'faith,'" by which she indicates an activism that is accompanied by critical and self-critical questioning in order never to settle into dogma (ibid.)
62. Ibid., 1158.
63. Lorde, *Our Dead Behind Us,* 15.
64. For a more extensive consideration of the metaphor of alchemy in relation to the innovative genres in which such poets as Rich write, cf. Diane P. Freedman, *An Alchemy of Genres.*
65. Rich, "The Hermit's Scream," 1158.
66. Ibid., 1158–59.
67. Lorde, "An Interview: Audre Lorde and Adrienne Rich," in *Sister Outsider,* 107–8. This passage is also quoted in Rich, "The Hermit's Scream," 1164; my ellipses.

Works Cited

Aiken, Susan Hardy. "Dinesen's 'Sorrow-Acre': Tracing the Woman's Line." *Contemporary Literature* 25, no. 2 (1984): 156–86.

———. *Isak Dinesen and the Engendering of Narrative.* Chicago: University of Chicago Press, 1990.

Allison, Alexander W., Herbert Barrows, Caesar R. Blake, Arthur J. Carr, Arthur M. Eastman, and Hubert M. English, Jr., eds. *The Norton Anthology of Poetry.* 3rd ed. New York: Norton, 1983.

Althusser, Louis. "Ideology and Ideological State Apparatuses (Notes toward an Investigation)." In *Lenin and Philosophy, and Other Essays,* translated by Ben Brewster, 127–86. London: New Left, 1971.

Altieri, Charles. "The Powers of Genuine Place." *Southern Humanities Review* 22 (Summer 1988): 205–22.

Anderson, Charles R. *Emily Dickinson's Poetry: Stairway of Surprise.* New York: Holt, Rinehart & Winston, 1960.

Anzaldúa, Gloria. *Borderlands: La Frontera.* San Francisco: Spinsters/Aunt Lute, 1987.

Arensberg, Mary, ed. Introduction. In *The American Sublime,* 1–20. Albany: State University of New York Press, 1986.

Austin, J. L. *How to Do Things with Words.* Edited by J. O. Urmson and Marina Sbisa. Cambridge: Harvard University Press, 1975.

Babcock, Barbara. "Mud Women and White Men." Lecture delivered at the *Arizona Quarterly Symposium,* University of Arizona, Tucson, 2 March 1989.

Bauer, Dale. "Gender in Bakhtin's Carnival." In *Feminisms,* edited by Robyn R. Warhol and Diane Price Herndl. 1988. Reprint, New Brunswick, N.J.: Rutgers University Press, 1991. 671–89.

Baym, Nina. *Woman's Fiction: A Guide to Novels by and about Women in America, 1820–1870.* Ithaca, N.Y.: Cornell University Press, 1978.

Beauvoir, Simone de. *The Second Sex.* Translated by H. M. Parshley. 1952. Reprint, New York: Vintage, 1974.

Bedient, Calvin. "How I Slugged It out with Toril Moi and Stayed Awake." *Critical Inquiry* 17 (Spring 1991): 644–49.

Benjamin, Jessica. *The Bonds of Love: Psychoanalysis, Feminism, and the Problem of Domination.* New York: Pantheon, 1988.

———. "A Desire of One's Own: Psychoanalytic Feminism and Intersubjective Space." In *Feminist Studies/Critical Studies,* edited by Teresa de Lauretis, 78–101. Bloomington: Indiana University Press, 1986.

Bennett, Paula. *Emily Dickinson: Woman Poet.* Iowa City: University of Iowa Press, 1990.

Benvenuto, Richard. "Words within Words: Dickinson's Use of the Dictionary." *English Studies Quarterly* 29, no. 1 (1983): 46–55.

Berg, Elizabeth. "The Third Woman." *Diacritics* 12 (Summer 1982): 11–20.

Berger, John. *Ways of Seeing.* New York: Viking Press, 1972.

Bergman, David. "Marianne Moore and the Problem of 'Marriage.'" *American Literature* 60 (May 1988): 241–54.

Bloom, Harold. *The Anxiety of Influence.* New York: Oxford University Press, 1973.

Browning, Elizabeth Barrett. *The Letters of Elizabeth Barrett Browning.* Edited by Frederick G. Kenyon. 2 vols. in 1. New York: Macmillan, 1897.

Brownstein, Marilyn L. "The Archaic Mother and Mother and Mother: The Postmodern Poetry of Marianne Moore." *Contemporary Literature* 30, no. 1 (1989): 13–32.

Buck, Claire. "Freud and H.D.: Bisexuality and a Feminine Discourse." *m/f* 8 (1983): 53–66.

———. *H.D. and Freud: Bisexuality and a Feminine Discourse.* New York: St. Martin's Press, 1991.

Burbick, Joan. "Emily Dickinson and the Economics of Desire." *American Literature* 58 (1986): 361–78.

Burke, Carolyn. "Getting Spliced: Modernism and Sexual Difference." *American Quarterly* 39 (Spring 1987): 98–121.

———. "Supposed Persons: Modernist Poetry and the Female Subject." *Feminist Studies* 11, no. 1 (Spring 1985): 131–48.

Burke, Kenneth. "On Methodology." In *The Philosophy of Literary Form: Studies in Symbolic Action*, 56–75. New York: Vintage Books, 1957.

Butler, Judith. *Gender Trouble.* New York: Routledge, 1990.

Cameron, Sharon. *Lyric Time: Dickinson and the Limits of Genre.* Baltimore: Johns Hopkins University Press, 1979.

Capper, Charles. *Margaret Fuller.* London: Oxford University Press, 1993.

Capps, Jack L. *Emily Dickinson's Reading: 1836–1866.* Cambridge: Harvard University Press, 1966.

Chisholm, Diane. "H.D.'s Auto*hetero*graphy." *Tulsa Studies in Women's Literature* 9 (Spring 1990): 79–106.

———. *H.D.'s Freudian Poetics: Psychoanalysis in Translation.* Ithaca,. N.Y.: Cornell University Press, 1992.

Chodorow, Nancy. *The Reproduction of Mothering: Psychoanalysis and the Sociology of Gender.* Berkeley and Los Angeles: University of California Press, 1978.

Cixous, Hélène. "Castration or Decapitation?" Translated by Annette Kuhn. *Signs* 7, no. 3 (Autumn 1981): 41–55.

———. "The Laugh of the Medusa." In *New French Feminisms: An Anthology*, translated by Keith Cohen and Paula Cohen, edited by Elaine Marks and Isabelle de Courtivron, 245–64. New York: Schocken Books, 1981.

Cixous, Hélène, and Catherine Clément. *The Newly Born Woman.* Introduction by Sandra M. Gilbert. Translated by Betsy Wing. Minneapolis: University of Minnesota Press, 1986.

Collecott, Diana. "Images at the Crossroads: H.D.'s 'Scrapbook.'" In *Signets: Reading H.D.*, edited by Susan Stanford Friedman and Rachel Blau DuPlessis, 155–81. Madison: University of Wisconsin Press, 1990.

Cooper, Helen. *Elizabeth Barrett Browning, Woman and Artist.* Chapel Hill: University of North Carolina Press, 1988.

———. "Working into Light: Elizabeth Barrett Browning." In *Shakespeare's Sisters: Feminist Essays on Women Poets*, edited by Sandra M. Gilbert and Susan Gubar, 65–81. Bloomington: Indiana University Press, 1979.

Costello, Bonnie. "The 'Feminine' Language of Marianne Moore." In *Women and Language in Literature and Society*, edited by Sally McConnell-Ginet, Ruth Borker, and Nelly Furman, 222–38. New York: Praeger, 1980.

———. *Marianne Moore: Imaginary Possessions.* Cambridge: Harvard University Press, 1981.

———. "Marianne Moore and the Sublime." *Sagetrieb* 6, no. 3 (Winter 1987, Marianne Moore Special Issue): 5–13.

Culler, Jonathan. *The Pursuit of Signs.* Ithaca, N.Y.: Cornell University Press, 1981.

De Lauretis, Teresa. *Alice Doesn't: Feminism, Semiotics, Cinema.* Bloomington: Indiana University Press, 1984.

———. "Eccentric Subjects: Feminist Theory and Historical Consciousness." *Feminist Studies* 16, no. 1 (Spring 1990): 115–50.

———. "The Essence of the Triangle or, Taking the Risk of Essentialism Seriously: Feminist Theory in Italy, the U.S., and Britain." *differences* 1, no. 2 (Summer 1989): 3–37.

———. "The Female Body and Heterosexual Presumption." *Semiotica* 67, nos. 3–4 (1987): 259–79.

———. "Feminism, Lesbianism, and the Fantasy of the Maternal Body." Lecture delivered at the School of Criticism and Theory, Dartmouth College, 20 June 1991.

———. "Film and the Visible." In *How Do I Look?: Queer Film and Video,* edited by Bad Object-Choices, 223–76. Seattle: Bay Press, 1991.

———. *The Practice of Love: Lesbian Sexuality and Perverse Desire.* Bloomington: Indiana University Press, 1994.

———. *Technologies of Gender: Essays on Theory, Film, and Fiction.* Bloomington: Indiana University Press, 1987.

Dellamora, Richard. *Apocalyptic Overtures: Sexual Politics and the Sense of an Ending.* New Brunswick, N.J.: Rutgers University Press, 1994.

———. *Masculine Desire: The Sexual Politics of Victorian Aestheticism.* Durham: University of North Carolina Press, 1990.

De Man, Paul. "Anthropomorphism and Trope in the Lyric." In *The Rhetoric of Romanticism,* 239–62. New York: Columbia University Press, 1984.

———. "Autobiography As De-facement." In *Allegories of Reading: Figural Language in Rousseau, Nietzsche, Rilke, and Proust,* 278–301. New Haven: Yale University Press, 1979.

———. "The Rhetoric of Blindness: Jacques Derrida's Reading of Rousseau." In *Blindness and Insight,* 102–41. Minneapolis: University of Minnesota Press, 1983.

———. "Semiology and Rhetoric." In *Textual Strategies: Perspectives in Post-Structuralist Criticism,* edited by Josué V. Harari, 121–40. Ithaca and New York: Cornell University Press, 1979.

Derrida, Jacques. *Of Grammatology.* Translated by Gayatri Spivak. Baltimore: Johns Hopkins University Press, 1976.

—————. *The Truth in Painting.* Translated by Geoff Bennington and Ian McLeod. Chicago: University of Chicago Press, 1987.

Dickie, Margaret. *Lyric Contingencies: Emily Dickinson and Wallace Stevens.* Philadelphia: University of Pennsylvania Press, 1991.

—————. "Reperiodization: The Example of Emily Dickinson." *College English* 52, no. 4 (April 1990): 397–409.

Dickinson, Emily. *The Letters of Emily Dickinson.* 3 vols. Edited by Thomas H. Johnson and Theodora Ward. Cambridge: Harvard University Press, 1958.

—————. *The Poems of Emily Dickinson.* 3 vols. Edited by Thomas H. Johnson. Cambridge: Harvard University Press, 1955.

Diehl, Joanne Feit. *Dickinson and the Romantic Imagination.* Princeton, N.J.: Princeton University Press, 1981.

—————. "In the Twilight of the Gods: Women Poets and the American Sublime." In *The American Sublime,* edited by Mary Arensberg, 173–214. Albany: State University of New York Press, 1986.

—————. *Women Poets and the American Sublime.* Bloomington: Indiana University Press, 1990.

Doane, Mary Ann. *The Desire to Desire: The Woman's Film of the 1940s.* Bloomington: Indiana University Press, 1987.

—————. "Film and the Masquerade: Theorising the Female Spectator." *Screen* 23, nos. 3–4 (September–October 1982): 74–88.

Dobson, Joanna. *Dickinson and the Strategies of Reticence: The Woman Writer in Nineteenth-Century America.* Bloomington: Indiana University Press, 1989.

Doolittle, Hilda. *Collected Poems, 1912–1944.* Edited by Louis L. Martz. New York: New Directions, 1983.

—————. *The Gift.* New York: New Directions, 1982.

—————. *Helen in Egypt.* New York: New Directions, 1961.

—————. *Tribute to Freud.* New York: New Directions, 1984.

—————. *Trilogy.* New York: New Directions, 1973.

DuPlessis, Rachel Blau. "The Critique of Consciousness and Myth in Levertov, Rich, and Rukeyser." In *Shakespeare's Sisters: Feminist Essays on Women Poets,* edited by Sandra M. Gilbert and Susan Gubar, 280–300. Bloomington: Indiana University Press, 1979.

—————. *H.D.: The Career of That Struggle.* Bloomington: Indiana University Press, 1986.

—————. "Language Acquisition." *Iowa Review* 16, no. 3 (Fall 1986): 252–83.

—————. "No Moore of the Same: The Feminist Poetics of Marianne Moore." *William Carlos Williams Review* 14, no. 1 (Spring 1988: Marianne Moore Special Issue): 6–32.

———. *The Pink Guitar: Writing As Feminist Practice.* New York: Routledge, 1990.

———. *Writing beyond Ending: Narrative Strategies of Twentieth-Century Women Writers.* Bloomington: Indiana University Press, 1985.

Durham, Carolyn. "Linguistic and Sexual Engendering in Marianne Moore's Poetry." In *Engendering the Word,* edited by Temma F. Berg, 224–43. Urbana: University of Illinois Press, 1989.

Eberwein, Jane Donahue. *Dickinson's Strategies of Limitation.* Amherst: University of Massachusetts Press, 1985.

Edmunds, Susan. "'I Read the Writing When He Seized My Throat': Hysteria and Revolution in H.D.'s *Helen in Egypt.*" *Contemporary Literature* 32, no. 4 (1991): 471–95.

Erkkila, Betsy. "Emily Dickinson and Class." *American Literary History* 4 (1992): 1–27.

———. *The Wicked Sisters: Women Poets, Literary History, and Discord.* New York: Oxford University Press, 1992.

Faderman, Lillian. "Emily Dickinson's Homoerotic Poetry." *Higginson Journal* 18 (1978): 19–27.

Felman, Shoshona. "Rereading Femininity." *Yale French Studies* 62 (1981): 19–44.

Fineman, Joel. "Shakespeare's Sonnets' Perjured Eye." In *Lyric Poetry: Beyond New Criticism,* edited by Chaviva Hosek and Patricia Parker, 116–31. Ithaca, N.Y.: Cornell University Press, 1985.

Fletcher, John. "Poetry, Gender and Primal Fantasy." In *Formations of Fantasy,* edited by Victor Burgin, James Donald, and Cora Kaplan, 109–41. London: Routledge, 1986.

Freedman, Diane P. *An Alchemy of Genres: Cross-Genre Writing by American Feminist Poet-Critics.* Charlottesville: University of Virginia Press, 1992.

Freud, Sigmund. *The Standard Edition of the Complete Psychological Works of Sigmund Freud.* Translated and edited by James Strachey. 24 volumes. London: Hogarth Press, 1953–74. Hereafter cited as *Standard Edition.*

———. "Feminine Sexuality." In *Standard Edition,* vol. 21.

———. "Fetishism." In *Standard Edition,* vol. 21.

———. "Medusa's Head." In *Standard Edition,* vol. 18.

———. "On Femininity." In *New Introductory Lectures on Psychoanalysis.* Translated by James Strachey. 1933. Reprint, New York: Norton, 1965. 99–119.

———. "Some Psychical Consequences of the Anatomical Differences between the Sexes." In *Standard Edition,* vol. 19.

———. "The Uncanny." In *Standard Edition,* vol. 17.

Friebert, Lucy. "From Semblance to Selfhood: The Evolution of Woman in H.D.'s Neo-Epic *Helen in Egypt." Arizona Quarterly* 36 (1980): 165–75.

Friedman, Susan Stanford. "Against Discipleship: Collaboration and Intimacy in the Relationship of H.D. and Freud." *Literature and Psychology* 33, nos. 3–4 (1987): 89–108.

———. *Penelope's Web: Gender, Modernity, H.D.'s Fiction.* New York: Cambridge University Press, 1990.

———. *Psyche Reborn: The Emergence of H.D.* Bloomington: Indiana University Press, 1981.

Friedman, Susan Stanford, and Rachel Blau DuPlessis, eds. *Signets: Reading H.D.* Madison: University of Wisconsin Press, 1990.

———. "'Woman is Perfect'": H.D.'s Debate with Freud." *Feminist Studies* 7, no. 3 (Fall 1981): 417–30.

Frye, Marilyn. "White Woman Feminist." In *Willful Virgin: Essays in Feminism, 1976–1992,* 147–69. Freedom, Calif.: Crossing Press, 1992.

Gallop, Jane. *The Daughter's Seduction: Feminism and Psychoanalysis.* Ithaca, N.Y.: Cornell University Press, 1982.

———. *Reading Lacan.* Ithaca, N.Y.: Cornell University Press, 1985.

Garber, Marjorie. *Vested Interests: Cross-Dressing and Cultural Anxiety.* New York: Routledge, 1992.

Gelpi, Albert. "Adrienne Rich: The Poetics of Change." In *Adrienne Rich's Poetry,* edited by Barbara Charlesworth Gelpi and Albert Gelpi, 130–47. New York: Norton, 1975.

Gilbert, Sandra M. "From *Patria* to *Matria*: Elizabeth Barrett Browning's Risorgimento." *PMLA* 99 (March 1984): 194–211.

———. Introduction. In *The Newly Born Woman,* by Hélène Cixous and Catherine Clément. Translated by Betsy Wing, ix–xviii. Minneapolis: University of Minnesota Press, 1986.

———. "Marianne Moore As Female Female Impersonator." In *Marianne Moore: The Art of a Modernist,* edited by Joseph Parisi, 27–46. Ann Arbor: UMI Press, 1990.

Gilbert, Sandra M., and Susan Gubar. *The Madwoman in the Attic: The Woman Writer and the Nineteenth-Century Literary Imagination.* New Haven: Yale University Press, 1979.

———. eds. *Shakespeare's Sisters: Feminist Essays on Women Poets.* Bloomington: Indiana University Press, 1979.

Gilligan, Carol. *In a Different Voice: Psychological Theory and Women's Development.* Cambridge: Harvard University Press, 1982.

Gilmore, Leigh. "The Gaze of the Other Woman: Beholding and Begetting in Dickinson, Moore, and Rich." In *Engendering the Word,* edited by Temma F. Berg, 193–207. Urbana: University of Illinois Press, 1989.

Guest, Barbara. *Herself Defined: The Poet H.D. and Her World.* Garden City, N.Y.: Doubleday, 1984.

Hadas, Pamela White. *Marianne Moore: Poet of Affection.* Syracuse, N.Y.: Syracuse University Press, 1977.

Hagenbüchle, Roland. "Precision and Indeterminacy in the Poetry of Emily Dickinson." *Emerson Society Quarterly* 20 (First Quarter 1974): 33–56.

Heath, Stephen. "Joan Riviere and the Masquerade." In *Formations of Fantasy,* edited by Victor Burgin, James Donald, and Cora Kaplan. 45–61. London: Routledge, 1986.

Hertz, Neil. *The End of the Line.* New York: Columbia University Press, 1985.

Heuving, Jeanne. *Omissions Are Not Accidents: Gender in the Art of Marianne Moore.* Detroit: Wayne State University, 1992.

Hines, Darlene Clark. "Rape and the Inner Lives of Black Women in the Middle West: Preliminary Thoughts on the Culture of Dissemblance." In *Unequal Sisters: A Multicultural Reader in U.S. Women's History,* edited by Ellen Carol DuBois and Vicki L. Ruiz, 292–97. New York: Routledge, 1990.

Hirsh, Elizabeth A. "Imaginary Eyes: 'H.D.,' Modernism, and the Psychoanalysis of Seeing." In *Signets: Reading H.D.,* edited by Susan Stanford Friedman and Rachel Blau DuPlessis. 1986. Reprint, Madison: University of Wisconsin Press, 1990, 430–51.

Hogue, Cynthia A. "(Re)Placing Woman: The Politics and Poetics of Gender in H.D.'s *Helen in Egypt.*" *American Poetry* 8 (Fall 1990): 87–99.

Hokanson, Robert O'Brien. "'Is It All a Story?': Questioning Revision in H.D.'s *Helen in Egypt.*" *American Literature* 64, no. 2 (June 1992): 331–46.

Holland, Norman. "H.D. and the 'Blameless Physician.'" *Contemporary Literature* 10, no. 4 (Autumn 1969): 474–506.

Holley, Margaret. *The Poetry of Marianne Moore: A Study in Voice and Value.* New York: Cambridge University Press, 1987.

———. "Portraits of Ladies in Marianne Moore and Elizabeth Bishop." *Sagetrieb* 6, no. 3 (Winter 1987: Marianne Moore Special Issue): 15–30.

Homans, Margaret. "'Oh, Vision of Language!': Dickinson's Poems of Love and Death." In *Feminist Critics Read Emily Dickinson,* edited by

Suzanne Juhasz, 114–32. Bloomington: Indiana University Press, 1983.

———. "'Syllables of Velvet': Dickinson, Rossetti, and the Rhetorics of Sexuality." *Feminist Studies* 11, no. 3 (Fall 1985): 569–93.

———. *Women Writers and Poetic Identity: Dorothy Wordsworth, Emily Brontë, and Emily Dickinson.* Princeton, N.J.: Princeton University Press, 1980.

Howe, Susan. *My Emily Dickinson.* Berkeley, Calif.: North Atlantic Books, 1985.

Hurtado, Aída. "Relating to Privilege: Seduction and Rejection in the Subordination of White Women and Women of Color." *Signs* 14, no. 4 (Summer 1989): 833–55.

Irigaray, Luce. *Speculum of the Other Woman.* Translated by Gillian C. Gill. Ithaca, N.Y.: Cornell University Press, 1985.

———. *This Sex Which Is Not One.* Translated by Catherine Porter. Ithaca, N.Y.: Cornell University Press, 1985.

Jacobus, Mary. *Reading Woman: Essays in Feminist Criticism.* New York: Columbia University Press, 1986.

Jaffe, Nora Crowe. "'She Herself Is the Writing': Language and Sexual Identity in H.D." *Literature and Medicine* 4 (1985): 86–111.

Jardine, Alice. *Gynesis: Configurations of Woman and Modernity.* Ithaca, N.Y.: Cornell University Press. 1985.

Jeffords, Susan. *The Remasculinization of America: Gender and the Vietnam War.* Bloomington: Indiana University Press, 1989.

Johnson, Barbara. *The Critical Difference: Essays in the Contemporary Rhetoric of Reading.* Baltimore: Johns Hopkins University Press, 1981.

———. *A World of Difference.* Baltimore: Johns Hopkins University Press, 1987.

Joplin, Patricia Klindienst. "Epilogue: Philomela's Loom." In *Coming to Light: American Women Poets in the Twentieth Century,* edited by Diane Wood Middlebrook and Marilyn Yalom, 254–68. Ann Arbor: University of Michigan Press, 1985.

———. "The Voice of the Shuttle Is Ours." *Stanford Literature Review* 1 (Spring 1984): 25–53.

Juhasz, Suzanne. Introduction. In *Feminist Critics Read Emily Dickinson,* edited by Suzanne Juhasz. Bloomington: Indiana University Press, 1983.

———. *Naked and Fiery Forms.* New York: Harper & Row, 1976.

———. *The Undiscovered Continent: Emily Dickinson and the Space of the Mind.* Bloomington: Indiana University Press, 1983.

Kahane, Claire. "The Gothic Mirror." In *The (M)other Tongue: Essays in Feminist Psychoanalytic Interpretation,* edited by Shirley Nelson Garner, Claire Kahane, and Madelon Sprengnether, 334–51. Ithaca, N.Y.: Cornell University Press, 1985.

Kahn, Coppélia. "The Hand That Rocks the Cradle: Recent Gender Theories and Their Implications." In *The (M)other Tongue: Essays in Feminist Psychoanalytic Interpretation,* edited by Shirley Nelson Garner, Claire Kahane, and Madelon Sprengnether, 72–88. Ithaca: Cornell University Press, 1985.

Kamuf, Peggy. "Penelope at Work: Interruptions in *A Room of One's Own.*" *Novel* 16, no. 1 (Fall 1982): 5–18.

Keating, AnnLouise. "Making 'Our Shattered Faces Whole': The Black Goddess and Audre Lorde's Revision of Patriarchal Myth." *Frontiers: A Journal of Women's Studies* 13, no. 1 (1992): 20–33.

Keller, Lynn. "'For inferior who is free?' Liberating the Woman Writer in Marianne Moore's 'Marriage.'" In *Influence and Intertextuality in Literary History,* edited by Jay Clayton and Eric Rothstein, 219–44. Madison: University of Wisconsin Press, 1991.

Keller, Lynn, and Cristanne Miller, "'The Tooth of Disputation': Marianne Moore's 'Marriage.'" *Sagetrieb* 6, no. 3 (Winter 1987: Marianne Moore Special Issue): 99–116.

Kenner, Hugh. *A Homemade World: The American Modernist Writers.* New York: Knopf, 1975.

Kloepfer, Deborah Kelly. *The Unspeakable Mother: Forbidden Discourse in Jean Rhys and H.D.* Ithaca, N.Y.: Cornell University Press, 1989.

Kofman, Sarah. *The Enigma of Woman: Woman in Freud's Writings.* Translated by Catherine Porter. Ithaca, N.Y.: Cornell University Press, 1985.

Kristeva, Julia. "From One Identity to an Other." In *Desire in Language: A Semiotic Approach to Literature and Art.* Translated by Thomas Gora, Alice Jardine, and Leon S. Roudiez, 124–47. New York: Columbia University Press, 1980.

———. "Motherhood According to Giovanni Bellini." In *Desire in Language: A Semiotic Approach to Literature and Art.* Translated by Thomas Gora, Alice Jardine, and Leon S. Roudiez, 237–70. New York: Columbia University Press, 1980.

———. *Nations without Nationalism.* Translated by Leon S. Roudiez. New York: Columbia University Press, 1993.

———. *Powers of Horror: An Essay on Abjection.* Translated by Leon S. Roudiez. New York: Columbia University Press, 1982.

————. *Revolution in Poetic Language.* Translated by Margaret Waller. New York: Columbia University Press, 1984.

————. "Women's Time." In *The Kristeva Reader,* edited by Toril Moi, translated by Alice Jardine and Harry Blake, 187–213. New York: Columbia University Press, 1986.

Lacan, Jacques. *Écrits: A Selection.* Translated by Alan Sheridan. London: Tavistock, 1977.

————. *Feminine Sexuality: Jacques Lacan and the école freudienne.* Edited by Juliet Mitchell and Jacqueline Rose. Translated by Jacqueline Rose. London and New York: Norton, 1983.

————. *Four Fundamental Concepts of Psycho-analysis.* Edited by Jacques-Alain Miller. Translated by Alan Sheridan. New York: Norton, 1978.

La Place, Marie. "Producing and Consuming Woman's Film: Discursive Struggle in *Now, Voyager.*" In *Home Is Where the Heart Is,* edited by Christine Gledhill, 138–66. London: BFI Press, 1987.

Laplanche, Jean, and Jean-Bertrand Pontalis. "Fantasy and the Origins of Sexuality." In *Formations of Fantasy,* edited by Victor Burgin, James Donald, and Cora Kaplan. 1968. Reprint, London: Routledge, 1986. 5–34.

————. *The Language of Psycho-analysis.* Translated by Donald Nicholson-Smith. New York: Norton, 1973.

Larsen, Jeanne. "Text and Matrix: Dickinson, H.D., and Woman's Voice." In *Engendering the Word,* edited by Temma F. Berg, 244–61. Urbana: University of Illinois Press, 1989.

Lerner, Gerda. *The Creation of Patriarchy.* New York: Oxford University Press, 1986.

Lévi-Strauss, Claude. *The Elementary Structures of Kinship.* Edited by Rodney Needham. Translated by James Harle Bell, John Richard von Sturmer, and Rodney Needham. Boston: Beacon Press, 1969.

————. *Structural Anthropology.* Translated by Claire Jacobson and Brooke Grundfest Schoepf. London: Basic Books, 1963.

Loeffelholz, Mary. *Dickinson and the Boundaries of Feminist Theory.* Urbana: University of Illinois Press, 1991.

Longinus. *Longinus on the Sublime.* Translated by W. Rhys Roberts. Cambridge: Cambridge University Press, 1989.

Lorde, Audre. "The Master's Tools Will Never Dismantle the Master's House." In *This Bridge Called My Back: Writings by Radical Women of Color,* edited by Cherríe Moraga and Gloria Anzaldúa, 98–101. New York: Kitchen Table Women of Color Press, 1981.

————. *Our Dead behind Us.* New York: Norton, 1986.

————. *Sister Outsider: Essays and Speeches.* Trumansburg, N.Y.: Crossing Press, 1984.

MacKinnon, Catharine A. "Feminism, Marxism, Method, and the State: An Agenda for Theory." In *Feminist Theory: A Critique of Ideology,* edited by Nannerl O. Keohane, Michelle A. Rosaldo, and Barbara Gelpi, 1–30. Chicago: University of Chicago Press, 1981.

Martin, Taffy. *Marianne Moore, Subversive Modernist.* Austin: University of Texas Press, 1986.

Martin, Wendy. *An American Triptych: Anne Bradstreet, Emily Dickinson, Adrienne Rich.* Chapel Hill: University of North Carolina Press, 1984.

McConnell-Ginet, Sally. "Linguistics and the Feminist Challenge." In *Women and Language in Literature and Society,* edited by Sally McConnell-Ginet, Ruth Borker, and Nelly Furman, 3–25. New York: Praeger, 1980.

McKinstry, S. Jaret. "'How Lovely Are the Wiles of Words!'—or, 'Subjects Hinder Talk': The Letters of Emily Dickinson." In *Engendering the Word,* edited by Temma F. Berg, 193–207. Urbana: University of Illinois Press, 1989.

Meese, Elizabeth A. *(Ex)tensions: Re-figuring Feminist Criticism.* Urbana: University of Illinois Press, 1990.

Michie, Helena. *The Flesh Made Word: Female Figures and Women's Bodies.* New York: Oxford University Press, 1987.

Miller, Cristanne. *Emily Dickinson: A Poet's Grammar.* Cambridge: Harvard University Press, 1987.

————. "Marianne Moore's Black Maternal Hero: A Study in Categorization." *American Literary History* 1, no. 4 (Winter 1989): 786–815.

Miller, J. Hillis. *The Linguistic Moment: From Wordsworth to Stevens.* Princeton, N.J.: Princeton University Press, 1985.

Miller, Nancy K. "Arachnologies: the Woman, the Text, and the Critic." In *The Poetics of Gender,* edited by Nancy K. Miller, 270–95. New York: Columbia University Press, 1986.

————. "Changing the Subject: Authorship, Writing, and the Reader." In *Feminist Studies/Critical Studies,* edited by Teresa de Lauretis, 102–20. Bloomington: Indiana University Press, 1986.

Mitchell, Juliet. *Women: The Longest Revolution.* New York: Pantheon Books, 1984.

Mitchell, Juliet, and Jacqueline Rose, eds. *Feminine Sexuality: Jacques Lacan and the école freudienne.* Translated by Jacqueline Rose. London: Norton, 1983.

Modleski, Tania. *The Women Who Knew Too Much: Hitchcock and Feminist Theory.* New York: Routledge, 1988.

Moi, Toril. "Reading Kristeva: A Response to Calvin Bedient." *Critical Inquiry* 17 (Spring 1991): 639–43.

Molesworth, Charles. *Marianne Moore: A Literary Life.* New York: Macmillan, 1990.

Montefiore, Jan. *Feminism and Poetry: Language, Experience, Identity in Women's Writing.* 2nd ed. London: Pandora Press, 1994.

Moore, Marianne. *The Complete Poems of Marianne Moore.* New York: Macmillan, 1967.

———. *The Complete Prose of Marianne Moore.* Edited and with an introduction by Patricia C. Willis. New York: Viking, 1986.

———. *A Marianne Moore Reader.* New York: Viking Press, 1961.

———. *Observations.* New York: Dial Press, 1924.

Morris, Adelaide. "The Concept of Projection: H.D.'s Visionary Powers." In *Signets: Reading H.D.,* edited by Susan Stanford Friedman and Rachel Blau DuPlessis. 1984. Reprint, Madison: University of Wisconsin Press, 1990, 273–96.

Morrison, Toni, ed. *Race-ing Justice, En-gendering Power: Essays on Anita Hill, Clarence Thomas, and the Construction of Social Reality.* New York: Pantheon, 1992.

Mossberg, Barbara Antonina Clarke. *Emily Dickinson: When a Writer Is a Daughter.* Bloomington: Indiana University Press, 1982.

Mulvey, Laura. "Afterthoughts on 'Visual Pleasure and Narrative Cinema' Inspired by King Vidor's *Duel in the Sun* (1946)." In *Visual and Other Pleasures.* 1981. Reprint, Bloomington: Indiana University Press, 1989, 29–38.

———. "Visual Pleasure and Narrative Cinema." In *Visual and Other Pleasures.* 1975. Reprint, Bloomington: Indiana University Press, 1989, 14–26.

Nathanson, Tenney. "Collage and Pulverization in Contemporary American Poetry: Charles Bernstein's *Controlling Interests.*" *Contemporary Literature* 33, no. 2 (Summer 1992): 302–18.

———. *Whitman's Presence: Body, Voice, and Writing in Leaves of Grass.* New York: New York University Press, 1992.

Nyquist, Mary. "Musing on Susanna's Music." In *Lyric Poetry: Beyond New Criticism,* edited by Chaviva Hosek and Patricia Parker, 310–27. Ithaca, N.Y.: Cornell University Press, 1985.

Oliver, Kelly. *Reading Kristeva: Unravelling the Double-Bind.* Bloomington: Indiana University Press, 1993.

Ostriker, Alicia Suskin. "Marianne Moore, the Maternal Hero, and American Women's Poetry." In *Marianne Moore: The Art of a Modernist,* edited by Joseph Parisi, 49–66. Ann Arbor: UMI Press, 1990.

———. *Stealing the Language: The Emergence of Women's Poetry in America.* Boston: Beacon Press, 1986.

———. "What Do Women (Poets) Want?: Marianne Moore and H.D. as Poetic Ancestresses." *Poesis* 6, nos. 3–4 (1985): 1–9.

Ovid. *The Metamorphoses.* Translated by Horace Gregory. New York: New American Libary, 1960.

Owens, Craig. "The Discourse of Others: Feminists and Postmodernism." In *The Anti-Aesthetic: Essays on Postmodern Culture,* edited by Hal Foster, 57–82. Port Townsend, Wash.: Bay Press, 1983.

Parker, Patricia. Introduction. In *Lyric Poetry: Beyond New Criticism,* edited by Chaviva Hosek and Patricia Parker, 11–28. Ithaca, N.Y.: Cornell University Press, 1985.

Parsons, Frank. *The Psychology of Dress.* 1920. 2nd ed. Garden City, N.Y.: Doubleday, Page, 1923.

Patterson, Rebecca. *The Riddle of Emily Dickinson.* Boston: Houghton Mifflin, 1951.

Peirce, Charles Sanders. *Collected Papers.* 8 vols. Cambridge: Harvard University Press, 1931–58.

Perkins, David, ed. *English Romantic Writers.* New York: Harcourt Brace Jovanovich, 1967.

Pollak, Vivian. *Dickinson: The Anxiety of Gender.* Ithaca, N.Y.: Cornell University Press, 1984.

Rajan, Tilottama. "Intertextuality and the Subject of Reading/Writing." In *Influence and Intertextuality in Literary History,* edited by Jay Clayton and Eric Rothstein, 61–74. Madison: University of Wisconsin Press.

———. "Romanticism and the Death of Lyric Consciousness." In *Lyric Poetry: Beyond New Criticism,* edited by Chaviva Hosek and Patricia Parker, 194–207. Ithaca, N.Y.: Cornell University Press, 1985.

Retallack, Joan. "Post-Scriptum-High-Modern." In *Postmodern Genres,* edited by Marjorie Perloff, 248–73. Norman: University of Oklahoma Press, 1988.

Rich, Adrienne. *Adrienne Rich's Poetry.* Edited by Albert Gelpi and Barbara Charlesworth Gelpi. New York: Norton, 1975.

———. *An Atlas of the Difficult World: Poems 1988–1991.* New York: Norton, 1991.

———. *Blood, Bread and Poetry: Selected Prose 1979–1985.* New York: Norton, 1986.

———. *Diving into the Wreck: Poems 1971–1972.* New York: Norton, 1973.

———. *The Fact of a Doorframe: Poems Selected and New 1950–1984.* New York: Norton, 1984.

———. "The Hermit's Scream." *PMLA* 108, no. 5 (October 1993): 1157–64.

———. *Of Woman Born: Motherhood As Experience and Institution.* New York: Bantam, 1977.

———. *On Lies, Secrets, and Silence: Selected Prose 1966–1978.* New York: Norton, 1979.

———. *A Wild Patience Has Taken Me This Far: Poems 1978–1981.* New York: Norton, 1981.

———. *Your Native Land, Your Life.* New York: Norton, 1986.

Riddel, Joseph. "H.D. and the Poetics of 'Spiritual Realism.'" *Contemporary Literature* 10 (Autumn 1969): 447–73.

———. "H.D.'s Scene of Writing: Poetry As (and) Analysis." *Studies in the Literary Imagination* 12, no. 1 (Spring 1979): 41–59.

Riviere, Joan. "Womanliness As a Masquerade." In *Formations of Fantasy,* edited by Victor Burgin, James Donald, and Cora Kaplan. 1929. Reprint, London: Routledge, 1986, 35–44.

Rose, Jacqueline. *Sexuality in the Field of Vision.* London: Verso, 1986.

Ross, Andrew. *The Failure of Modernism: Symptoms of American Poetry.* New York: Columbia University Press, 1986.

Rubin, Gayle. "The Traffic in Women: Notes on the 'Political Economy' of Sex." In *Toward an Anthropology of Women.* Edited by Rayna R. Reiter, 157–210. New York: Monthly Review Press, 1975.

Rukeyser, Muriel. *Breaking Open.* 1944. Reprint, New York: Random House, 1973.

Russo, Mary. "Female Grotesques: Carnival and Theory." In *Feminist Studies/Critical Studies,* edited by Teresa de Lauretis, 213–29. Bloomington: Indiana University Press, 1986.

Saldívar-Hull, Sonia. "Wrestling Your Ally: Stein, Racism, and Feminist Critical Practice." In *Women's Writing in Exile,* edited by Mary Lynn Broe and Angela Ingram, 181–98. Chapel Hill: University of North Carolina Press, 1989.

Schweickart, Patrocinio P. "Reading Ourselves: Toward a Feminist Theory of Reading." In *Gender and Reading: Essays on Readers, Texts, and Contexts,* edited by Elizabeth A. Flynn and Patrocinio Schweikart, 31–62. Baltimore: Johns Hopkins University Press, 1986.

Sedgwick, Eve Kosofsky. *Between Men: English Literature and Male Homosocial Desire.* New York: Columbia University Press, 1985.

Sewall, Richard. *The Life of Emily Dickinson.* 2 vols. New York: Farrar, Straus & Giroux, 1974.

Shurr, William H. *The Marriage of Emily Dickinson: A Study of the Fascicles.* Lexington: University of Kentucky Press, 1983.

Sielke, Sabine. "Snapshots of Marriage, Snares of Mimicry, Snarls of Motherhood: Marianne Moore and Adrienne Rich." *Sagetrieb* 6, no. 3 (Winter 1987: Marianne Moore Special Issue): 79–97.

Silverman, Kaja. *Male Subjectivity at the Margins.* New York: Routledge, 1992.

Slatin, John M. "Advancing Backward in a Circle: Marianne Moore as (Natural) Historian." *Twentieth Century Literature* 30, nos. 2–3 (Summer–Fall 1984): 273–26.

———. *The Savage's Romance: The Poetry of Marianne Moore.* University Park: Pennsylvania State University Press, 1986.

Smith, Martha Nell. *Rowing in Eden: Rereading Emily Dickinson.* Austin: University of Texas Press, 1992.

Smith-Rosenberg, Carroll. *Disorderly Conduct: Visions of Gender in Victorian America.* New York: Oxford University Press, 1985.

St. Armand, Barton Levi. *Emily Dickinson and Her Culture: The Soul's Society.* Cambridge: Cambridge University Press, 1984.

Stapleton, Laurence. *Marianne Moore: The Poet's Advance.* Princeton, N.J.: Princeton University Press, 1978.

Stonum, Gary Lee. *The Dickinson Sublime.* Madison: University of Wisconsin Press, 1990.

Sword, Helen. "Leda and the Modernists," *PMLA* 107, no. 2 (March 1992): 305–18.

Vickers, Nancy J. "Diana Described: Scattered Women and Scattered Rhyme." In *Writing and Sexual Difference,* edited by Elizabeth Abel. 1981. Reprint, Chicago: University of Chicago Press, 1982, 95–109.

Walker, Cheryl. *Masks Outrageous and Austere: Culture, Psyche, and Persona in Modern Women Poets.* Bloomington: Indiana University Press, 1991.

———. *The Nightingale's Burden: Women Poets and American Culture before 1900.* Bloomington: Indiana University Press, 1982.

Warner, Marina. *Alone of All Her Sex: The Myth and the Cult of the Virgin Mary.* 1976. 2nd ed. New York: Wallaby-Simon & Schuster, 1978.

Watts, Emily Stipes. *The Poetry of American Women from 1632 to 1945.* Austin: University of Texas Press, 1977.

Webster, Noah. *American Dictionary of the English Language.* 1841. Reprint, Amherst: J.S. and C. Adams, 1844.

Weiskel, Thomas. *The Romantic Sublime: Studies in the Structure and Psychology of Transcendence.* Baltimore: Johns Hopkins University Press, 1976.

Willis, Patricia. "The Road to Paradise: First Notes on Marianne Moore's 'An Octopus.'" *Twentieth Century Literature* 30, nos. 2–3 (Summer–Fall 1984): 242–66.

————. ed. *Marianne Moore: Woman and Poet.* Orono, Maine: National Poetry Foundation, 1990.

Woolf, Virginia. *Between the Acts.* 1941. Reprint, New York: Harcourt Brace Jovanovich, 1969.

————. *Orlando: A Biography.* 1928. Reprint, New York and London: Harcourt Brace Jovanovich, 1956.

————. *A Room of One's Own.* 1929. Reprint, New York: Harcourt, Brace, & World, 1957.

Wolff, Cynthia Griffin. *Emily Dickinson.* New York: Knopf, 1986.

Yeats, W. B. *The Collected Poems of W. B. Yeats.* 1956. Reprint, New York: Macmillan, 1972.

Zonana, Joyce. "The Embodied Muse: Elizabeth Barrett Browning's *Aurora Leigh* and Feminist Poetics." *Tulsa Studies in Women's Literature* 2, no. 8 (1988): 241–62.

Zwinger, Lynda. *Daughters, Fathers, and the Novel: The Sentimental Romance of Heterosexuality.* Madison: University of Wisconsin Press, 1991.

Index

apostrophe, xviii, 5, 7, 88
Aldington, Richard, 143
Althusser, Louis, 227n10, 232–33n8
Anzaldúa, Gloria, xx

Benjamin, Jessica, 214n73
Berg, Elizabeth, 231n84
Beauvoir, Simone de, 165, 204n30
bisexuality, 12, 151, 154–55.
   See also H.D.
Browning, Elizabeth Barrett, 10–12, 13–14,
   28, 31–32, 43, 67, 195
Bryher (Winifred Ellerman), 117, 135, 142,
   154
Buck, Claire, 117, 118, 130
Burke, Carolyn, 75, 107

Cameron, Sharon, 204n24, 227n24
castration, 119, 128, 131, 134–35, 141–42,
   148, 151
   and femininity, 38, 61, 106, 137–38, 143,
     147, 154–55
   and Lacanian ethics, 146, 156
   and subjectivity, 11–12, 18–19, 229n44.
   See also H.D., Lacan

Chisholm, Diane, 119, 126, 150
chora, semiotic, xix, 22, 63
   as maternally connoted, 19–21, 24, 176.
   See also Kristeva
Cixous, Hélène, 131, 135, 142
Collecott, Diana, 230n64
consciousness,
   mestiza.
     See Anzaldúa
   raising, 27, 189, 198
     See also Rich
Costello, Bonnie, 74, 76, 79, 104, 218n33
Culler, Jonathan, xviii, 5, 8

De Lauretis, Teresa, xx-xxi, 8, 16, 29, 106,
   130, 186
   critical of Kristeva, 22, 25
   on cultural feminism, 161, 224n90
   on gender and subjectivity, 4, 9–10, 14,
     17, 25–28, 140, 149–50, 202n7
   on lesbian, desire, 22, 183
     subjectivity, 188–91, passim
De Man, Paul, xxi, 8, 17, 20, 26, 28, 122
   on poetic writing, 13–15, 16, 29.
   See also rhetoric
dialogism. *See* heteroglossia
Dickie, Margaret, 67, 213n67

255

herethics, 22, 24–25, 144, 175–76, 188, 199–200, 213n65.
  See also Kristeva; poetic, practice
Hertz, Neil, 41, 54–57, 68, 134
Heuving, Jeanne, 85, 86
heteroglossia (dialogism), 83, 86, 165
heterosexuality, 22, 153, 157, 189, 226n10
  construct of, xxi, xxii, 118, 123, 144, 150, 152, 162, 233nn11,15
  hegemony of, 163, 182, 189
  institution of, xx, xxii, 9, 38, 48, 151, 164, 178, 183
  and poetic tradition, 83
Higginson, Thomas Wentworth, 32, 40–43, 50, 71
Hill, Anita, 190
Hines, Darlene Clark, xx
Hirsh, Elizabeth, 125, 131, 151–52
Hitchcock, Alfred (*Rebecca*), 177–78
Holley, Margaret, 111, 113
Homans, Margaret, 4, 129, 161, 179
Horney, Karen, 166
Howe, Susan, 211n39
Hurtado, Aída, xx, 187–88
hysteria, 29, 168, 181, 214n71, 231n71
  female, alternative to, 153, 207n88, 221n62
  male, 12, 129, 145, 231n70

Image, concept of, 152
Imaginary, 21, 151, 159, 227n19
  maternal, 164–65, 170, 176, 180
Irigaray, Luce, 2, 4, 5, 6, 86, 133, 137, 143, 146, 211n40
  on the gaze, 127, 204–5n38
  mimesis, feminist concept of, 88, 121, 134, 169, 204n34
irony, 29, 128

Jacobus, Mary, 15, 231n71
James, Henry. *See* Moore
Jardine, Alice, 8, 16, 17
Jeffords, Susan 127, 155, 231–32n85
Johnson, Barbara, 2, 14, 16, 17, 113
jouissance, 21, 97, 215n2
Juhasz, Suzanne, 213n63

Kahane, Claire, 61

Kahn, Coppélia, 145
Kamuf, Peggy, 233n12
Kant, Immanuel, 41, 54
Keats, John, 85
Keller, Lynn, 78, 217n25, 221n63
Kenner, Hugh, 110, 120, 217n25
Kloepfer, Deborah Kelly, 164, 235n43
Kofman, Sarah, 34, 37–39, 118, 141, 147, 151, 155, 223–24n76
Kristeva, Julia, xix, xx, 28, 89, 156, 175, 176, 184, 186, 200, 235n43
  and mother, figure of, xx, 16, 21–23, 24, 180, 183
    abjection of, 17, 53–56
  and poetic practice, revolutionary, xx, xxiii, 20, 24–25, 27, 144, 175–76, 189.
    See also herethics; poetic, ethical practice
  and sexual difference, 22–24
  and subjectivity, 16, 17–25, 56, 160, 180, 183, 188, 205n49

Lacan, Jacques, 18, 21, 22, 26, 78, 119, 156
  and linguistic subject, xxi–xxii, 19, 145–46, 232n86
  and woman, 1, 3, 12, 16–17, 168, 202n2
La Place, Marie, 39
Laplanche, Jean, 227n19
Larsen, Jeanne, 42
lesbian, continuum, 164, 178, 182
  desire, 182–84
  existence, 178–80, 182
  feminism, 162
  sexuality, 142, 147
  subjectivity, xxii, 182–85.
    See also De Lauretis; Rich
Lévi-Strauss, Claude, 4
Locke, John, 161
Loeffelholz, Mary, 32, 33, 39, 196
Lorde, Audre, 180, 185, 187, 198, 199–200
lyric, xxi, 83, 161, 227n26
  gendered tradition of, xviii–xx, 2–12, 126, 165, 167–68.
    See also poetic tradition

MacKinnon, Catharine A., 9, 27, 228n34
man, as symbol, xx, 2, 16, 71, 100, 119, 123
Martin, Taffy, 85, 216n16